LISTEN UP!

Stories of Pearl Harbor, Vietnam the Pentagon, CNN and Beyond

PERRY M. SMITH, JR.

outskirts
press

TABLE OF CONTENTS

PREFACE

Since I was seven years old, I have been telling stories of interesting and sometimes remarkable happenings in my life. I love telling stories and, over the years, many family, friends and colleagues have asked me to write them down.

The following are stories of someone who, before the age of thirteen, watched the Japanese attack on Pearl Harbor, learned about the rationing of life on an evacuation ship in the Pacific Ocean, made his first public speech at age seven, observed a food riot in Naples, Italy, shortly after World War II, and visited Greece during the Greek Civil War. My long life has been marked by successes, setbacks, a truly exceptional marriage, two kids, four grandkids and enough adventure to fill many lifetimes.

Perhaps the most interesting stories are some of my major setbacks. I will describe the failures and try to draw lessons from each. Also included are many Air Force flying stories, some of which are quite dramatic. Saving a commercial airliner is perhaps the most unusual of them all. In addition, I will tell you lacrosse stories, media stories, combat stories, Pentagon stories, and a few stories from everyday life, some which are quite funny.

For those who do not recognize my name, I am probably best known for my years as a military analyst for CNN, NBC TV, CBS TV and CBS radio from 1991 through 2003.

During the Persian Gulf War of 1991 (Operation Desert Storm), I served as one of two full-time military analysts for CNN. During that six-week war, there were periods of time when more than a billion people were watching CNN. Although I did not know it at the time, top officials in Washington and in Saudi Arabia were watching me. My fifteen minutes of fame actually lasted for forty-two days. The CNN story and why I resigned from that network in protest over CNN's ethical failure are described in this memoir.

Note to the Reader

I have highlighted what I believe are the more interesting stories in **bold**. You may wish to skip over the discussion of my family, my various jobs, and my forty moves from place to place. If so, I suggest you skim the table of contents or text until you see some **bold** printing. I hope this approach works for those who may be short on time.

Thoughts from the Editor
(AND A LOVE LETTER FROM A DAUGHTER)

I have been asking my dad, for years, to write down all of his stories. He certainly has experience with writing. His first book, published when I was a little girl, was the result of an award for his Columbia University PhD dissertation. He has written a book on leadership in large organizations, a how-to guide on working in the Pentagon, and a snapshot of his time working for CNN during the First Gulf War. He is a regular contributor to his local newspaper, The Augusta Chronicle. He even has experience with biography. He wrote a book, plus crafted a DVD, about my grandfather, Jimmie Dyess, who is the only person to have been awarded the highest military and civilian recognitions of bravery, the Congressional Medal of Honor and the Carnegie Medal. He also authored several DVDs, one about my great uncle, Hervey Cleckley, M.D., a Rhodes Scholar, author of the international bestseller, *The Three Faces of Eve* and a world-renowned psychiatrist credited with first describing the psycho/sociopathic personality.

I think it is high time for Major General Perry McCoy Smith, Jr., USAF retired, to get down on paper (or get up in the cloud?) what he has been voicing since he was 7 years old when he first described his eye witness impressions of the bombing of Pearl Harbor.

My life has been filled with Perry Smith stories. So have the lives of just about anyone he meets. NOT included in this book, with the exception of "The Pope Joke" in the Jeff Rosensweig/Emory section, are ANY of his mostly terrible "Dad jokes." "The General," as many lovingly refer to him, is a wonderful storyteller but an awful joke teller! He tells both stories and jokes with equal enthusiasm to friends and acquaintances and many people he meets. It is a good thing he pursued a career in the Air Force, a PhD in International Relations, a second act as a speaker and educator, and a third act as promoter of good causes. He would have failed miserably as a comedian. My, mostly, patient mom gets to hear the poorly delivered jokes over and over and over again. She sometimes has to remind him of the punchline! Although bad at jokes, many of his stories are funny, so you will enjoy reading those.

I very much enjoyed editing this, my dad's memoir. Since my life has been filled from the start with Perry Smith, my life has also been gifted with his stories. I must brag a moment and say that I am responsible for the inclusion of quite a few of the stories. It was wonderful to ask him, "What about the one when…?" By the way, you are welcome, Verfurth family and flying school friends, for the Pete-Verfurth-eats-a-jar-of-jalapenos story. Who knew that the larger-than-life man, in my dad's flying school story, which I had heard since a child, would end up being my father-in-law?

Perry Smith's stories are worth hearing/reading, as they are not just entertaining, but also educational. His life went in a number of interesting directions. His mother, from a prestigious Pennsylvania family, grew up on the Upper West Side of Manhattan, a neighbor of Humphrey Bogart. His father, a West Point graduate and career officer, grew up in a farming town in Ohio. Born at West Point during the depression, young Perry's only choice in an undergraduate education was the United States Military Academy. There was no money for college. His childhood was sculpted by the Depression and World War II years and his family lived in Europe immediately after the war. He not only attended West Point, like his father, but his family lived on campus when he matriculated.

He was an unlikely varsity athlete, with friends who would become famous, and joined the Air Force rather than the Army after graduation. He was a professor at the Air Force Academy, asked to lead the Political Science department, but chose to try to get back to fighter jets instead. He flew a combat tour during the Vietnam war, and taught at, then led, the National War College. He worked at the Pentagon, in various jobs, on two different occasions and was unceremoniously fired the first run through. For a short time, he had his dream job, commanding a wing in Germany with the best fighter jets of that time, but then was sent off to charm military leaders of European allies. After his Air Force career, he was a familiar face on CNN and a valued teacher of leadership and strategic planning to many organizations, large and small. Finally he has become more and more involved in improving his adopted hometown and other areas of interest.

During all of this, he has maintained his enthusiasm for learning, meeting people, and forming, refining and reforming his positions on any topic. When someone challenges him on an idea, he doesn't get angry, dogmatic or defensive, he gets interested. He is a "liberal" thinker in the broadest of terms. He is always looking to learn something new. He was one of the first people I knew to buy a Mac computer, an iPhone and a Kindle. He was an early fan of Amazon, likely because of his love of books.

A favorite memory of my childhood is when the Encyclopedia Britannica salesperson came to our house and Dad bought a set. He then proceeded to read the twenty or so volumes, flipping through to the sections that interested him, during his middle of the night reading sessions. He was my "google.com" before there was Google. Whenever I had a question about something, he usually knew the answer. It was a bit of a disappointment when my husband, Rob, didn't have the answer to all my children's questions. Having grown up with Perry Smith as a father, I thought that was part of "a father's" role. Thank goodness for the internet, if you can't have Perry Smith living with you all the time.

When my brother, McCoy, and I were growing up and especially when we lived in Europe as teenagers, my dad would plan wonderful family trips. There is a list of some of the places he took his kids and my mom in the following pages. Looking back, I saw a remarkable amount of Europe before leaving my teen years.

Perry Smith is a man of his times, which you will see in this book. I tried to make the book as readable as possible for future generations without editing out his perspective. He grew up, of course, with male white privilege, but I don't think he or my mother ever felt their race was above any other. (This is remarkable, really, as my mother is a southerner and spent a good deal of her childhood in the South, with some family members who were outwardly racist.) Although the military was racially integrated in the 1940s, Perry's first time rooming with an African American was in 1991. As far as gender roles, my brother was encouraged to study engineering, while I was encouraged to go to college and study what interested me, with no career in mind. During <u>his</u> time, most college educated women got married and then stayed at home with the kids. I once overheard him say to a friend "I'm a little worried that Serena will never find a husband because she is just so smart." On the flip side, he was very impressed with my academic and career accomplishments, as well as those of his friend's children. I remember when his classmate's daughter, Lissa Young, went to West Point and eventually became a professor there. He was so very proud of her and still corresponds with her.

I hope you enjoy GDa's stories as much as I have. His grandchildren call him GDa, because my mom announced upon the birth of my first child, that she was to be called "GG" for gorgeous grandma and he was to be called "G Daddy." Dyess, my oldest, couldn't say G Daddy, so he is forever, now, GDa.

I dedicate my efforts in editing this book to my favorite human. Can you tell I am a "daddy's girl"? I love you Dad!!

<u>Listen Up</u>, because the following are some great stories.

Chapter One:

PARENTS, ANCESTORS, AND MY CHILDHOOD

BORN AT WEST POINT, New York in the depth of the Great Depression, I was fortunate to be in a family where my dad had a full-time job. He was a captain in the Army and taught English to cadets at the United States Military Academy at the time of my birth. I was born on Beethoven's birth date (16 December). It snowed hard that cold December day in 1934. For my mother and dad, I was their second child. My sister, George Anne, had been born eighteen months earlier also at the West Point hospital. Sadly, my sister lived a short and unhappy life, dying at age 53 in 1986.

MY MOTHER: MARY EMILY PORTER SMITH

My mother, Mary Emily Porter Smith ("Meps" was her nickname), had had a fascinating life before she married my father in September, 1929. Her father, George Porter, was the assistant treasurer of the New York Central Railroad throughout the early years of the 20th Century. Railroads were king in America in those days and George Porter was well paid and well connected in New York City and beyond. Her mother was Anna F. Phyffe who married George Porter when she was 21 and he was 45. The small family lived in Manhattan on West 80th street near the Hudson River. They had an apartment in a nice part of town.

My mother's family was originally from Harrisburg, Pennsylvania. She was a direct descendent of a Revolutionary War officer, Colonel Andrew Porter. Her great grandfather was David Rittenhouse Porter, the governor of Pennsylvania in the 1840s.

1

Born in 1903 in New York City, Meps Porter was an only child. One of her early memories was playing with Humphrey Bogart. Bogart was the son of a prominent physician. As a young boy, he was a bully and my mother could not stand to be with him.

As a small girl Meps would often visit rehearsal sessions at the Metropolitan Opera. She had a friend whose father worked there.

Enrico Caruso, the famous Italian tenor, took a liking to little Mepsie Smith and gave her a hug every time he saw her. She heard Caruso sing on many occasions.

As a teenager Meps had a good friend who had a summer home on Long Island. Coming back from a weekend with her friend, she was told to lie down on the floor of the back seat of the car. When she arrived at home, Meps told her dad how exciting it was to know that her friend's Dad was being targeted by a member of the Mob. Her Dad became extremely angry that his daughter would be exposed to danger. He never let her play with that friend again.

Mary Emily Porter Smith attended a private, all girls, school in Manhattan. Saint Agatha's was located on West End and 87th street. Upon graduation from Saint Agatha's in 1921, she studied to become a secretary (very few women in the 1920s attended college). After secretarial school she obtained a job working for the renowned newsman, Grantland Rice. During the time that Meps worked for Rice, he became the "Dean of American sports writers."

Meps's father died of kidney failure on June 6, 1923. His death hit the small family very hard. The loss of a loving husband and father was difficult. Anna Porter was 42 and Meps only 20 when George Porter died. Quite soon economic factors caused Meps and her mother to move to 155 East 54th Street. Anna remained a widow for the rest of her life. When the Great Depression hit, her New York Central Railroad stock declined by more than 90%.

The 1920s were often called "The Golden Age of Sports." Part of the reason was there were so many outstanding American athletes and coaches during those heady years after World War I. Babe Ruth, Lou Gehrig, Bobby Jones, Bill Tilden, Knute Rockne and Jack Dempsey to name just a few. Grantland Rice's towering prose and poetic gifts helped lift these sports figures to iconic status. Meps got to meet many of these athletes. She also met the members of the famous "Algonquin Round Table." This informal group of authors and reporters included Ring Lardner, Dorothy Parker, Robert Benchley, George Kaufmann, Alexander Woollcott, and, on occasion, Grantland Rice himself.

MY FATHER: PERRY McCOY SMITH, SR.

My father, Perry McCoy Smith, a native of Zanesville, Ohio, was born on 22 February, 1900. He was the son of attorney, Perry Smith, and Juliet Kane McCoy. As a young boy Perry spent his summers working on a farm near Zanesville. By the time he was fourteen, he was skilled as a driver of tractors, trucks and automobiles. Once he heard the grinding of gears outside his window. He looked out to observe his dad trying to get his new model T Ford started. Young Perry ran outside and gave his father a lesson in how to start and how to drive an automobile.

Perry Smith was born in 1864 in Zanesville. He was the last of thirteen children. He loved to tell stories from his youth. For instance, when chicken was served at dinner, he claimed that he always was given the neck. Not wishing to go into the family business, he went to college and became an attorney. He received his law degree from the University of Michigan. A kindly man, he was known for the pro bono work he did for folks who could not pay for his services. He had a shortened leg as a result of childhood polio. One of his shoes was highly elevated. He walked with a limp and used a cane to get around.

Perry Smith died at age 72 in 1946 leaving Juliet a widow. She was not in good financial shape and had to sell the family home on Ashland Avenue. For nineteen years her three children sent her monthly checks until her death at age 92. Her brother Will was a delight while her sister Helen was a bit of a grouch. In 1965, Helen and Juliet died three weeks apart in Zanesville, Ohio

When I attended my great aunt Helen's funeral, I visited my grandmother, Juliet, in a nursing home. At that time she was ninety two years old. As soon as I entered the room, she looked up and said. "I don't know who you are but you are handsome so give me a kiss." I may have been the last person to give her a kiss. Three weeks later she died.

My grandmother, Juliet "Gaga" Smith was a delightful, perky person. At age 83 in 1956 she would attend some of my lacrosse games at West Point. While sitting in the hard, wooden bleachers, she cheered for me and the Army team throughout these games. Her deep and loud voice could be heard by players and spectators alike.

Perry and Juliet Smith had three children. Perry (my father), Cornelia and Wilbur. They were nicely spaced five years apart. Cornelia married the Reverend Elwood Haines in 1933. Haines later became the Episcopal Bishop of Iowa. Bishop Haines died at age 56 of cancer. I remember him well. He came all the way from Iowa to Richmond, Virginia to confirm me as a member of the Episcopal Church. My family was headed to Italy so he confirmed me even though I was quite young (only 12 years old).

Cornelia and the Reverend Haines had one child, Juliet, who was born in 1935. Much later Cornelia married John Marshall. Both had been widowed. Cornelia Haines Marshall's two marriages were happy and rewarding ones. Incidentally, my first cousin, Juliet Mofford, a talented writer, has published eighteen books.

My father's brother Wilbur Smith married Jane Bailey in the late 1930s. They lived in southern California for many years. In the worst crash in aviation history in 1977, 583 people in two aircraft were killed when two aircraft collided in the Canary Islands. Both Wilbur and Jane died that day. The Wilbur Smith's had two children, Bailey and David. Both of my first cousins from the Wilbur Smith family live with their families in southern California.

Upon graduating from Lash High School in Zanesville in 1918, my father, Perry McCoy Smith, received an appointment to the United States Military Academy at West Point, New York. He entered West Point on 11 November, 1918, the day World War I ended. While he was a cadet, he had a chance to graduate early but he chose to stay for the full four years. His most famous classmate was Maxwell Taylor. Taylor had a brilliant military career. In the 1950s he became the Chief of Staff of the Army. In 1961, President Kennedy brought him back from retirement and made him Chairman of the Joint Chiefs of Staff.

Perry McCoy Smith graduated from West Point in 1922 and

decided to make the military his career. He chose as his branch, the Coast Artillery Corps. Since Perry was an accomplished horseman, it is unclear why he did not pick the Cavalry. However, protecting American ports was an important mission of the Army and duty at places like Panama, Hawaii and the Philippines was quite attractive.

Mary Emily Porter of the Pennsylvania Porters married First Lieutenant Perry McCoy Smith, of the Ohio Smiths in the Plaza Hotel in New York City in September, 1929, one month before the stock market crash. As the Great Depression deepened, Lieutenant Smith took a 15% pay cut. However, he was able to stay in the military - this meant a steady paycheck throughout the 1930s and beyond. During the 1920s and 1930s, promotions were slow. Perry was a lieutenant for eleven long years. By the time my sister and I were born, our dad was stationed at West Point, NY, the location of the United States Military Academy, where the cadets attend four years of college. While at the Military Academy in the 1930s, Captain Perry Smith served as an English professor and later as a tactics instructor.

Baby McCoy's First Adult Friend - Omar Bradley

At West Point in the mid-1930s, our family lived in a small home on a historic Army post. The house was located three blocks from the main campus. In those days, officers and their families lived on military posts, forts or bases. Their neighbors and friends were all military families. On December 16th, 1934, Perry McCoy Smith, Jr. arrived on a snowy day in the West Point hospital.

A certain nearby neighbor just loved babies. On his way home from work, this Army officer of the West Point class of 1915 would stop by and visit his littlest friend, "McCoy" Smith (for the first seventeen years of my life I was called McCoy, my middle name).

At that time, this neighbor, Omar Bradley, was an over-aged Army major who had a fair chance of being promoted to lieutenant colonel before he retired. Ten years later he was a four-star general in command of more than a million troops in active combat in Europe. When he was promoted again in 1950, he became the last of the American military leaders to be promoted to the five-star rank. Hence my very first adult friend became a famous American. I have no recollections at all of Major Bradley because, when I was just six months old, my Dad received a new assignment.

PANAMA, VIRGINIA, AND KANSAS

Our family left for Panama in the summer of 1935. This was my first move - to be followed by 39 more. Our family life in Panama was idyllic; war clouds had not yet appeared on the horizon. My dad's job was to protect the Panama Canal from enemy attack. During our two years in Panama we lived on both sides of the Isthmus. In each case we lived in military quarters on Army posts.

As a baby in Panama, I was underweight. A doctor gave the following advice: little McCoy should drink two ounces of beer each day. This formula worked as I slowly gained weight. I had my beer at noon each day; that led to a nice nap shortly thereafter. When our family left Panama in the summer of 1937, the officer's club threw a party for their smallest and most regular customer, two-and-a-half-year-old McCoy Smith.

In 1937, my dad's new posting was at Fort Monroe, Virginia - his job was to help protect and defend the vital Hampton Roads area of southeastern Virginia. Two years later, in 1939, Captain Perry Smith was most pleased when he received the news that he had been selected to attend the prestigious Army Command and General Staff College at Fort Leavenworth, Kansas. Graduating in the fateful year of 1940, Captain Smith took our small family to Hawaii. War had broken out both in Europe and in Asia by the time we sailed under the Golden Gate Bridge in June, 1940 and headed west. I was five and a half years old.

My mother's mother, Anna "Nan" Porter, had lost almost all of her money during the Great Depression. By the mid-1930s my Dad had worked on the paperwork to bring Nan officially into our family. Nan was designated an official military dependent. She was an integral part of the Perry McCoy Smith family from 1935 until she died in the late 1940s. Nan believed in reading books to children, so George Anne and I greatly benefitted from the loving care of "Nanny" Porter. Also, Nan Porter loved to party. She was the first person I observed in an inebriated state. She would not be the last.

My first recollection in life was the smooth ride on the Ocean Liner (the term "Cruise Ship" was not used in those days) from San Francisco to Honolulu in the summer of 1940. But my most vivid memory of that trip was the arrival of our ship at the port in Honolulu. From an upper deck of the ship we watched young Hawaiian boys dive for pennies thrown off the ship by the passengers. As a boy of five, I was amazed at how clear the water was and how deep these small boys would dive to grab the quickly descending pennies. On occasion, someone would toss a nickel or a dime in the water - to the great delight of the Hawaiian boys.

My formal education had begun back in Virginia quite early, when I was only three years old. When my older sister, George Anne, went off to kindergarten, I felt lonely, sad and desolate. After noticing my distress, my mother got permission from the school to let a three-year-old boy enter kindergarten. I had a second full year of kindergarten in Kansas. Having so much early schooling probably helped me do well as a student from elementary school through high school. By the time I was seventeen, I had attended eleven different schools throughout the Territory of Hawaii, the United States and Italy.

After settling down with my family in a small house in Honolulu in 1940, I entered the first grade at age five. We lived on Fort Ruger which was on the slopes of Diamond Head mountain. The open-air schools I attended were local schools so military kids and Hawaiian kids were my classmates.

Life in Hawaii in 1940 and 1941 was very special for everyone in our family. There were only three hotels on Waikiki Beach, so the broad beaches were never crowded. The biggest excitement came about once a month when an ocean liner would arrive from the mainland. On many occasions our whole family would go down to the dock to greet the arrival of the ship. On each ship there was at least one person whom our family had known on previous military assignments. The United States Army was small in those days and friendships were close.

Since there was no air conditioning in Hawaii in the early 1940s, the work schedule was arranged appropriately. Work for military and civilian workers started at 6 AM and most were able to return home by

1 PM. Folks would eat a late lunch and either go to the beach or take a nap. On the weekends, Sunday school would start promptly at 8 AM. This early start for Sunday school led to an important and dramatic moment in the lives of my sister and me.

Our family lived in three separate homes on the island of Oahu from the summer of 1940 until February, 1942. The first house was on Fort Ruger, the second house was on an Army base (Fort Kamehameha) and the third house was back in Honolulu - but this time within the civilian community. As my father received each new assignment, it was required that we move. In those days, we had very few household goods (most of the furniture was provided by the government) so family moves were easy. In the summer months, kids mostly were barefooted, although shoes were required at school and on Sunday mornings.

In the first and second grades, I was the smallest and youngest child in my class. The biggest kids were those with Polynesian blood. Most were good-natured and not bullies. However, if a large boy wanted to get his way with a smaller kid, he would just state, "I am going to sit on you." To avoid being sat upon, I was always careful to be nice to my huge classmates.

CIGARETTE SMOKING AT AGE FIVE

The first time my sister and I got into real trouble we were very young. Our good friend and neighbor, David Potts, was 8, George Anne Smith was 7 and I was 5. David found a package of matches and a package of cigarettes. We climbed to the attic of David's house and our adventure began. David brought along a baby's silver cup and filled it halfway with water.

After taking a puff or two, David took his cigarette and jammed it into the cup. My sister, George Anne, followed his lead, took a couple of puffs, and into the cup went her cigarette. Now it was my turn. I was a shy, unadventurous five year old. I had no interest in their little game. However, I was shamed into giving it a try. I took one puff, coughed and placed a perfectly good cigarette into the cup. I did not smoke another cigarette. This exercise continued with George Anne and David until twenty cigarettes filled the cup. We left the attic feeling good - we had done something that we knew was wrong and had

managed to avoid getting caught - or so we thought.

However, David Potts made a major mistake. He left the cup full of soggy cigarettes in the attic.

A few weeks after our smoking adventure, our parents called a family meeting. It did not go well. George Anne and I were read the riot act for doing something that was dumb and dangerous. My sister took the heat for smoking and for encouraging me to join in. I had three advantages. I was very young, not at all adventurous and was led astray by David and George Anne. My parents were gentle in their criticism of me.

This is a good example of a bad mistake leading to a good result. That cigarette which I smoked in 1940 was the only one I smoked for the rest of my life. Sadly, my sister did not learn a lesson in 1940. She took up smoking when she was in high school. Like my dad, she became a lifelong chain smoker. She died at age 53 while my dad died at age 55. My wife, Connor, smoked moderately for a while but gave smoking up completely in 1962 when she was pregnant with our son McCoy. Happily, none of our kids or grandkids ever smoked.

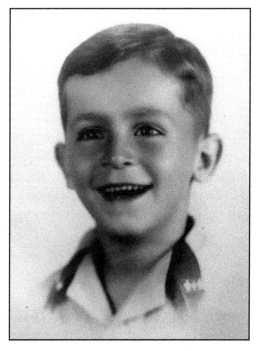

Although George Anne and I were very young, we learned an important lesson in 1940. Telling the truth had a big payoff. Our parents forgave us for our mistakes since we told the whole truth and did not try to deny any of our activities. They realized that this was an important learning opportunity for the whole family.

McCoy Smith in Hawaii at age 6, 1941.

When we were stationed at Fort Kamehameha my dad was a battery commander of a coast artillery unit that had a number of large, sixteen-inch guns. The mission of the gun battery was to protect Pearl Harbor from attack from the sea by enemy battleships, cruisers, destroyers and other combatant ships. I remember going out to watch the firing of these big guns. I would put my fingers in my ears and, when a gun fired, I could watch the large projectile race out toward the target. The targets were barges towed by a ship (usually a destroyer). If you had binoculars you could see the splash even though the target was fifteen miles offshore.

There was a major problem with this mission of coastal defense. These large guns did not have the range to reach aircraft carriers which might operate one hundred miles or more offshore. Hence there was a need for anti-aircraft guns which could shoot down enemy airplanes. The Coast Artillery Corps had a secondary mission of anti-aircraft artillery; my father was qualified in both missions.

As the weekend of 6-7 December, 1941 arrived, most people in Hawaii were unprepared for how much our lives would soon change. Within a period of six months, I would witness an air attack, be evacuated on a ship with 2000 people on board, be stranded in San Francisco with no permanent place to live, move to cold, snowy Saint Cloud, Minnesota, make my first public speech and lead my entire school in the pledge of allegiance.

It is often stated by historians and journalists that the day of the attack on Pearl Harbor was the most important single day for America in the 20th Century. It certainly was an important day for me. Please remember - I was 9 days short of my seventh birthday. I was quite young, but my memories of that day remain vivid.

Pearl Harbor: A Crazy Trip to Sunday School and Back

The morning of 7 December, 1941 started out as just another Sunday morning for our family. We lived in a small rented home in Honolulu. My dad and mother loved to party on Saturday nights so the routine for Sunday morning was as follows. My eight-year-old sister, George Anne, and I were served breakfast by our mother.

Then we went out to our front yard and were picked up by an Army truck about 7:00 AM. My folks would go back to bed as soon as the truck left.

We were always some of the first kids to be picked up. The truck would pick up other kids from military families along the way to the chapel at Fort DeRussy. The trip was timed so we would arrive at the fort in time for our 8 AM Sunday School class. Since I had a problem with motion sickness, I was allowed to sit in the back of the truck so I could look outside. This kept me from becoming "truck sick."

On that fateful December day, the routine described above ended abruptly at about 7:55 AM. As the truck, by this time full of kids, pulled up to the main gate at Fort DeRussy something very unusual happened. Instead of being waived through by the military policeman at the front gate, the truck was stopped. I remember leaning out of the truck to try to find out why we had stopped short of the chapel.

What I saw was an Army captain in a fatigue uniform. He was wearing a World War I type helmet and had a pistol in a holster at his waist. He was very animated and was shouting at our driver. Soon thereafter, the truck turned around and it sped off back into the city of Honolulu. It became clear that the driver was dropping the kids off at their homes. No one told those of us in the back what was going on but some of the older kids figured it out.

Being in an Army truck during the first wave of the Japanese air attack was not the best place to be. Luckily, no Japanese fighter or bomber saw us as a target of opportunity, so no bombs or bullets came our way. As the truck sped through the narrow streets, I was frightened and crying. My sister remained calm. She tried to comfort me. She helped me hang on to the bench in the truck so we would not be tossed out the back. It was a wild and scary ride. I saw plumes of smoke and a few airplanes, but the only noise I remember was the noise of the truck's engine as the driver drove at a very fast rate.

When we reached our home, my mother was out in the front yard. She was delighted to see us. She gave us each a big hug before she led us down to the basement of our small home. I did not understand why I was being hugged. I had not made it to Sunday school, and I had no stories to tell her. Also, we were Yankees; we were not a hugging family. Up to that time, I had not had a hug from my mother in a number of years.

Leadership Lessons from the Pearl Harbor Attack

When I became an adult, I studied the attack on Pearl Harbor with the idea of drawing some lessons from an event that shaped my life in so many ways. When I conduct workshops on executive leadership, I make the following points. From the Japanese perspective, the attack was a success at the <u>tactical</u> level, only a modest success at the <u>operational</u> level and a major failure at the <u>strategic</u> level. Tactically, everything went well for the Japanese.

The Americans were caught by surprise. Dozens of ships and hundreds of aircraft were destroyed or badly damaged. The Japanese lost no capital ships. They sailed home in triumph.

At the operational level, the attack was less successful. No American aircraft carriers were struck (all of the American aircraft carriers were out at sea). The oil supplies were not targeted nor were the American dry dock facilities.

At the strategic level, the attack was a colossal failure. The Americans got very angry, became unified in a common cause, and created what Roosevelt would call the "Arsenal of Democracy." In less than four years three fascist nations were defeated, including the Japanese Empire.

As I emphasize in my leadership workshops, decisions which do not take into account the medium and long-term goals often fail. The most successful leaders are those who maintain a strategic perspective. Two great questions to ask during the decision-making process are, "What are the long-term implications?" and "How does this decision fit within our strategic plan?"

On that fatal day so many years ago, my dad sped off to work. We did not see him for about three days. The big concern throughout the Hawaiian Islands was whether the Japanese were going to follow up their air attack with a ground invasion. There was also some concern that Japanese parachutists might support the invasion.

School was cancelled for the rest of 1941. Everyone wanted to contribute to the war effort. My project was helping our next-door neighbor dig a bomb shelter. I was six years old so my shovel was small and my contributions to the digging were minuscule. Nine days after the Japanese attack I celebrated my seventh birthday. I remember nothing about that day except the fact that I received one gift (it was a combined birthday and Christmas gift). Like most families, we had been a frugal family throughout the Great Depression.

My mother was convinced that the Japanese would not invade the islands and she wanted to stay in Hawaii. Having been an executive secretary prior to her marriage, she quickly obtained a job as a secretary to an admiral. While she was at work, our grandmother, "Nanny" took care of George Anne and me. My mother and my dad (by now an Army major) tried to convince authorities that she was an essential person and should not be evacuated. Their pleas failed.

There were a number of reasons why the military dependents were required to leave Hawaii and return to the mainland. First, if the Japanese invaded and captured the Hawaiian Islands, the military dependents would be in grave danger. Second, there was soon to be a major surge of American troops from the mainland into Hawaii and there would be a need for housing for these troops from all of the military services. Third, military troops remaining on the island would be working long hours, seven days a week and having to worry about their families would be an extra burden. Finally, food and other supplies that had to be imported from the mainland needed to be reserved for the troops, the native Hawaiians and other civilians (including many Japanese Americans).

EVACUATION: WHEN LIFE WAS RATIONED - FEBRUARY, 1942

In late February, 1942, my mother, grandmother, sister and I climbed aboard an ocean liner, the SS Lurline. The ship was a grand luxury liner which was commissioned in 1932. It was the top liner in the Pacific throughout the 1930s. On 7 December, 1941, it was underway on a voyage from Honolulu to California. Upon learning of the attack, the Lurline proceeded at top speed to San Francisco to drop off her passengers so she could rush back to Hawaii. The SS Lurline was designed to carry 715 passengers. As you will see, that was a problem as two thousand women and children climbed up the gangplanks.

Ahead of us was a trip across the North Pacific from Pearl Harbor to San Francisco. There were enough life preservers for everyone, but not enough lifeboats on the ship for 2000 passengers. Hence, my grandmother, who was in her sixties, was not assigned a seat on a lifeboat. She was issued a life preserver. If we had been sunk by a Japanese submarine, she would have gone down with the ship. In the cold water of the North Pacific, she would have perished quickly.

As I recall the rules, no one over the age of forty was assigned a seat on a lifeboat. The policy was clear - older people did not count as much as children and young adults. At age seven I learned about the rationing of life.

The lesson was not clear to me at the time. However when I reached adulthood I realized that there are some situations where there are no good answers, yet decisions need to be made. For instance, a combat medic who is dealing with many wounded soldiers sometimes has to leave someone who is unlikely to survive in order to treat others who, if given rapid treatment, have a better chance of survival.

The voyage on board the SS Lurline was an arduous one as we "zig zagged" our way through the rough seas of the North Pacific. These evasive maneuvers were designed to reduce the chances of a successful submarine attack. I was seasick throughout the twelve-day voyage and spent the entire time in our stateroom. The stateroom was designed to accommodate four people. Since fourteen were assigned, we slept in shifts. Some of the adults and older children slept on the floor. On this memorable trip, the SS Lurline was escorted by destroyers for most of the way.

BACK ON THE MAINLAND - WHERE DO WE LIVE?

When we finally sailed into San Francisco Harbor, most of the passengers assembled on deck. As we passed under the Golden Gate Bridge, patriotic music was played on the ship's loudspeaker system. I remember looking up and noticing that most of the adults (almost all were women) were crying. At age seven I did not understand that there could be tears of joy - I thought people cried only when they were sad or in pain.

We had friends in San Francisco who greeted us. They arranged for an apartment for us to stay in until my mother could decide where we might settle down until my father was reassigned back to the mainland. We had always accompanied my dad in his previous assignments. Now we needed a low cost place to live until we could be together again. We had no idea how long it would be before Major Perry Smith could return to the mainland.

Because San Francisco was an expensive city we could not afford to stay there for an extended period of time. My father's aunt, Helen Storer, was contacted by telephone at her home in Saint Cloud, Minnesota. Helen McCoy Storer was the younger sister of my father's mother, Juliette McCoy Smith.

Richard and Helen Storer lived in a large home in a nice part of town. They were in their 60s, had no children of their own and had plenty of room for us. Mr. Storer was in the granite business and was quite wealthy. In fact, he was the only member of our family who came out of the Great Depression in good financial shape. The Storers agreed to take care of us until my father returned from Hawaii.

St. Cloud, Minnesota is Different from Hawaii

In late March, 1942, my mother, grandmother, sister and I travelled by train from San Francisco to Chicago. We changed trains and continued on to Minneapolis. On the train trip to Chicago, my sister, who was always quite adventurous, jumped off the train in Denver to make some snowballs. After almost two years in Hawaii, snow and snowballs were really fascinating to small kids. When the train started to move, my mother jumped off the train, grabbed my sister and leaped back onto the train.

On many occasions George Anne was in trouble - while her quiet, shy little brother avoided trouble and seldom needed discipline. In any case, my sister's off-the-train adventure provided an exciting moment in a long, rather boring, train ride. My only other recollection of the train trip was playing cards with a sailor. He was patient and taught me a number of card games.

In Minneapolis, we were met by Richard Storer at the train station; he drove us to Saint Cloud in his big, and very impressive, Buick car.

It was late March, 1942. The weather was still cold and snowy. A few days later my sister and I entered elementary school in Saint Cloud. We instantaneously became mini celebrities having witnessed the Pearl Harbor attack. This led to two activities in which I did not want to participate.

Just before a Memorial Day event in May of 1942, I was asked to lead my elementary school in the pledge of allegiance. Please remember, I was seven years old and in the second grade. The entire student body was assembled outside the school. My directions were clear - go out in front of the kids, turn toward the flag and yell out the first few words of the pledge of allegiance. I was told that everyone would join in soon after I started. However, I made a big mistake. I walked out in front of the assembled group, turned around and there was no flag to be seen. I had walked to the wrong end of the group. I then made the long walk to the other end while many of the kids giggled at my goof.

My First Public Speech at Age Seven, 1942

That same spring (1942) gave me another unwanted challenge. My second-grade teacher asked me to tell the class my Pearl Harbor story. I had never given a speech before and I really did not want to do it. My mother helped me decide what to tell and how to tell it. I practiced a few times. My talk was rather short but then the next challenge popped up. The teacher started asking me questions. Why weren't we ready? Was it a failure of intelligence? Was it a failure of leadership? Was Roosevelt at fault? I did not know how to answer these questions. However, I think I stated that I thought the attack on Pearl Harbor was the fault of the Japs (in 1942, I cannot recall anyone using the word Japanese).

The transition from barefoot Hawaii to cold and snowy Saint Cloud in the spring of 1942 was memorable and quite exciting. But within three months we were off to Wilmington, North Carolina. My dad had been reassigned from Hawaii to Camp Davis which was just to the north of Wilmington. He got the job he really wanted - the command of an Anti-Aircraft-Artillery Group. By now he was a full colonel and his job was to train the group and prepare it for deployment to Europe. We arrived in Wilmington in the late summer of 1942.

Finding a house to rent in the Wilmington area was a challenge. With the large flow of troops and their families into the area, there were very few houses available for rent. Happily, the mayor of Wilmington, Bruce B. Cameron, came up with a creative idea. He had two homes, one in downtown Wilmington and the other on Wrightsville Beach. He rented his summer home to us in the wintertime and his winter home to us in the summertime.

The house on the beach was heated by potbelly stoves. The bedrooms were cold, but the rest of the house was quite toasty. I attended the entire 3rd grade in Wilmington; once again, I was the youngest in my class.

The summer of 1943 rolled around and we were off to Richmond, Virginia. To the great disappointment of my dad, he received orders to go to the Anti-Aircraft-Artillery Headquarters to become the operations officer for this large military organization The Anti-Aircraft-Artillery Group which he had trained for a year sailed to Europe in the summer of 1943 with a new commander, a very sad day for my father.

Our family rented a home in a delightful suburb of Richmond. For three years, my sister and I attended the same school, Westhampton Elementary School on Patterson Avenue. Our home was near the corner of Patterson Avenue and Three Chopt Road (6903 Emondstone Avenue). Just beyond Three Chopt Road there was nothing but trees. My sister and I rode to school each morning on our bicycles, a distance of about a mile.

During our years in Richmond, everyone was involved in supporting the war effort. On Saturday mornings, kids walked around neighborhoods and collected newspapers and tin foil. We also had a small "victory garden" where we grew vegetables. Gasoline and meat were rationed and many other items were in short supply.

WAR RATIONING: THE RACE FOR FIVE BANANAS

On Thursday mornings the whole family would get up early, go to the local grocery store and enter just as it opened (I think it was 7 AM). My job was to run to the banana area and grab five bananas (we were allowed one banana per person in the family). If I did not move fast, all the bananas would be gone and there would be no chance to get more for another week. In short, there was both formal and informal rationing. Bananas (one per family member) fit into the informal category.

Gasoline was rationed during the war. We received an allocation of three gallons per week. Our family had one car and my dad went to work in a carpool. Almost everywhere we went my sister and I travelled via bicycle.

I was bullied quite badly my first day of school in the fourth grade. The playground behind the school was not supervised during recess periods. I faced my first experience in dealing with an older and bigger boy who loved to be mean to little kids. This boy came up to me and poked me in the chest. He said, "Where are you from, kid?" I told him I did not know. He insisted that I give him a place. My dad was from Ohio, so I said that I thought I was from Ohio.

The bully then said, "Does that mean you are a Yankee?" When I said, " I guess so," the bully pushed me hard in the chest. In the meantime, another kid had knelt down directly behind me. I flipped over backward and landed on my head, to the delight of the bully and his friends. I learned in the 4th grade in Richmond, Virginia in September, 1943, how to identify and avoid bullies. For my entire life, I have had a low tolerance for bullying.

In 1944, when I was nine years old, my father received an assignment that would take him to Italy for six months. Dad sat me down and, in a very serious voice, told me, "McCoy, you are the man of the house and I expect you to take care of your sister, mother and grandmother while I am away in the combat theater."

He reminded me of all the family duties that he was responsible for and emphasized that these duties were now mine. Some examples follow: At 6 AM every morning I had to go down to the cold, dark basement to shovel a certain amount of coal into the base of the furnace. I was also required to check the furnace at least three times each day. Just before bedtime, I had to tamp the fire down and prepare the furnace so it would continue to provide heat for the entire night.

Another chore was mowing the grass with a hand mower. Since our home in Richmond had a large and hilly lawn, this was a tough job for a skinny nine-year-old. I would mow the lawn in sections. About the time I finished the last section, it was time to start again. Soon after my father left for Italy in the fall of 1944, I realized that I had to become an adult. Shortly after he left, I celebrated my tenth birthday.

During my third year in Richmond (1945-1946), I was in the sixth grade and doing quite well. I even had a girlfriend, although I was so shy that I never told her how much she meant to me. I was a serious student and I had a wonderful homeroom teacher, Mrs. Fields. On my first report card, I received straight As. Even though I was a good student, this had never happened to me before.

Very few students received straight As. I was mighty proud as were my parents and my grandmother. Some of my school chums were given a dime for every A on their report card. I suggested to my mother that this was a really good idea. She strongly disagreed and told me that our family expected good grades and would not pay for As.

Shortly thereafter I made what seemed like a wild proposal. I said, "Mom, if I get straight As in all six of my report cards will you give me $5?" Assuming that this was highly unlikely, she reluctantly agreed. A few days later I approached Mrs. Fields and told her of the arrangement. In very firm terms, she told me that my penmanship was not very good and that if I were to get straight As, I had to work hard to improve in this area. Long story short, I got straight As for the entire year and received the $5, a large sum in 1946. In 2021 dollars this would be about $100.

THE MOVE TO ITALY, 1946

By the spring of 1946, World War II was over, and my dad received a permanent assignment to Italy. His was an important job. He was to be the operations officer (G-3) for the military government of Italy. Although Italy had become an ally towards the end of World War II, the British and Americans formed a military government until such time as a peace agreement with Italy could be finalized. The Soviets were a problem over the issue of Trieste. The issue was clear: would this important port city on the Adriatic Sea be part of Italy or part of the communist controlled nation of Yugoslavia?

Our family sailed for Naples in June, 1946. "See Naples and die" (*Vedi Napoli e poi muori*) is an Italian saying of unknown origin and authorship. The idea of the proverb is that after one has seen the port city of Naples there is nothing else worth seeing, comparatively speaking.

Naples occupies one of the most beautiful sites in Europe and has been a favorite with tourists for centuries. It is known for the bright sunshine, the deep blue waters of the Tyrrhenian Sea, the Bay of Naples, the Isle of Capri, and the panoramic beauty of the city itself on the north shore of the bay. Added to this was Mount Vesuvius, four thousand feet high and forty miles in the distance, smoking by day and glowing by night. All of this has long been famous in song and story.

After receiving a warm welcome, we were driven through the rubble of that city to our new home on the grounds of the Royal Palace of Caserta. The British and US governments had requisitioned the palace as well as its extensive gardens and grounds.

Located twenty miles north of Naples, Caserta had been the capital of the Kingdom of Two Sicily's (1815-1860). Our home was not fancy. It was a metal Quonset hut with a couple of pot-belly stoves strategically placed to keep everyone reasonably warm. It had a living room, one bathroom and three bedrooms. There was an electric hot plate in the living room but no kitchen. The winter of 1946-1947 was the coldest in southern Europe in decades. The impact on the Italians was severe. There was heavy snow in southern Italy and many of the ponds were frozen. Since there was no kitchen in our house, we ate our meals at an officer's club which was a few blocks from our home. Two important events occurred in my life at Caserta.

RUNNING AWAY FROM A FOOD RIOT

My mother, my sister and I were shopping in a large open arcade in Naples in October, 1946. My dad's driver, an Army sergeant, was also with us. On both sides of the arcade were rows of small shops. We were inside a shop when we heard a series of very loud thuds that shook the ground under our feet. We ran out into the arcade and what we saw was frightening.

A few hundred yards away a mass of men was running towards us. Each thud that we heard was the sound of a shopkeeper pulling down a steel door that would protect his store from looters. What we were witnessing was a major food riot. We ran to our car. As we drove away, I looked out the back and observed that the rioters were tipping over streetcars. At age 11, I could not understand why hungry men would want to tip over streetcars.

A few weeks later I had a chance to observe a remarkable musical production. Our family attended a performance of La Boheme at the San Marco opera house in Naples. Playing Rodolfo was Beniamino Gigli. Gigli had been a fascist and was soon to be thrown out of Italy. This was to be his last performance on Italian soil. After the performance, members of the large audience would shout out an aria and Gigli would sing it without notes. For more than an hour the audience stood in awe as the greatest tenor since Caruso, sang at least a dozen arias. The applause after each solo was deafening. My mother explained to me later that we had just witnessed something very special.

Back at Caserta an incident almost cost my sister and me our lives. In the dead of winter of 1946-1947 George Anne and I were walking back to our house from dinner at the officer's club. We had to cross over a fast running stream. I had come up with the idea of making paper airplanes, lighting their noses on fire and sailing them over the stream. It worked quite well until we ran out of paper. We decided to try to retrieve some of the planes that were floating down the stream. This turned out to be a very bad idea.

When George Anne reached down to grab a plane, she slipped on the mossy bank and, SPLASH, into the water she went. As I reached down to try to rescue her, I slipped and fell into the water beside her. The banks of the stream were covered with cold, wet moss and were very slippery. The water was so cold that there was ice on the edge of the stream. We had a really hard time pulling ourselves to safety. Fortunately, George Anne managed to climb out. She then helped me out and we ran back to our house and stripped out of our cold, wet clothes.

The big decision we had to make was whether to tell our parents about our stupidity. After some debate we decided to fess up and tell them the whole story. My dad, mom and grandmother were wonderful. They praised us for telling the truth, asked us if we learned a lesson, and let the issue drop.

During the eight months we lived in Caserta, George Anne and I attended a very small elementary school. From grades 1 through 8 there were about twenty-five American kids. All the kids were white. Integration of the military by President Harry Truman was still a year away. I was eleven years old and in the seventh grade. There were only two seventh graders: the very pretty, Gail Jayne, and me. My homeroom teacher had to cover a number of subjects, but her expertise was as a math teacher. She kept feeding me books to read and exercises to accomplish. In eight months, I worked my way through seventh and eighth grade math and halfway through ninth grade algebra. There was nothing to slow me down. This turned out to be a hugely important period in my academic life - I will explain later.

During the months from the summer of 1946 to the spring of 1947 our family took many trips. Whenever we travelled in Italy, we always stayed in hotels which were outstanding - the very best hotels in the great cities of Italy. For instance, the Excelsior Hotel in Rome and the Royal Danieli Hotel in Venice. The reason we could do this was because the British and American military had requisitioned a number of five-star hotels which had not been destroyed during the war.

When we went shopping, which we did often, the currency of choice was a carton of cigarettes. As I recall Chesterfields were the most coveted. Although my dad smoked heavily (this would lead to his premature death at age 55) my mother and grandmother did not. Each adult could buy a specific number of cartons (almost everything was rationed).

In any case, there seemed to be plenty of cartons available for our shopping trips. I remember my mother purchasing, in Florence, a complete silver service for the price of three cartons of cigarettes. This sliver service included a large silver tray, a silver pitcher, a silver bowl, and some large silver serving spoons and forks. Its value today would be at least $2000.

On a trip to Athens, Greece in August, 1946, I had my first lesson in economics - watching how people dealt with the problem of runaway inflation. At the time, there was a civil war going on, with most of the fighting taking place in northern Greece. The economy was in shambles and the government was printing money at a great rate. During the airplane flight from Italy to Athens, we bought, using American dollars, a number of small gold coins. I had never seen a gold coin before, and I was fascinated by how small they were, quite a bit smaller than a dime.

Soon after we arrived at the Hotel Grande Bretagne in downtown Athens, we found ourselves out on the street exchanging our gold coins for drachmas, the Greek currency at that time. For an American dollar we received 17,000 drachmas. If we traded in a gold coin, we received a much better rate - 35,000 drachma per dollar. Of course, we chose the gold coin route. When we departed Athens three days later, we traded our leftover Drachmas for American dollars. Hence, the whole trip cost us very little. I should point out in times of great economic uncertainty gold coins were coveted more than any paper currency.

Because of the inability of a bankrupt Britain to do much to help Greece, America came forward in 1947 with an economic rescue package which was labeled the Truman Doctrine (Turkey was also helped). This was the forerunner of the Marshall Plan. One part of the trip to Greece was very unpleasant, my parents required us to eat Greek food. While the other kids on the trip ate hamburgers, we had to eat sour meat wrapped in grape leaves - uggh.

After eight months living in Caserta, Italy, it was time to move again. By the spring of 1947, the military government of Italy moved north to the city of Leghorn on the west coast of Italy. Most of the families moved to the resort town of Viareggio, which was an hour's drive north of the port city of Leghorn. There was no school to attend in Viareggio, so kids spent much of the time on the beach from May, 1947 until we left Italy for good in October, 1947.

In March, 1947, while our family was visiting Venice, my Dad received permission for me to observe the trial of German Field Marshal Kesselring. Kesselring had been the commander of all German troops in Italy. He was being tried for war crimes, specifically for the murder of Italian partisans by German SS troops. Kesselring's attorney was making the case that certain SS units were not under Kesselring's command and he had no knowledge or control of their activities. Although we stayed at the trial for only an hour or two, I remember the solemn nature of the proceedings and the skill of the attorneys on both sides.

May 1st, 1947 was a memorable day for my entire family. We were visiting Milan and staying at a luxury hotel near the center of the city. Our rooms were on an upper level, around the 6th or 7th floor. At this time in history, the Communist party was very strong in Italy and the mayors of most of the cities in northern Italy were members of the Italian Communist Party.

During the late 1940s, May 1st was a very important day for socialists and communists. Labeled "May Day," it was the day that workers celebrated their labor as the engine of modern society. A huge, all-day demonstration took place in Milan that day. Our family got a close-up look at the joy and excitement in the crowd. Our hotel was guarded by a number of well-armed American soldiers. In the hallways near the windows there were large piles of sandbags and the troops had zeroed in their machine guns in case the mob attacked our hotel.

The demonstrations were peaceful, but I will never forget the noise of the singing and chanting. In retrospect, this was probably the high point of the Communist movement in Italy. When the Marshall Plan kicked in and the economies of Italy and France began to revive, the attraction of communism slowly diminished. It has been said that the Marshall plan saved Western Europe from communism. I would agree with that assessment. In fairness, it should be pointed out that the leader of the Italian communists, Palmiro Togliatti, was willing to operate within a democratic process.

In mid-May, 1947, at age 12, I experienced terrible stomach pains, which turned out to be appendicitis. My problem was misdiagnosed for a number of days and my appendix ruptured. In previous years this would have meant certain death. However, the new miracle drug, penicillin, which was not available for widespread use until 1945, saved my life.

I spent two weeks in an American military hospital in Leghorn. Every three hours for the entire two weeks I received a very painful penicillin shot in my bottom. For those two weeks there was an open wound in my lower abdomen. Out of that wound was a drain which allowed the poison to drain out. To this day, I have a scar which my kids and grandkids have called my "second belly button." Throughout those two weeks, my mother stayed by my side to give me support and comfort.

In the summer of 1947, the family took an idyllic train trip through Switzerland. We stopped in Lugano, Zurich, Bern and Geneva. We binged, drinking milk, eating ice cream, munching on salads, and pouring milk in our cereal. This was very special since none of these delicacies had been available to us in Italy for over a year. We all fell in love with the Swiss people and wonderfully clean, well-ordered Switzerland on that marvelous ten-day trip.

We lived in northern Italy from April, 1947 until October, 1947. In the resort town of Viareggio, the Army had requisitioned the most historic and elegant hotel in the town. Only two blocks from the beach, the Principe di Piemonte Hotel gave us the very best service. Our family lived in a suite of rooms on an upper floor. We took all of our meals in the hotel restaurant. In my more than eighty years on this planet, only twice did I live the life of great luxury: the six months in Viareggio and, many years later, when I served as an enrichment speaker on twenty voyages on Crystal Cruises. (more about that later).

Colonel Perry Smith, McCoy (age 12), Lieutenant General John C H Lee, George Anne (age 14), 1947.

Our Family Returns to the
United States - October, 1947

As the autumn of 1947 approached, it was time to pack up for our return to the States. I was approaching my thirteenth birthday by this time. I had moved twelve times and many more moves were to come. The trip home was memorable. International airline travel was not yet the norm so we travelled on an Army troop ship. We ran into a North Atlantic hurricane and our round bottomed ship rolled so much that at times you had to brace yourself in bed to avoid being tossed out. Like my trip from Hawaii five years earlier, I was seasick most of the way. How pleased I was to sail into calm New York harbor in late October, 1947.

Those who immigrate to America are inspired by the Statue of Liberty and its wonderfully welcoming message. Having been out of the country for sixteen months our family was uplifted when we viewed Lady Liberty from the port side of our ship. Like our arrival in San Francisco in February, 1942, this was an emotional moment for each of our family members and most of our fellow passengers.

My Dad had received an assignment to the Pentagon, so we moved to Washington, D.C. I was about to have my second lesson in economics. My parents found a wonderful house on Cleveland Avenue in the northwest part of the city. Our home was less than a block from the grounds of the National Cathedral and in the winter there was fine sledding on the Cathedral grounds. The school district was the best in the District of Columbia.

The house cost $23,000 but there was a problem. My family did not have enough money to pay the down payment. My Dad's father had passed away in June, 1946 and throughout the late 1940s, he was supporting his mother as well as his mother-in-law. None of them had social security and none was employed. To help find enough money for the down payment on the house my Dad asked me how much money I had saved.

I had been a frugal boy and, although my allowance was small, I had saved up $400 (in today's terms that would be about $5000). My dad asked me to give it all to him with the promise that when we left Washington and the house was sold I would get my four hundred dollars back with interest added on. I was fourteen years old at the time.

When we left DC in the summer of 1949, there was a slump in the housing market. Dad sold the house at a loss, so he was not able to pay me back. I don't remember being upset or mad about it - the economics were explained to me and I understood. Somehow it felt OK. I had helped the family in a time of need.

For the eighteen months we lived in Washington, I attended Alice Deal Junior High School. Students were in the 6th, 7th and 8th grades. Segregation in the District of Columbia meant that there were no black students in any of my classes. My sister attended Woodrow Wilson High School. In the 1940s, these schools were ranked as the best public schools in the District of Columbia.

We would walk the five blocks from our home to the trolley stop on Wisconsin Avenue. The special student tickets cost three cents each. We would get off the trolley at the Nebraska Avenue stop and walk to our schools. I graduated from Alice Deal in the spring of 1949. I had done well academically, especially in math. I was small for my age, a quiet fellow and one of the youngest in my class. I would not become an outgoing person until my junior year at West Point.

MY SECOND STOP AT WEST POINT

In the summer of 1949, we were off to West Point, New York, where my dad was to serve on the staff of the Superintendent of the United States Military Academy for the next four years. He and my mother were delighted with the assignment. We lived on the grounds of the academy in Quarters 66. This brick home was located near the West Point football stadium and beautiful Lusk Reservoir. Directly across from our home were two red clay tennis courts. My love for tennis, which has lasted a lifetime, started in the summer of 1949. I was fourteen years old.

On many mornings in the summer months I played tennis with Mrs. Heiberg. She was a colonel's wife who was in her mid-40s. As a young person she had played at Forest Hills, New York, in the US Open championships. She had great tennis skills and I never came close to defeating her. I think she enjoyed playing with me because I was very energetic and chased down most of the balls she sent my way.

In the fall of 1949, I entered the tenth grade at Highland Falls High School. There were fifty-five girls and boys in our class. About a dozen of our class members were highly motivated, studied hard and hoped to go to college.

In the spring of my senior year, our math teacher would drive a few of us down to New York City on a Saturday morning. At New York University we would take examinations in math and science. If we scored well, our small high school would get an "excellence" grant from the State of New York.

The brightest kids in New York State would represent their high schools. This turned out to be a lesson in humility for me. Although our school earned a small grant, my score put me well below the average. I never made it into the top one thousand. When we analyzed the results, we saw that kids from the elite schools in New York City were head and shoulders above all of us. However, high school classmates Mike Esposito and Sam Gates did better than I did. A few years later they both graduated higher than me in the West Point class of 1956.

During one month each summer of my high school years at West Point, I was a camp counselor at Round Pond Boys Camp. My pay was $50 for the month of work. The camp, which was on the West Point reservation, welcomed kids whose families had a West Point connection. At age 15 in 1950, I was the youngest counselor, so I got the youngest boys to supervise. The campers would stay for a full month, live in tents and learn skills such as canoeing, swimming, riflery, and hiking. Their parents, all of whom lived on the West Point post or in one of the nearby towns, could visit the campers once a week.

This was my first leadership opportunity. I would have many more. With twelve seven-year-old kids to supervise, I had quite a challenge. Some were wise guys; others were painfully shy; still others cried at night because they missed their mothers so much. In the evenings when the campers were in bed, my fellow camp counselors and I would play various games. Canoeing on a moonless night was great fun. With two of us in each canoe we would try to ram other canoes. The rules were clear. Just before the crash, the aggressor canoe would shout out DING DING.

We got in trouble on one occasion. One of the older camp counselors had a car. He would sneak off and bring back a few bottles of beer. Ballantine was the beer of choice - at age 15 drinking beer in a canoe at night was quite exciting. Long story short - we got caught. The beer drinking stopped the next day.

Little Vince Lombardi's Big Goof

One of my small campers was Vince Lombardi, Jr. He was much like his dad: chunky and full of life. He was being raised in a very strict Catholic family. Young Vince enjoyed the relative freedom of the camp. He was very popular with his fellow campers. The name Vince Lombardi had not yet become well known throughout America. He was an assistant coach to Red Blaik, the famous Army football coach. Coach Lombardi left West Point to join the coaching staff of the New York Football Giants in 1953. He then moved on to become the head coach of the Green Bay Packers. Vince Lombardi soon gained the reputation as the best football coach in America. In his honor, the Lombardi Trophy is presented each year to the winner of the Super Bowl. However, back in the early 1950s, he was known as an assistant coach who was highly skilled at motivating young athletes.

Seven-year-old Vince Jr. picked up some profanity at camp. On the morning that his dad was scheduled to pick him up, I heard little Vince say, "shit." I pulled him aside and told him, in very strong terms, that he should never use that word around his dad. He looked up at me and broke out in tears. My guess is - he followed my advice.

The man in charge of the Round Pound Boys Camp was a large, impressive Army lieutenant colonel named Jerry Sage. His nickname was "Silent Death Sage." During World War II, he was assigned to the OSS. He spent much of the war behind enemy lines in Europe. He was captured and spent some time in Stalag Luft III. He escaped from captivity on more than one occasion. His book, *Sage*, is still available on amazon.com. He was a humble man. All of us at the boys camp were in awe of him. In the movie, *The Great Escape*, Steve McQueen played his role. This was the first time I had the opportunity to spend some time with a military hero. It would not be my last.

In my senior year in high school, I had the opportunity to visit

Princeton University. My dad arranged for me to ride in the bus with the Army lacrosse team. In 1952, Army and Princeton were the two top-rated college lacrosse teams in the nation. The game was a great one, and the Princeton campus was beautiful. Spending some time with college lacrosse players was a special treat. A few days after I returned from Princeton, I suggested to my dad that I was considering going to Princeton. His answer was quite firm. "Son, you go to West Point or you go to work. We have no money for college."

In the spring of 1952, my dad pulled me out of high school and sent me to a prep school called Bradens. For three months, my Highland Falls High School classmates, Mike Esposito and Sam Gates, joined me. We spent day and night learning how to take tests. Both of my friends were smart but we needed to score high on the West Point exam if we were to be accepted into the United States Military Academy. All three of us were accepted.

My three years at Highland Falls High School were memorable mostly for what I did not accomplish. Even though I was one of the tallest boys in my school. I did not make the varsity basketball team. I did not win one match as a member of the tennis team. I did not graduate at the top of my class (I was 11th out of a senior class of 55). I was not elected to any leadership positions. I was not an impressive physical specimen. (I was six foot three inches tall and weighed 145 pounds - the skinniest boy in my class). With the initials of PM, I acquired the nickname of "Pea Muscles."

My high school class graduated on 26 June, 1952. Less than a week later I would enter West Point. I was seventeen and a half years old and was one of the youngest members of the West Point class of 1956. On graduation night from high school, there were many parties to attend. At each party a different alcoholic beverage was served: champagne, scotch, bourbon, wine and beer. Knowing I was going to be locked up at West Point for the next year, I decided this was time to party. The drinking age was eighteen in New York but bar owners in the vicinity of West Point did not check IDs in those days. Fortunately, I was not driving. When I was deposited back at my home at about midnight I was drunk as a skunk.

The next day was pure hell. This was the day that I learned what a hangover was. I did not want to get out of bed. The parents of my girlfriend, Carol Carson, were scheduled to pick me up and take us to Lake George in upstate New York for a few days of relaxation. Carol's parents thought it was hilarious that I was so badly hung over. I did not share their mirth. Incidentally, soon after I entered West Point, Carol left me for an upper-class cadet, so I was without a girlfriend for my entire plebe year.

Chapter Two:

⌇⌇⌇

A West Point Cadet: 1952 - 1956

THE WEST POINT experience in the 1950s was memorable in many ways. Considered the best engineering school throughout the 19th century, the United States Military Academy had produced many of the top leaders in the American wars from the Civil War through World War II. Two West Point graduates were destined to be American presidents, Ulysses S. Grant and Dwight David Eisenhower. Attending an institution at a time when a graduate, Eisenhower, was serving as the president of the United States, made every West Point cadet feel special.

The first year was the toughest. We were "fourth classmen" and called "plebes." During our third class year we were called "yearlings." Our second class year was especially hard academically - we were called "cows." As first classmen or seniors we were called "firsties." As seniors we had many leadership opportunities.

Each class at West Point has unique features which differentiate them from other classes. For instance, the class of 1915 will forever be known as "The class the stars fell on." Many graduates of the class of 1915 reached the general officer rank including five star generals Eisenhower and Bradley. The class of 1956 arrived in July, 1952 as the first class to enter West Point after the cheating scandal of 1951.

The cheating scandal started with the football team. A few outstanding cadet athletes did not have the intellectual ability to pass some of the tough academic courses. Slowly a system was devised that would give them, ahead of time, answers to upcoming examinations. Within a year, most of the football team and a few athletes from other sports were taking advantage of this cheating system. A cadet on the swimming team reported this cheating to his cadet honor representative.

This led to a major investigation. Ninety cadets were expelled for either cheating themselves or assisting others as they cheated. Hence all of us in the class of 1956 got a double dose of honor and ethics. This special education served us well throughout our lifetimes.

A second factor of importance for our class was the West Point Heart Study. We lived an especially healthy life as a direct result of the biennial feedback we received on the state of our health. (see Appendix C for details,)

The summer period of my first year as a cadet at West Point was known as "Beast Barracks." Our class of 1956 entered with 660 young men on the first of July, 1952. When we graduated four years later our class size had dwindled to 480. That first summer was very tough. We were exposed to the severe discipline of military life, but we were never hazed. No upperclassmen were allowed to hit us, touch us, shove us or take any direct physical action against us. Upperclassmen were allowed to make us stand at attention for long periods of time, shout at us, make us run up and down many flights of stairs, give us quizzes and hand out demerits.

From early morning reveille until the time we collapsed into bed, we were never allowed to walk - every move was at double time. Discipline during meals was especially severe. We had to sit on the front half of our chairs and practice high standards of etiquette. However, we were not required to eat "square meals." In other words, the fork could go directly from the plate to the mouth. Women were not allowed entry until 1976. In the class of 1956, there was only one African American. Roger Blunt was a very sharp cadet who later became a general officer. I got to know him well on the lacrosse field.

Each of the cadet companies during Beast Barracks consisted of about 110 plebes. Since I was six feet three inches tall, I was assigned to the company with the tallest new cadets. Within our cadet company, when we lined up for various events, we were usually placed in alphabetical order. Hence, on many occasions, I lined up immediately behind a tall, burly cadet named Norman Schwarzkopf.

The name Schwarzkopf was well known throughout America in the 1940s and 1950s. Norm's father had created a very popular radio show called "Gang Busters." It was based on his experience as the head of the New Jersey State Police. Young Norman was constantly harassed by the upperclassmen and was asked often to shout out the "Gangbuster Poop." Each week, to introduce the radio show and to grab the attention of all the listeners, there were loud, dramatic words. Because Cadet Schwarzkopf had such a deep, strong voice, you could hear the following throughout the whole central area of the West Point barracks.

"Dum, Dum, Dum, Dum D Dum, from the files of the New Jersey State Police, CBS Presents GANG BUSTERS!"

SWEATING AND SINGING WITH SCHWARZKOPF

At the end of each long day during Beast Barracks, the new cadets were assembled in long lines in the basement of the cadet barracks. Called a "shower formation," all of the new plebes were expected to sweat through our cotton bathrobes before we were ushered into a precisely timed, two-minute shower. Each evening I would line up next to Norm Schwarzkopf. At six three and 230 pounds, he could sweat through his bathrobe in about 15 minutes. At six three and 150 pounds, I always was the last to be sent to the showers. Not once did I sweat through my bathrobe. Norm also beat me in singing. We all tried out for the cadet choir. New cadet Schwarzkopf had a powerful bass voice. I had no voice at all. He also scored higher in academics and military aptitude.

Many years later, four-star General H. Norman Schwarzkopf was the top commander during the 1991 war with Iraq (Desert Storm). I had retired and was serving as a military analyst for CNN. Having known Norm quite well when we were cadets helped me as I described on TV his background, personality, and accomplishments at West Point.

The plebe year for the class of 1956 lasted from 1 July, 1952 until June, 1953. It was a year of constant harassment by the upperclassmen of the plebes. Since plebes were outnumbered, three to one, there was always an upper-class cadet who would catch us doing something wrong. After Beast Barracks, each plebe was assigned to one of twenty-four cadet companies. I was fortunate to be assigned to Company M-2. Consisting of cadets who were all quite tall (six foot, two inches and taller), M-2 had the reputation as being the most laid-back company in the entire Corps of Cadets.

Plebes were not harassed as often and as vigorously in M-2 as in the other companies. Also, many of the upper-class cadets were involved in varsity athletics so they did not have the time or the inclination to give plebes a hard time. By the time I joined Cadet Company M-2 in September 1952, I had acquired a new nickname. It was based, in part, on the first two initials of my name, P and M.

An upperclassman found out that I had lived at West Point during my high school years. He asked me if I knew a certain young woman who lived in the local area. She was a large, outgoing woman who was about three years older than me. She had been a friend of my sister. She had a reputation of being extremely forthcoming when on dates with cadets. When I told them that I did know her, I immediately got a new nickname, "Pleasant Moments." It really did not apply since I never had any "pleasant moments" with her.

Many of my fellow classmates in M-2 company struggled with academics during their plebe year. Fortunately, because I had such a fine education from pre-kindergarten through high school, academics seemed rather easy for me.

Since my high school girlfriend, Carol Carson, had dumped me for an upperclassman, my only dates were blind dates. All upper-class cadets got to go home for Christmas, but plebes had to stay on Post. Since my dad was still stationed at West Point, I had a chance to spend some pleasant evenings with my family. This was a huge bonus for me that only a few other cadets, who also had fathers stationed at West Point, enjoyed.

A FASCINATING MONTH IN EUROPE

By the time plebe year ended, my parents had moved back to Naples, Italy. This was to be my father's last assignment in the military. I decided to take the month's break in Europe, so I travelled to an Air Force Base on the East Coast and caught a military cargo aircraft that took me to Frankfurt, Germany. A visit to Berlin was followed by a visit to Paris in June, 1953. During the first two weeks in Europe, I travelled with a fellow cadet classmate, Jerry Amlong.

When Jerry and I jumped off the train which took us from Frankfurt to Paris, we were met by many young people who were distributing leaflets. *SAUVEZ LES ROSENBERGS* (Save the Rosenbergs). Julius and Ethel Rosenberg were scheduled to die in Sing Sing prison on June 19th. Both had been found guilty of being spies for the Soviet Union. The Rosenbergs would leave behind two small children.

Each leaflet highlighted the upcoming demonstration that was to be held the next day in front of the American Embassy. The French Communist party was quite active in the early 1950s. This party had a strong anti-American agenda. All over Paris in the summer of 1953 was graffiti. EISENHOWER THE ASSASSIN: RIDGWAY THE BUTCHER. In 1953, Eisenhower was our President and Ridgway was the Supreme Allied Commander of NATO. Ridgway's headquarters were in the suburbs of Paris. Jerry and I decided that observing an anti-American demonstration might give us a good story to take back home. We were disappointed that, because of heavy rain, the demonstration fizzled out - only a few angry Frenchmen showed up.

The Kindness of Cadet Leroy Suddath

After returning from our holiday in early July, 1953, our entire class spent two months conducting field exercises at Camp Buckner. The camp was located about six miles west of the main campus. This large West Point reservation was an ideal location for military maneuvers. The camp included rigorous training, but it felt like a vacation when compared to our plebe year.

One of the field exercises was a two-day trek through a large expanse of trees and brush. Each cadet carried a field pack, a rifle, and a canteen as well as an additional piece of equipment. My task was to carry the base plate of a 57 mm mortar. This large, round steel plate weighed about forty pounds.

At the time I was 18 years old, six foot three inches tall and I weighed 155 pounds. I was super-skinny and not very strong. With the initials of P and M, I had gained a nickname of "Pea Muscles" at Round Pound Boys Camp. This nickname followed me to West Point. Unlike the Pleasant Moments nickname, the Pea Muscles nickname made sense.

On this demanding two-day hike, about every hundred yards on the uphill slopes, I would drop the base plate. Totally wiped out, I felt I would not make it to the end of our hike. My West Point classmate, Leroy Suddath, was in my squad. Leroy was larger and stronger than me. He was a fine athlete. When he saw how much I was struggling, he said something like, "Perry, I will give you a break, let me carry it for a while." Leroy picked up the base plate and carried it for the rest of the way - never even suggesting that he might give it back to me. I have never forgotten his kindness that day, more than 67 year ago.

In 2014, I learned that Dr. Randy Smith had nominated Leroy for a high honor in Augusta, Georgia, my current home town. Remarkably, it turns out that Leroy went to high school in the same town I would choose as my permanent home many years later. In the fall of 2015, Leroy was inducted into the Hall of Fame of the Academy of Richmond County. Leroy was honored for his distinguished military service by the high school he had attended in the late 1940s. He had been a star basketball player in 1948 and 1949 and received All State honors.

I had the pleasure of telling Leroy about this Hall of Fame honor. He was surprised and absolutely delighted. He thought that the Academy of Richmond Academy had totally forgotten about him. At the Hall of Fame event were many of his family members and friends. Army Major General Leroy Suddath joined a list of past inductees which included James Longstreet, Judy Woodruff, Carl Sanders, Doctor Hervey Cleckley and Medal of Honor recipient Jimmie Dyess.

In 2020, at a moving memorial service at Saint John's Episcopal Church in Savannah, Leroy was honored by family and friends. Admired by thousands, this esteemed southern gentleman had died at age 89. Leroy was older than most of his classmates. After graduating from high school, he attended Auburn University for two years. In 1951 he joined the US Army. He was 21 years old when he entered West Point with the class of 1956.

I made many friends during the summer encampment at Camp Bunker in 1953. We were housed in open bay barracks. It was nice to be grouped during the summer with cadets of different heights. This way we got to know more than just the same sized cadets in our regular companies. In my barracks at Camp Buckner was a short, skinny cadet named Don Morelli. He and I quickly became good friends. Don had a great sense of humor and he often came up with crazy ideas.

Since lining everything up in proper order was important at West Point, Don decided that the two skinniest cadets in our company should line up, side-by-side. Since Don was five feet six inches small and I was six foot three inches tall, lining up anything smartly might be a problem. Don had a magic formula - he suggested that we line up our athletic shorts. He told me to pull my shorts way down. Then he pulled his shorts way up. A picture was taken to show that, by golly, we found a way to look super sharp - our shorts were lined up. Nothing else, of course.

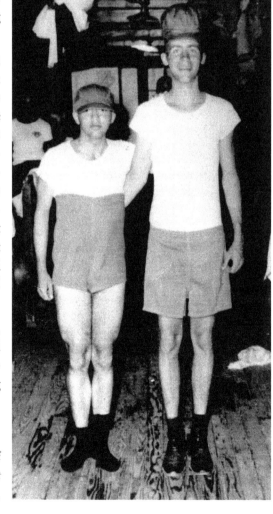

Well, it did not turn out especially well. Don pulled his shorts up too high and I pulled mine down too low. This was planned as a goofy photo. It fully met our expectations. In order to make the photo even sillier, Don suggested that we emphasize our height differential. He pulled his cap down low and I went high with my cap.

So there we were, two eighteen year old West Point cadets giving posterity something

Cadets Don Morelli and Perry Smith at Camp Buckner, 1953.

memorable. Little did I know that twenty seven years later, at an important meeting in the Pentagon, this picture would appear displayed on a large screen. Two silly cadets ended up as two major generals, one Army and one Air Force. That day Don Morelli gave a group of senior officers a good laugh.

ROOMMATES SELECTED

That same summer, something happened that had a profound and lasting impact on my life. It turned out to be one of the greatest blessings I would receive. As the cadets of the class of 1956 got ready to return to the main West Point campus and to start our yearling (sophomore) year, we were told that we could choose our roommates. If we desired, they could remain our roommates for the next three years.

Two of the most outstanding cadets from Cadet Company M-2 approached me - I will never forget the moment. They asked me to be their roommate. One was Don Holleder and the other was Jerry Amlong. Both had solid leadership skills and both were fine athletes. "Holly" would become a first team All American football player by his junior year. Jerry would soon become a varsity lacrosse player. They were muscular, handsome jocks: me, not so much.

I could not understand why they would want me to be their roommate. I had survived our plebe year but there was nothing outstanding about me. I had tutored a couple of my company mates during my

West Point roommates: Jerry Amlong,
Donald Holleder, and Perry Smith, 1955.

plebe year but one had flunked out. After I quickly agreed to their proposal, I asked them, "Why did you pick me?" They said (I am not sure of the exact words), "Perry, you are smart and we are dumb. We want you to help get us through this place."

In the 1950s all cadets, during the first three years, took the same courses (except for foreign languages). We were divided into academic "sections" of about 18 cadets each. The smart cadets were in the first section, the ones who really struggled were in the 9th and 10th sections. Within each section, we sat in accordance with how well we were doing in any particular course. I usually sat in one of the last seats in the first section or somewhere in the second section. My roommates tended to be in one of the last three sections. We were graded nearly every day and our grades were posted on a bulletin board about every six weeks.

My roommates struggled in math, science, and engineering courses as well as in English. In the evenings, I would look over the lesson for the next day and then sit down with both roommates. I would try to hit the highlights and have them do a couple of sample problems.

By the time I got to class I had already taught the lesson and was able to do quite well. Hence, helping them helped me, <u>a valuable lesson indeed.</u> My class standing improved over the course of our last three years. Eight years later, this relatively high class standing enabled me to get into a first-rate graduate school, Columbia University. I should point out that our classmate, Bob Richards, was a better academic coach than I was - he helped my roommates and many others.

YEARLING AND COW YEARS: 1953 - 1955

During a weekend at Camp Buckner, at the end of the summer of 1953, a dance was held. A large number of single girls attended. Many of us had a chance to meet and dance with them. The informal rules allowed us to cut in on a dancing pair. There was one girl who gained lots of attention. She was petite, pretty and was a graceful dancer.

I danced with her just once but managed to get her address. She lived in the Queens borough of New York City. I wrote to her and asked her to come to West Point for a football weekend. To my surprise and delight, she agreed to come. She had received fourteen letters from cadets. I was both pleased and humbled that she chose me.

Her name was Myra Murphy. She came from an Irish Catholic family. Soon, I had a steady girlfriend. Although she was just sixteen and a junior in high school, she was quite mature. Since I was eighteen, the age differential was not an issue.

Yearling year was a delight from start to finish. Jerry Amlong also had a steady girlfriend from New York City, Nancy Sullivan. After two dismal years, the Army football team came roaring back. By defeating nationally ranked Duke early in the season and later by defeating an excellent Navy team, Army was boosted way up in the national football rankings. That year the Army football team earned the coveted Lambert Trophy. We were the best in the East.

By the time the spring of 1954 arrived I was playing junior varsity lacrosse. As an attack man I scored goals quite often. Late in the season, my thumb was shattered. As I walked to the hospital I got dizzy and almost passed out. When the doctor showed me the X ray, he was able to count 25 separate pieces of bone. He seemed surprised that none of the bone fragments had penetrated my skin.

I was admitted to the hospital. My memory of those three days was pain. To reduce the throbbing, I would lie in bed and elevate my right hand way above my heart.

In the hospital ward there was a television set. I watched the Army-McCarthy hearings on television. Observing Senator Joseph McCarthy and his sidekick, Roy Cohn, berate witnesses was my first exposure to congressional hearings. It would not be my last.

As the 1954 lacrosse season ended, the Army coach, Morris Touchstone, pulled me aside. He told me to work hard on my lacrosse skills in the months ahead. He explained that he planned to make me a starting attackman of the 1955 lacrosse team. It appeared that my dreams would come true. Best of all, Myra visited West Point often and she accepted my gift of an "A" pin. Now she was more than just a girlfriend. By golly, we were "pinned."

In the summer of 1954, our entire class visited a number of Army and Air Force bases. Two magic moments occurred for me at two Air Force bases. At Maxwell Air Force Base, I received a ride in the back seat of a jet aircraft. It was a thrilling experience. A week later, I watched an Air Force firepower demonstration at Eglin Air Force Base, Florida. As the end of this impressive display of airpower approached, the announcer calmly stated, "Ladies and Gentlemen, The Thunderbirds." Five seconds later at a low altitude, at high speed and with thunderous noise the Air Force precision aerobatic team flew over the stands from the rear. Flying F-100s, this team, in very close formation, put on an impressive show. As I watched, I said to myself - one day I would want to fly that airplane. Four years later that dream would come true.

That day in 1954, I decided that when I graduated from West Point, I would choose the Air Force rather than the Army. To make the Air Force list, I had to have near perfect eyesight and I needed to graduate in the top two thirds of the class of 1956. Both seemed likely since I had entered West Point with 20/20 vision and my academics were in good shape.

The fall of 1954 started out fine. We were the equivalent of college juniors and all three of the roommates had been promoted to the rank of "Cow Corporal." This was a good indication that we ranked high in the area of military aptitude and leadership. In M-2 company, there were twenty cadets in the class of 1956. Nine gained the rank of cadet corporal.

Also, Holly was slated to be the starting end on both defense and offense on the football team. Quarterback Pete Vann was a fine passer who was especially skilled at throwing the long ball. Holly had fine speed and excellent pass catching skills. He would get open, catch a pass at full speed and race farther down the field. In the football season of 1954, the Vann to Holleder combo got the attention of sports writers and commentators. Despite missing the first two games of the season, Holly was named a first team All American on five polls. Pete Vann was named a first team All American on three polls.

Earlier that fall, bad news had arrived. Holly was busted from cadet corporal to cadet private. Even worse, he was suspended from the football team for the first month of the season, which is why he missed those first two games. His offense was making a phone call to a girl while he was on duty as a cadet in charge of quarters. This violation occurred while we were at Fort Benning during the summer of 1954. An especially rigid Army officer had turned him in for this offense.

Once Holly was back playing football, the team did well. However, losing to Navy made the 1954 football season a disappointment. In the 1954 Army-Navy game, Pete Vann, Holly and the entire Army team played well. However, Navy, led by quarterback George Welsh and All American end Ron Beagle played better.

MY FATHER DIES

In the spring of 1955, my dad died of a massive heart attack at age 55. His health was poor during his last few months. He was in Florida at the time of his death. Neither George Anne, who was working full time at a bank in Highland Falls, nor I were able to be with him as death approached.

The funeral was held at the Old Cadet Chapel on a cold and rainy day. Colonel Perry McCoy Smith, graduate of the West Point class of 1922, was buried very close to the chapel. Knowing how much the United States Military Academy meant to him, my mother felt that this was perfect for his final resting place. My dad, who had retired from the Army nine months before his death, never had a chance to enjoy his well-earned retirement.

Soon after my father's death, my mother moved into a small apartment in Highland Falls. She would live there until after my graduation in 1956. I saw her often and she attended all of our home lacrosse games. She and my sister were two of the strongest supporters of Army lacrosse in 1955 and 1956.

In the spring of 1955, there was more bad news for me and also for Jerry Amlong. Jerry and the lovely Nancy Sullivan broke up. Jerry took the separation very hard. Jerry's bad news was followed by bad news for me. Myra Murphy sent me a "Dear John" letter and returned the "A" pin I had given her the previous year. She had fallen in love with a man who was the president of his class at Fordham University. The news from Myra was unexpected and devastating. Twenty months of a joyful life with her came crashing down.

What was helpful for me during this difficult time was the game of lacrosse. I was especially busy in the spring of 1955. Lacrosse had become a big part of my life by this time. I started every game for the Army lacrosse team. My coach and my team counted on me to score many goals in each game. I focused my attention on lacrosse but unfortunately, the Army lacrosse team had a losing season in 1955 and lost to Navy at Annapolis.

After the third game that year, I had dealt with a leg pain whenever I ran. I had not played well and felt partially responsible for the poor performance of the team. Early in the summer, I entered the West Point hospital with an infected leg. An X-ray showed that I had played most of the season with a hairline fracture of my leg. When the lacrosse coach learned about my leg, he was pleased. He felt that with a well-healed leg, I would play better during the 1956 season.

Back to Camp Buckner - Summer, 1955

After completing my junior year at West Point, I was off to Camp Buckner once again. As a first classman, I received two summer assignments. I was the cadet-in-charge of "The Platoon in Attack" exercise which each member of the class of 1958 had to complete. The officer-in-charge was a charismatic Army officer with combat experience during the Korean War, Major Hal Moore.

My second assignment that summer was as the executive officer of a cadet company. The company commander was classmate Norman Schwarzkopf. Both Hal and Norm would move on to distinguished careers in the Army. Working for and with these two outstanding men was a pleasure - I learned much about leadership from each of them. Incidentally, Hal Moore (along with co-author, Joe Galloway) tells his story in the bestselling book, *We Were Soldiers Once...and Young*. This book is one of the best books on combat during the Vietnam War. Mel Gibson played the role of Lieutenant Colonel Moore in the movie of the same name.

Who Will Lead Company M-2?

In the fall of 1955, three cadet roommates in cadet company M-2 and a US Army captain found themselves involved in a series of friendships and accomplishments. Of the cadets, Donald Walter Holleder was the best athlete, Ransom J. Amlong was the most outgoing, and I was the most studious. Captain Hank Emerson, our company tactical officer, was a human dynamo.

Every cadet at West Point during the mid-1950s knew who Holly was. His football and basketball exploits gained him lots of attention and praise. To remind, football at West Point during the 1940s and 1950s was a big deal. Starting with the national championship teams in the mid-1940s, Army football was ranked high nationally most years from 1944 through 1959 (the exception was 1951 and 1952 in the aftermath of the West Point "cribbing scandal" when most of the football team was dismissed for cheating on academic examinations).

Before the days of widespread TV coverage there were two sports that held the wide attention of the American public: professional baseball and college football. Interest in these two sports was sustained through radio and through popular magazines like *Sport* and *Sports Illustrated.*

Most young men and other sports fans throughout America recognized the names of Army football greats: Doc Blanchard, Glenn Davis, Arnold Tucker, Hank and Dan Foldberg, Barney Poole, Arnold Galiffa, Pete Vann, Don Holleder, and Pete Dawkins.

As the start of the 1955 football season approached, Holly, a first team All American end, was switched to quarterback. The famous Army football coach, Red Blaik, had made that controversial decision. It was labelled by the press the "Great Experiment." Quarterback Pete Vann had used up his eligibility and Blaik was looking for the best leader for the Army football team. Holly turned out to be a good choice to be the quarterback and team leader.

Football All American Donald Walter Holleder, 1955.

When Holly's picture graced the cover of *Sports Illustrated* in the fall of 1955, it was an extraordinary moment for Don, the Army football team, the Corps of Cadets and everyone else associated with West Point.

Jerry Amlong and I basked in Don's reflected glory. To be Don Holleder's roommate was special. The friendship among the three of us was based on mutual support and respect. Jerry was super gung-ho, very sharp militarily and quite emotional. When a dumb edict would come down from on high, Jerry would often get mad or upset. Jerry cared deeply about West Point and was admired for his commitment to this historic institution.

Don was mature beyond his years. He handled his fame with aplomb. When he did get a little high on himself, it was usually Jerry who would say, "Oh, come on Holly" or "Knock it off, Don." The term we used often was, "You still put your trousers on one leg at a time."

Holly got lots of fan mail and was expected to answer each letter. The athletic department provided a stack of pictures of Holly in his football uniform. He would sign each picture. On his behalf, I would answer the letters. I would then give the letters and signed pictures to the athletic department who took care of the mailings.

Our cadet company, Company M-2, had a terrible time from the early autumn of 1954 to the late spring of 1955. M-2 was ranked at the bottom among the twenty-four cadet companies at West Point. The cadet leaders of Company M-2 from the class of 1955 had many problems. A number got busted down to cadet private as a result of disciplinary problems. Others were so busy playing varsity sports they devoted little time and effort providing leadership to the underclassmen in the company. It was clear to all of us in the company that M-2 needed strong cadet leadership as the 1955-1956 year commenced.

On to the scene in the summer of 1955 came Captain Hank Emerson, a 1947 West Point graduate and Korean War veteran. He would be the M-2 Tactical Officer for our senior year at West Point. Someone who enjoyed challenges, Captain Emerson had volunteered for the job of tactical officer for M-2 Company. His role was to straighten the goof-off M-2 Company. He threw his considerable energy into that task.

Hank was a confirmed bachelor who had dedicated his life to the Army. Hank "gunfighter" Emerson later became a highly respected lieutenant general in the Army. As cadets, we did not know what to make of this super gung-ho officer. He seemed to spend both day and night hanging around our company area. Our previous tactical officers had been hands-off men so the arrival of Captain Emerson was a shock to us all. It took us a while but, over time, we learned to respect him.

One of Captain Emerson's first tasks was the selection of the cadet leadership for M-2 company. There were four likely candidates for the position of company commander. Holleder, who had been busted from cadet corporal to cadet private in the fall of 1954, was not one of them. To the surprise of everyone in company M-2, Emerson picked Don - a good and popular choice especially among the underclassmen of M-2 Company.

Captain Emerson, who had the skill of recognizing leadership potential, realized that Holleder would be the best man to take M-2 company to high levels of performance. By the time our class graduated in 1956, M-2 company was ranked in the top half of the cadet companies. Much credit goes to Cadet Captain Don Holleder and Army Captain Hank Emerson.

It should be noted that the class of 1957 in company M-2 was an especially talented group. It included Bill Huckabee, Don Kutyna, Jerry Scott, and Bill Yates. By the time June, 1957 rolled around, M-2 Company was ranked the top cadet company in the Corps of Cadets. Hank Emerson played a big role taking a cadet company from dead last to first in two years.

Upon graduation in June, 1956, Holly and Jerry joined Hank as officers in the US Army. I was off to the Air Force but eighteen months after our West Point graduation I would rejoin Holly for a special event. Don had fallen in love with Caroline Pierce of Alexandria, Virginia. A wedding was to be held in the iconic Fort Myer chapel in Arlington, Virginia. When Don called me to discuss the upcoming wedding, I received some big news.

Don had many close friends so it was a surprise when he asked me to be the best man in his wedding. I was delighted. What a blessing that invitation turned out to be! Two days before the wedding of Donald Holleder and Caroline Pierce in Arlington, Virginia, Don introduced me to the maid of honor, a lovely, talented lady from Augusta, Georgia, Connor Cleckley Dyess. She has decorated my life for more than 61 years.

Returning to the West Point years, when the Army lacrosse team played Navy at Annapolis in the spring of 1955, I noticed a large "M" burned on the field. The Maryland lacrosse team had done the deed earlier that year. That fall, the thought occurred to me and others that this trick might work for us. In those years, the Army-Navy football rivalry was of broad sporting interest. An "A", burned on the field at Veterans Stadium in Philadelphia, would send a powerful message. It would be viewed by 102,000 fans at the post-Thanksgiving Army-Navy football game and the millions who would watch the game on TV.

The plan was developed by classmates Bill Crites, Jimmy Ellis, Bob Richards and others. I was a key player because I had access to an automobile, my mother's Plymouth. Although we were in our senior year at West Point, we were not yet authorized to own automobiles.

Bill, Jimmy, Bob, and I drove down on Thanksgiving Day in 1955 to Philadelphia. That evening we parked near the football stadium at about 10 p.m. With cans of gasoline in hand we approached our goal. The first problem we faced was a tall fence which surrounded the entire stadium. Two of us managed to scale the fence. Our next obstacle was a heavy canvas tarp that covered the entire playing field. Our third problem was the cold rain.

After about two hours of work, the tarp was rolled back far enough for a large "A". We carefully spread out the gasoline but we could not get it to burn. The grass was short and damp and it refused to catch fire. Our efforts were not in vain however. The grass ended up being stained black by the gasoline. The large "A" was there for all to see on that marvelous day in late November when Army beat the Navy 14 to 6 in football.

When we returned to retrieve our car, dawn was breaking. We faced a new problem - my mother's car was gone. Unwisely we had left the car keys, our money and our IDs in the car. It had been impounded by the police and taken across town.

That turned out to be a two-dimensional problem. We could not pay the cab driver who had taken us to the police station. Also, we could not prove to the police that the car was ours. In a great stroke of luck, we had left an envelope in the car with "Don Holleder" written on it. Holly's picture had been on the cover of *Sports Illustrated* the previous week so some of the policemen knew who he was.

When I explained that Don Holleder was my roommate and when we confessed our deed at the football stadium, the police gave us the car keys. They seemed impressed that we had managed to climb the high fence at Veterans Stadium. As we departed, they wished the Army team the best in the upcoming game. Incidentally, the cab driver got paid.

In the *Sports Illustrated* issue that was published before the big game there was an article by the well-known sportsman, Herman Hickman. Hickman had been a guard on the Tennessee football team, an All American on the Grantland Rice All American football team, the football coach at Yale, a sports reporter and a professional wrestler (over 500 matches). Although the Navy team was heavily favored, Hickman's words were prophetic.

"Colonel Blaik's Great Experiment was designed primarily for use against Navy. Holleder, one of the greatest competitors football has ever seen, may be a bear at his new position in the game that matters. … Colonel Blaik probably wants this one more than any game since his first victory over Navy in 1944. Psychologically, the outcome favors Army. It certainly would be a personal triumph for him and Don Holleder if the Cadets came through."

In the 1955 football game, Army beat Navy 14-6. Quarterback Holleder threw two passes - neither one was complete. Holly, like most of his teammates, played both offense and defense. When Pete Lash scored Army's second touchdown, the victory was sealed. Two days later, Don was on the basketball court with the Army team. Never a starter in basketball, Don got lots of playing time as a power forward, a strong defensive player and a top rebounder.

For those who wish to learn more about Holly, you may want to read, *The Spartan Game* by Terry Tibbets or watch the 60-minute video, *When Duty Calls, the Life and Legacy of Don Holleder*. This video is available on YouTube. The video includes footage from the 1955 Army-Navy game as well as interviews with Jerry Amlong, Butch Harbold, Doc Bahnsen, Pete Lash, Pete Vann, Leroy Suddath, and John Foss.

My athletic record at West Point was a mixed one. I had learned a little hockey and lacrosse on pick-up teams during my high school years. However, I was not proficient in either sport. At West Point, I made the plebe team in both sports but was a scrub. I got almost no playing time on the hockey team and was a fourth team midfielder in lacrosse.

A big breakthrough came through just before our last plebe lacrosse game in the spring of 1953. The coach of the plebe team asked me to play as an attack man. Because I was tall, he told me to play directly in front of the opponent's goal (the position was called "crease attack man"). In that last game, I scored three goals against a weak opponent. From that day on, I would always play lacrosse on the crease.

During my second year at West Point, I played on the junior varsity hockey team. Of all the hockey players at West Point in the 1950s, I may have been the worst. Sometime around January, 1954, I approached the Army hockey coach, Jack Riley, and asked for his advice. I told him I was considering two options: playing both hockey and lacrosse or giving up hockey and concentrating on lacrosse. With a smile he said, "Smith, I think you would make a fine lacrosse player."

With sadness, I turned in my hockey gear. The advice that Coach Riley gave me that day turned out to be first-rate. I focused my full attention on lacrosse, played on the junior varsity team my yearling year and was a varsity player my junior and senior years. During those last two years, I was the starting crease attack man on the varsity team. If I had tried to play both sports, I probably would never have made the varsity on either team. Incidentally, Jack Riley was the head coach of the 1960 United States Olympic ice hockey team. In a big upset, America won the gold medal that year.

In addition to the good advice I received from Coach Riley, I received helpful advice from my roommate, Don Holleder. I asked Don what his secret to success as a football player was. He told me that he worked harder than anyone else on his team. He went on to tell me that I could be an outstanding lacrosse player if I worked hard all year long to perfect my skills.

During the long, cold winters at West Point I would spend many weekend hours alone in a squash court. The purpose was to perfect my "stick work," to learn to catch and throw with power and accuracy both right-handed and left-handed, and to work on my "quick stick" skills. One of the important skills for someone who hangs around the front of the goal is the ability to receive a pass in the stick and shoot the ball very, very quickly. The idea was to get rid of the ball before you were hammered by one or more defense men. Many of the goals that I scored those last two years were the result of receiving a pass from behind the goal and very quickly hurling the ball into the net. On many occasions I was knocked to the ground and only knew I had scored when one of my teammates would give me a congratulatory tap on my helmet.

Lacrosse played a very important part in my life. Having been a terrible athlete in high school, it was both unexpected and rewarding to play at the varsity level at West Point. Our 1955 season, my junior year, was a disappointing one - we lost more games than we won. However, 1956 was a much better year for Army lacrosse. Our record was seven wins and four losses, but we beat Navy for the first time since 1952.

We also beat other powerhouse teams including Princeton, Yale, Hofstra and Syracuse. The star player for Syracuse was Jimmy Brown. An All-American in both football and lacrosse, Brown also

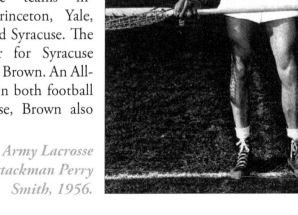

Army Lacrosse Attackman Perry Smith, 1956.

competed on the Syracuse track team. In 1956, Brown played lacrosse and ran for the Syracuse track team on the same day - that may help explain how we managed to hold him scoreless. Upon graduation from Syracuse University in 1957, Jimmy Brown starred as a running back for the Cleveland Browns. He is listed as one of the greatest American athletes of the 20th Century.

Our lacrosse coach was Morris Touchstone. The fine players on the 1956 team included John Snodgrass, Butch Harbold, Pete Lash, John Higgins, Jerry Amlong, Stainton Smith, Bill Schrage, Paul Winkel, Jack Sharkey, Mitt Shattuck, Ted Dayharsh, Art Boudreau, Bob Caron, Bob Sullivan, Ben Glyphis, Ed Valence, Moon Mullins, Ray Riggins, Bill Yates, Mike Harvey, and Jack Wiegner. The most impressive quality of the team was how unselfish each player was. We had no "hot dogs" whose only desire was to score goals. When in doubt my teammates would pass the ball and let someone else take the shot.

My Most Memorable Lacrosse Game

The game was a very tight one. Two nationally ranked teams were playing. It was a tied game. The score was 4 to 4 with 12 seconds to go in the game. Everyone on both teams was anticipating an overtime period. The game was college lacrosse. The date was April, 1956. The location was New Haven, Connecticut and the teams were Yale and West Point. The Yale team was moving the ball towards the Army goal when Army defenseman Ben Glyphis intercepted a Yale pass.

On the field was an official with a gun raised above his head pointed straight up. He was loudly counting off the remaining seconds in the game: 12, 11, 10, 9. Glyphis passed the ball to an Army midfielder, Jack Wiegner, who was streaking down the field: 8, 7, 6, 5.

As Wiegner raced toward the Yale goal, I was sure he would just fire away. But when my defenseman left me to pick up Jack, Wiegner passed the ball to me: 4, 3, 2. I caught the ball, turned quickly and fired at the goal. The ball hit the back of the net just as the gun went off. The referee threw up his arms indicating that the goal was good. Army won, 5 to 4.

Pandemonium followed.

My teammates rushed me, knocked me down and everyone (except our elderly coach) piled on top of me. With 25 players burying me, I held my breath. I hoped the pile of players, lacrosse sticks, gloves and helmets would all untangle soon.

INTIMIDATION ON THE LACROSSE FIELD

In the spring of 1956, the Army lacrosse team was playing a nationally ranked team - Rutgers. In the first half, I scored four goals and Army was ahead. In the second half, Rutgers sent in a really tough, mean defenseman. Clearly his job was to shut me down. When the referee was not looking, he beat me up with his stick. No one had done this to me in the past on the lacrosse field and I did not know how to handle his intimidation.

I did not score in the second half and Army lost the game. I learned three powerful lessons that day. Beware of the bullies, do not let yourself be intimidated and do not be someone who intimidates others. Later in my life I encountered two people who tried to intimate me. I immediately recognized what was going on and took action to prevent the intimidation from taking place. In both cases, a tough guy threatened to prevent my promotion. I reacted by saying, "Be my guest sir, and I will be sure that you never again have any interaction with anyone who works for me."

THE ARMY-NAVY LACROSSE GAME OF 1956

In 1956, the Army Navy lacrosse game was played at West Point. A crowd of about five thousand lined the field. Once again, both teams were ranked in the top ten of Division I lacrosse teams. One of the stars for Navy was a midfielder named Ron Beagle. For two years he had been a first team All American football player and in 1956, he was a second team All American lacrosse player. In the mid-1950s the two greatest college athletes were Jimmy Brown and Ron Beagle. In 1956, I had the unusual honor of playing against them both.

My most memorable moment in that Army Navy game was when I hurled my skinny body at Ron Beagle. It felt like running into a Mack truck. I managed to knock him down along the sidelines. The crowd cheered. Beagle jumped up right away. My rise from the turf was much slower.

The Army team fell behind but in the second half, we came roaring back. We won the game 8 to 5. In the last few minutes when it was clear that Army was going to be the winner, the applause began. When the gun went off, the crowd rushed the field. My mother approached the team captain, Johnny Higgins, to give him a big kiss. But she was too quick. Johnny still had his helmet on. Her face banged into the metal cage in the front of the helmet. She got quite a bruise.

It is hard for me to explain how important the victory over Navy that spring afternoon was. For the next week, cadets from throughout the academy would pat me on my back, shake my hand, and congratulate me on the grand victory. I was honored, humbled and pleased to represent a team which had performed so well on its biggest stage. For that one week, I understood what life was like for Holly - but for Holly the attention he received lasted for two full years.

Being selected to play in the North-South lacrosse game which was held in Geneva, New York just after our graduation and later named

All American recognition.

a member of the 1956 lacrosse All American team (second team) was frosting on the cake. I had never dreamed that I could be a starting player of a nationally ranked lacrosse team - to realize this dream was very special.

Throughout my years of playing ice hockey and lacrosse, my body took a regular beating, both at practice and during games. During my plebe year a hockey puck hit me just above the eye and within a few hours my eye had completely closed. The whole area around the eye turned black, then blue, then yellow. After a couple of days, I could see out of the eye - but I had quite a shiner!

My lacrosse injuries were also quite substantial. Because I played just in front of the goal, I was hammered quite often both in practice and in games. Our helmets were leather with a medal cage that was supposed to protect the face. While playing lacrosse, my leg was broken as was my right thumb. A hit to my brow in a game in Baltimore led to lots of stitches. At the game, the trainer gave me some butterfly stitches and I soon went back on the playing field. After the game, I was taken to Johns Hopkins hospital to receive some more permanent stitches. By the next morning the swelling was so bad that my eye had completely closed.

The morning after most lacrosse games I could barely get out of bed. However, my battered body recovered quickly, and I was ready for practice on Mondays. I should point out that many of my goals were "garbage goals." In other words, when one of my teammates would shoot at the goal and the ball would bounce off the chest or the stick of the goalie, I would goose it with my lacrosse stick into the goal for a score. My teammate did all the work, yet I got credit for the score. I was kidded for my garbage goals by teammates and observers alike. However, my coach, Morris Touchstone, never complained - his attitude was "a goal is a goal." And you can't win unless your team scores often.

CHOOSING OUR FUTURES

One of the most memorable moments of the senior year for the West Point class of 1956 occurred when the entire class (480 cadets) assembled in a large auditorium during the late spring of 1956. With graduation approaching, it was time for each member of the class to select his career path. The choices were: Engineers, Infantry, Armor, Artillery and Signal Corps - or the Air Force. Since the Air Force Academy would not graduate its first class until 1959, both Annapolis and West Point allocated 25% of its class to the Air Force from 1947 through 1958.

The selection process was quite simple. It was done using class standing. The top man in our class got first choice and the last man in the class got whatever was left. Class standing was based on a formula that included academics, athletics and military leadership. Since there were many slots for each branch, the first one hundred cadets in our class got their very first choice. The first branch to run out of slots was Engineers. From this point forward the drama increased. My roommate Don Holleder wanted to go Air Force but by the time his name was called out, all 119 Air Force slots had been taken. Incidentally, you could not pick Air Force unless you had excellent vision - 20/20 or better in both eyes. I picked the Air Force when my name was called out.

Out of a graduating class of 480, my class standing was 76. As mentioned above, this score was based on three factors: academic performance, athletic performance and military aptitude. Academic rating was the most important factor. What helped my overall class ranking the most was my academic performance. In athletics and military leadership my scores were OK - probably a bit above average in both. Being a cadet lieutenant as well as a letterman on the varsity lacrosse team probably helped raise my overall score. To explain the cadet rank breakdowns, there were about 40 cadet captains and about 120 cadet lieutenants in the senior class. Hence, as far as military aptitude, I was somewhere in the top third of my class.

As graduation day approached, I decided to ask two young ladies to join me for the weeklong festivities. This decision turned out to be a big mistake; it caused both my mother and one of the ladies to cry. The first young lady I invited had a fulltime job in Ossining, New York. I invited her for the weekend and assumed she could not stay for the festivities after the weekend because she would need to get back to work on Monday. My assumption was wrong. She had taken a week off from work but had not told me. The second young lady arrived on

Sunday evening. She was scheduled to stay in the same dorm room at the Thayer Hotel as the first girl. Telling the first girl that she had to leave and explaining the issue to my mother was what led to the tears. The only person who did not seem to be upset was the second girl.

One of the special moments during our last week as cadets was the graduation parade. The entire corps of cadets honored our class as they "passed in review" on the plain at West Point. The first Company to be saluted was Company A-1. After all of the companies in the first regiment were saluted, the companies of the second regiment were saluted. A-2 was first and our company, M-2 was last. In fact, in every parade conducted by the Corps of Cadets, M-2 was always last. The tall cadets of Company M-2 would declare, "West Point always saved the best for last."

Company M-2 first classman at the
West Point Graduation Parade, May, 1956.

Secretary of the Army, Wilbur Brucker, was our graduation speaker. He handed out 480 diplomas on June 1st, 1956. Those who received the loudest cheers were Bob Stewart (top graduate) and our finest athletes: Bob Farris, Pete Lash, Butch Harbold, Don Holleder, and Ralph Chesnaukas, However the loudest cheers of all came when the "goat" of our class, Jack Sloan, received his diploma.

Being the last man was quite an honor. It meant he barely made it, but he made it. Two stories of note. Charlie Glenn graduated just behind Holly. The cheers for Holleder were so loud that Charlie worried that his parents could not hear when his name was announced. Also, when the hats were tossed high in the air, they had to come down somewhere. A descending hat hit John Stevenson's father and broke his nose. Who knew that a West Point graduation was a contact sport?

Secretary of the Army Brucker presenting diploma to Cadet Perry Smith, Graduation Day at West Point, June, 1956.

Four hundred and eighty young men were commissioned into the Army and Air Force on June 1st, 1956. 361 joined the Army, 119 joined the Air Force. Eight would be killed in Vietnam and nine in aircraft accidents. More than seventy percent would serve a full career in the United States military.

Jerry Amlong, was scheduled to be married soon after graduation. His bride to be was the lovely Nancy Sullivan. Jerry and Nancy had broken up during our junior year, but when Nancy's brother, Paul, graduated in June, 1955, the romance rekindled. However, there was a major problem. The parents on both sides could not stand each other. The possibility of fisticuffs was a real one. Colonel and Mrs. Amlong were strongly opposed to the marriage. They both felt Nancy Sullivan was "below the Amlong station." Mr. Sullivan was a high school teacher and football coach whereas Colonel Amlong was a high-ranking officer in the Army. I knew both families and it was clearly my job to mediate between two angry men. My solution worked pretty well, I made sure that each family had consumed plenty of booze before they got together. When both sets of parents saw how much Jerry and Nancy loved each other, their hearts melted, and the marriage ceremony was conducted without a hitch.

Chapter Three:

OFF TO THE AIR FORCE, 1956

AFTER TWO GLORIOUS months of vacation, where I played in the North-South lacrosse game, attended weddings, and hung out at the beach, it was time to head to Arizona for flying school. I drove my new car down to Mobile, Alabama to hook up with classmate, Fred Dent. The class of 1956 was not allowed to own cars until two months before graduation. If I was going to be a pilot, I felt I should get a jazzy car. The best one I could afford was a Ford convertible ($2400). Fred Dent really splurged and purchased a 1956 Thunderbird for $3600.

Before graduation, Fred and I devised a plan for the summer. After meeting up in Alabama we would drive our two cars in formation to Marana, Arizona, where we would commence flying school. When I arrived in Mobile, Fred was already there staying with his dad and mother. Fred's father was an active duty major general in the Air Force. He commanded a large logistics depot at Brookley Air Force Base near Mobile.

During my stay on base, Fred and I had a big night in downtown Mobile. At the end of the evening we decided to race each other back to the base. The bet was - who could get back to Fred's home first. We both raced through the main gate - not stopping even when signaled to do so. We got chased down and given citations by the security police. The next day we had to report to Major General Dent - a rather austere figure. My thoughts as we prepared for the meeting - "I have been an Air Force officer for less than two months and I am already in trouble" - and with a two-star general, no less.

General Dent asked us to explain exactly what happened. It was not a pretty picture as we told the full story. Too much to drink, speeding through Mobile, racing through the main gate at Brookley Air Force

Base even though the security policeman had signaled that we should stop, more speeding on base until the police car turned on its siren and its flashing lights.

General Dent listened quietly and then said something like. "Now young men, what you did was very serious - but I must tell you a story. When I was a young second lieutenant going through flying school at Randolph Field, I raced through the main gate and the Military Police took a couple of shots at my car. At least you did not get shot at. So, get out of here. I am sure you have learned your lesson." I will never forget the kindness of General Dent that day.

In fact, we had not learned our lesson. Driving in formation from Alabama to Arizona, we decided to have a race from one small town in West Texas to another. It was not a fair contest. Fred Dent drove a brand-new Thunderbird with a top speed of 135 miles per hour. My Ford convertible could do only 120 mph. Fred won the race.

Later we were cruising along at about 90 miles per hour when we were both pulled over by the Texas state police. They led us to a county official. We tried to convince him that we would soon be flying airplanes at a very high speed and hence we were very safe at 90 miles per hour on an empty highway. He was not impressed by our most persuasive arguments and fined us both!

FLYING SCHOOL AT MARANA, ARIZONA

Our flying school class (57-T) consisted of exclusively Naval Academy and Military Academy graduates. The first seven months of flying training was called Primary and the next six months was called Basic. We reported for Primary in early August, 1956. Located about 30 miles to the north of Tucson, Marana Air Base was run by civilian contractors. Most of the student pilots were bachelors who lived in barracks on base. The weather was hot but very dry. Each day the temperatures in the afternoon were in the 100s. Everyone preferred early morning flying and afternoon academics. Having arisen each morning at 5:50AM for the four years at West Point, we all were used to early get ups. At Marana Air Base, we rolled out of bed at 4:30 AM since the first flight briefings were at 5:30 and first flights, at 6:30 AM.

There was a strong motivation for everyone to excel in Primary flying school. Class standing was a major factor in determining whether we would move on to jets or to go to basic flying school in prop airplanes. The majority of our class wanted jets. Jet airplanes had been introduced into the Air Force shortly after World War II. By 1957 most of the fighters and bombers were powered by jet engines while most of the tanker and cargo aircraft were powered by propellers.

After a few days of ground school at Marana, each one of us had our first flight. This flight was called the "dollar ride." The airplane was the Air Force T-34 - a single engine, propeller-driven, two-seat airplane made by the Beech Aircraft Corporation. The afternoon of my "dollar ride" was a disaster for me. It was very hot and very bumpy. My instructor pilot was named Stranberg. He was big, burly and mean; the classic tough guy. He looked and talked like the actor, Earnest Borgnine. In those days everyone knew who Borgnine was. A pudgy, gapped-tooth middle aged man, he had earned the best actor Oscar in 1955 when he starred in the movie, *Marty*.

As Mr. Stranberg gave me an air tour of the local area, I quickly got very airsick. He headed home, climbed out of the aircraft and said to me, "Son, some people can fly airplanes, and some cannot." He then walked off. It was very clear that he thought I was in the second category. Since he was a top dog among the instructor pilots, I thought my chances of getting my wings were extremely low.

Happily, I was assigned to a different instructor pilot, Bill Goedeke, who was a lowkey, kind and considerate man. Like all of the instructor pilots, he was a civilian with thousands of hours of flight time. The rules in Air Force flying schools regarding air sickness were very strict. If you got sick five times you would be washed out - simple as that.

I got sick about sixty times during that seven months of primary flight training, but I did not wash out. When Bill Goedeke realized how badly I wanted to be a pilot, he came up with a brilliant strategy. After I got sick, he would open up the canopy and we would bomb the desert with my barf bag. He would not report me for being sick. I thanked him many times for his kindness. Sadly, I lost track of him after a few years.

Take offs and landings were easy and I soon soloed. My next trial came when I had about fifteen hours of flying time. It started at ten thousand feet. Following the directions of my instructor pilot, Bill Goedeke, I reduced the power to idle, pulled the control stick way back and I pushed the right rudder to the stop. The airplane shuddered, stalled, and quickly proceeded to go into a spin. The nose soon was pointed toward the stark dirt of the Arizona desert. As the aircraft continued to spin, I counted off the turns, one, two, three etc. etc. By the time I reached ten, I was dizzy, and the desert was much closer.

I neutralized the controls and slowly pushed the throttle forward. The aircraft smoothly came out of the spin. I had lost five thousand feet of altitude but was still four thousand feet above the ground. Airsickness followed immediately.

Why in the world would we be required such a dangerous and disorienting maneuver? The answer was easy. Air Force student pilots had to learn how to deal with emergencies and other difficult situations. Successfully conducting a ten-turn spin followed by a smooth recovery was one of the flying school requirements.

Other challenges were barrel and aileron rolls, loops, Cuban eights, Immelmanns and lufberries. Each of these aerobatic flight maneuvers was great fun for most of the student pilots. None of this boring straight and level flying for an eager student pilot. However, these maneuvers were real problems for those of us with motion-sickness issues. We did not look forward to these maneuvers, nor did we carry them out well.

The rules were clear. After a student pilot got air sick for the fifth time, he had to report to a flight surgeon. The doctor would pour ice-cold water into an ear. If the eyes fluttered for two minutes or more, the pilot had an overly sensitive middle ear. This was usually the cause of motion sickness of every type.

I was a classic eye flutterer. Both ears caused my eyes to flutter long past the two-minute mark. This was bad news. Any more air sickness would lead to elimination from flight school. My flight instructor came to my aid. Bill Goedeke's evaluation of me was as follows: after I got sick, I seemed able to fly pretty well. If I really, really wanted to be an Air Force pilot, Goedeke would not report the air-sickness episodes.

Although I got airsick in primary flying school, I slowly learned how to maintain my orientation during all flight maneuvers. There were only two episodes of airsickness in the follow-on program in the T-33 jet trainer. Once I became a full-fledged fighter pilot, the airsickness problem went away. I will always remember the kindness of my instructor pilot, Bill Goedeke.

SILLY SHENANIGANS AT MARANA AIR BASE

Having been locked up for four years at West Point and Annapolis, you might assume that we would engage in some wild activities. We sure did. Here are three of the most memorable ones: the Arizona toads, the pogo stick, and the obstacle course.

Chuck Young, my company mate from West Point was constantly complaining about the toads which hung around outside our barracks. At night, under the outdoor lamps, lots of bugs would fly around. This was feast time for the Arizona toads. On occasion a toad would wander into our barracks. One evening as Al Renshaw and I were driving from Tucson to Marana, we stopped for gas. Around the well-lit gas station were hundreds of toads.

In a moment of inspiration, we collected about 30 toads, placed them inside two cardboard boxes and brought them to Chuck's barracks. All of the toads were given their freedom in his barracks. We closed the doors on both ends of the building so the toads could not escape.

During the course of the night, the toads found places to hide - shoes and slippers were favorite venues. When the twelve officers woke up the next morning they were greeted by the sounds of toads (trilling) and the fury of Chuck Young. At first, he blamed one of his barrack mates for leaving a door open. Later that day he learned of our dastardly deed. Led by Chuck, retaliation followed in unremembered ways.

Another wild (but actually quite mild) event involved a pogo stick which was on sale at a local store. Al and I couldn't resist. Our first challenge was learning how to "pogo." After many crashes and near crashes, we learned the skill. Our next decision got us in trouble. On the upcoming weekend a formal dance was scheduled. Both the student pilots and our military supervisors were invited. Since neither Al nor I had a date, we decided that the pogo stick would be our date and our dance partner. It seemed like a good idea to have our newly purchased pogo stick join the festivities. It was a big hit.

Some of us were able to pogo with one hand on the stick and dance with a willing partner with the other hand. We were breaking new ground - no one had ever engaged in pogo dancing in the past. The trouble arrived when the inebriated First Lieutenant Ellis, our military supervisor, asked to try out the pogo stick. A man of limited talent and skills, Ellis fell off the pogo stick on his first try. He badly injured his ankle. Al and I left the dance fairly early. Walking down the road was Lieutenant Ellis's angry wife - her husband had made a fool of himself once again. We picked her up and dropped her off at the main gate.

On the following Monday, I was called into Lieutenant Ellis's office. He was in considerable pain and was using crutches. He admonished me for bringing the pogo stick to a dance. I was tempted to remind him that it was his idea to try pogoing. I did not remind him of the anger of his wife.

Another wild activity involved an obstacle course. After imbibing at the officer's club on a Friday evening, someone came up with the idea of a competition between ex cadets and ex midshipmen. Each long barracks building housed twelve officers. Unlike open bay barracks, these buildings gave each of us a certain degree of privacy. There was a partition separating each semi private room. Open at the bottom and at the top, these wooden partitions allowed air conditioning and toads free access to the next room.

The rules for the obstacle course were simple, climb over the first wall, race across the first room, dive under the next wall, climb over the next - and so forth. When reaching the far end of the building, the competitor would immediately reverse course. As the competitor left the barracks, he had to run over to a complex of bars and accomplish some unremembered tasks.

Climbing under a bed did not disturb the resident, but as we came over the top, we had to be careful to avoid the bed just under us. Even though we were pretty sloshed, we managed to miss landing on any of the residents. However, the noise woke them all up. Some got a kick out of our shenanigans - others not so much.

Who won is lost in memory. The barracks residents were unhappy with our disruptive activities but seemed to tolerate the drunken activities of a bunch of their friends. They asked us not to engage in this activity again. We agreed.

Crazy Days and Nights in Tucson

Tucson, Arizona in 1956 and 1957 was a medium-sized city with a population of about 150,000. The two biggest centers of population were the University of Arizona and Davis Monthan Air Force Base. Unlike our training base at Marana, Davis Monthan was a fully operational Air Force Base where bombers were assigned. We had very little contact with these bomber aviators. Most were married so they gave us little competition as we checked out the girls at the University of Arizona.

Most of us going through primary flying school were bachelors so chasing girls at the University of Arizona was a weekend routine. We had a solid income which included flying pay. We were clean cut, polite and relatively athletic. Hence, we could compete well with the male undergraduates and graduate students of the University of Arizona.

The Big Five and the Memorable Bet

During our days at Marana Arizona, five bachelors got together on weekends to chase girls, play golf or tennis, visit Mexico and generally have a grand time. Chuck Young, Al Renshaw, Fred Dent, Pete Verfurth and Perry Smith were the five West Pointers who composed "The Big Five." We used to kid each other about who might get married first and who might be last. A bet was made. The last one to get married would have the honor of having his ass kissed by all under the clock tower in the Central Cadet Area at West Point. This last man would also receive four bottles of his favorite whiskey.

One by one the marriages took place, first it was Fred, then Pete, then Chuck and then Al. I was the last to tie the knot. But when the key moment occurred and we were all present at West Point for a class reunion in 1996, the long-discussed deed did not take place. I never encouraged it nor did anyone else. I cannot imagine the reaction of the West Point authorities if we had actually carried out the dirty deed. I did expect to get four bottles of booze. That did not happen either.

Pete Verfurth's Jalapeno Challenge

The most adventurous member of the big five was Pete Verfurth. Pete just loved Mexican food; the "spicier" the better. As the big five were sitting around a table in a restaurant in Nogales, Mexico, Pete drew our attention to a bowl of jalapeno peppers which was sitting in the middle of the table.

Pete stated quite boldly that he could eat all of the peppers at one sitting. A bet was established with the following rules. Each of us would toss in a dollar. If Pete ate them all in rapid succession, he would get our money. If not, he would have to pay us one dollar each. Please remember we made $350 per month so a dollar was a pretty big number.

Another rule was that Pete could consume every beverage on the table, but not until he had swallowed the last pepper. In the bowl were about fifteen rather large Jalapenos.

Pete seemed to enjoy the first four or five - he smiled and radiated joy. The next few were not so welcome. Perspiration appeared on his face. The last few clearly caused him pain, but, by golly, he consumed them all. On the table were glasses of water, an orange drink and a beer or two. Pete chug-a-lugged the whole lot.

Sadly, in 2020, we lost Pete. Thousands of his friends miss his bubbly personality and, yes, his crazy ideas. Whenever I order Mexican food, I think of him.

The hangout of choice in Tucson was a bar/restaurant called *The Green Shack*. On Friday afternoons there was a two-hour happy hour and drinks were half price. A martini cost a quarter and a good steak meal could be had for $2.50.

One warm Friday evening in the late fall of 1956, someone suggested that we pile into a couple of cars and go skiing. I was game, but

*The Big Five: Fred Dent, Al Renshaw, Chuck Young,
Pete Verfurth and Perry Smith, 1990.*

I thought we were off for a session of water skiing. The route took us north to Flagstaff and to what was then a primitive ski area. The only route up the slopes was a cold and slippery rope tow. All of us crashed dozens of times but we fell in love with snow skiing that weekend. For the next forty-five years, skiing would be an important part of my life and the life of our family.

Shooting Al Thelin Through the Leg

Over a long weekend a bunch of us took a trip to Mexico. Someone came up with a really bad idea - shooting at jack rabbits with a pistol from our car in the dead of night. We had been consuming lots of beer, so our accuracy was marginal at best. After missing many times, I passed the 22-caliber pistol to my friend and West Point classmate, Al Thelin. As he commenced to reload, he somehow pulled the trigger and BANG - he shot himself in the leg. The bullet went all the way through his calf and the bleeding was quite extensive. Someone in the car wrapped a tight bandage around his leg - that slowed the bleeding, but the pain continued. We drove at a very fast pace to the city of Hermosillo and found a hospital where he was well taken care of.

Al Renshaw, who had brought the pistol along, felt responsible for the gunshot wound. I also felt bad since when I handed the pistol to Al Thelin, I told him it was not loaded. It was Al Renshaw and Perry Smith who took care of Al Thelin while the others proceeded on in another car for a weekend on the beach.

After crossing the border back into Arizona the next day, we dropped our wounded friend by the Air Force hospital at Davis Monthan Air Force Base. Needless to say, Al Renshaw and I got into big trouble. My training report on our final departure from Marana Air Base was quite negative - it claimed that I was immature. Considering my activities during my seven months at Marana, this was a fair assessment.

Knowing I was not likely to get high marks in the flying stage because of my air-sickness problem, I worked especially hard on academics. By the spring of 1957, we had graduated from primary and were off to basic. Out of about sixty in my class, I graduated near the middle. This meant I could go on to jets - but there was a possible hitch. Much depended on the judgment of the instructor pilot.

Mr. Goedeke asked me for my preference. I told him - "jets." I wanted to be a fighter pilot in the worst way. The rationale I provided him was as follows. First, I was not getting airsick as often. Second, when someone else was flying the airplane, I often would get sick, but when I was flying the aircraft and knew ahead of time what maneuvers I was going to undertake, I seldom got sick. In those days, jets meant that for most of your flying career you would be flying by yourself.

My kind instructor pilot recommended me for jets. Hence, I was off to Big Spring, Texas - to Webb Air Force Base and the single engine jet, the T33. Those who were recommended for multiengine aircraft also moved to West Texas, to Lubbock (Reese Air Force Base) - about eighty miles north of Big Spring. Those assigned to Reese would train on the B-25, a twin-engine aircraft, a stalwart combat aircraft of World War II. About half of our class at Marana went to Reese Air Force Base, including Al Renshaw and Pete Verfurth.

From that point forward, I would see fighter pilots often through the years but would have little contact with those who went on to fly bombers and cargo aircraft. The two exceptions were Al Renshaw and Peter Verfurth. They will appear often in this book.

On arriving at Webb Air Force Base, I quickly learned what life would be like in the stark, semi-desert environment of West Texas. When I checked into my room, I picked up the pillow from my bed. Where the pillow had been, the sheet was white. A layer of brown dust covered the rest of the bed - and the whole room. As I began to unload my car, an afternoon thunderstorm caught me outside. I experienced a "mud storm." As the rain fell through the dust storm, I was spattered by tiny clumps of mud.

Flying jets was great fun. I got airsick only twice. The T-33 trainer had room for two pilots. Usually the instructor sat in the back and the student in the front. I had to lower the seat to the very bottom - the airplane was not designed for tall people. When we were learning to fly on instruments, we strapped into the back seat. There was a canvas hood which the student pilot would slide along the inside of the aircraft canopy. This training helped get us ready for flying in bad weather. Often called "blind flying," piloting under the hood required total dependence on the flight instruments. Of all of these training missions, I enjoyed flying in formation with other aircraft the most. For the next twenty-five years, most of my flying involved formation flying with two, three or four aircraft.

After being spoiled by the university town of Tucson, finding single girls in Big Spring, Texas was nearly impossible. Hence on most weekends it was off to Dallas for the bachelors in our class. There were some apartments near Love Field where flight attendants lived (in those days they were called airline hostesses). Back in the 1950s, all of the hostesses were young, female and single. They had to meet certain height, weight and appearance guidelines. Many were very attractive; some were knock-you-down gorgeous.

On our first trip to Dallas, four of us drove around an apartment area in hopes of finding lovely young ladies. Bingo - we spotted a swimming pool where about a dozen women were hanging out. I was driving and was so entranced with the view that I drove right up onto the sidewalk. Everyone at the pool noticed my bad driving and my focus on the pulchritude at the pool.

We quickly donned our swimsuits and walked into the pool

Lieutenant Perry Smith proudly wearing brand new pilot wings.

area. The airline hostesses welcomed us warmly. Friendships were formed and many weekend trips to Dallas followed. With the exception of Ellen "Cole" Brown, who later married Chuck Young, I have not kept up with any of these lovely ladies.

Graduation from flying school was, of course, a very special day. We received our pilot wings in September, 1957. A trip to an advanced flying school soon followed. Again, class standing was important. Those who were at the top of the class were assigned to Williams Air Base, near Mesa, Arizona, to check out in the best fighter in the Air Force, the F-86. Those who were in the middle of the class got to go to Luke Air Force Base (just north of Phoenix) to check out in the F-84F. Those who were near the bottom of the class were assigned to the Air Training Command to fly T-33s and become flight instructors. Graduating number 17 out to a class of 60, meant that I missed the cut for F-86s. Hence, it was off to Luke Air Force Base to fly the underpowered, "bent wing," fighter-bomber, the F-84F.

A MEMORABLE WEDDING: THE GETAWAY CAR IN THE LOBBY

In the time period between Webb AFB and Luke AFB, a bunch of brand-new pilots drove 1000 miles from West Texas to Brawley, California to attend the wedding of our close friend, Fred Dent. Fred was marrying the spectacularly lovely and glamorous Marion

Hausmann. They had met in Tucson while she was an undergraduate at the University of Arizona. Fred quickly fell head over heels in love with her. Whenever he was not with her, he was quite mopey. Marion agreed to marry Fred as soon as he graduated flying school.

When it was time for the wedding to commence there was a problem. The mother of the bride could not be found. Someone suggested that she might be having a cocktail at the bar in the hotel across the street from the church. Sure enough - I found her and her boyfriend enjoying a pleasant drink at the hotel bar. When I suggested that it was time to go to the wedding, they had little interest in leaving the bar. In fact, they graciously offered to buy me a drink so we could discuss the upcoming nuptials.

Knowing I had to take fast action, I grabbed both of their drinks and headed for the church. They dutifully followed their drinks and the brash lieutenant who was carrying them. As we entered the church, I poured the cocktails into a couple of potted plants near the church entrance. The ceremony started about 15 minutes late - but the marriage worked and worked well.

The wedding reception of Fred and Marion was memorable. Our bunch of cocky Air Force pilots felt especially mischievous. Someone had the wild idea of taking the nicely decorated getaway car, a Volkswagen beetle, and carrying it to the hotel lobby. Ten strong men picked up the car, walked it up a long flight of stairs and placed it carefully in a prominent spot in the hotel lobby. Up to that time, I had never even thought of picking up an automobile, much less carrying it some distance. It seemed like a fine idea at the time and it worked. It was the talk of everyone at the wedding reception.

Wedding guests applauded our audacity and admired the witty slogans written on the car. With a HIP HIP HURRAY, they toasted us for our ingenuity. Everything was going along swimmingly until the hotel manager showed up. He grabbed me and asked me if I had brought the VW into his hotel. I told him, yes, that with the help of some others, I had done so. He angrily demanded that I immediately remove the car. I told him I would be happy to help, but my colleagues seemed to have drifted away. I suggested that this was a memorable experience for his hotel. Why not celebrate the occasion and take some pictures to highlight the ingenuity of members of the wedding party? His anger was something to behold.

Not long after my confrontation with the hotel manager, Fred arrived with the car keys. He unlocked the car and placed Marion gently into the passenger seat. Fred climbed in on the driver's side, started the engine and drove out the front door of the hotel. Many cheered as the VW bumped down the stairs and headed off into the night.

Knowing his mischievous friends well, Fred assumed that he would be followed after he left the hotel. Fred had an escape plan that was quite creative - but it did not work. He drove to a secret location where another VW was parked. He and Marion jumped from one car to the next and off they went towards Yuma, Arizona. Four cars were in hot pursuit. When Fred hit the main highway, we joined up in close formation on each side of his car. Our plan worked well until the flashing lights of a couple of police cars appeared behind us. We pulled over and Fred and Marion made their escape.

Fred and Marion Dent were married for 58 years. Sadly, handsome, humorous, humble Fred died at age 80 in 2015. He was buried near his dad, who had admonished Fred and me those many years ago, at West Point in late June, 2015. Many friends and family were in attendance at a moving graveside ceremony at the West Point cemetery. A reception was held at the headquarters of the Association of Graduates, on the grounds of the Military Academy. Funny stories were told as we celebrated the life of a dear friend, Frederick Rogers Dent.

FLYING STORY: GOING SUPERSONIC

The F-84F fighter was a disappointment. Severely underpowered, it took forever to take off on a hot day in Arizona. Jet engines are much less efficient on hot days. The F-84F had a single cockpit which meant that no one could show you how to fly the aircraft. What a feeling of accomplishment it was to fly an airplane that no one had taught you how to fly. Not only did we teach ourselves how to take off, land, fly formation, and perform acrobatics, but we also taught ourselves how to drop dummy bombs, shoot the gun and hit targets in the air and on the ground.

One day, when I was flying solo, I decided to fly faster than the speed of sound. I climbed to a high altitude, pushed up the power and pointed the nose toward the ground. It was early in 1958 and, by golly, I had flown supersonically. A really big deal at that time.

On graduation, I received the top gun award. My class was small, only about 20 pilots. After so many bouts of airsickness to be named the top gun in my class was special. Fred Dent was in a sister class - he also was named top gun.

Soon after graduating from gunnery school at Luke, it was off to Nellis Air Force Base which was located just outside of Las Vegas, Nevada. Learning to fly the supersonic supersabre (the F-100A) was great fun. A nice bonus was a chance to enjoy the attractions of Las Vegas. In 1958, tickets to shows were cheap and there was no charge at all for most of the lounge shows. The big show I enjoyed the most was Nat King Cole. Louis Prima and Keely Smith was our favorite lounge show. Louis's performance of "Just a Gigolo" was classic.

BAILING CLASSMATES OUT OF JAIL

One of my challenges as a young Air Force officer was getting involved with jails in Mexico and Las Vegas. Chuck Young and Fred Dent were tossed into a Mexican jail, at some point, but I don't remember the details. All I remember was finding the jail, paying the fines and being thanked by my friends. However, the Las Vegas story is still fresh in my mind.

When Chuck and I were attending F-100 school in Las Vegas in the spring of 1958, we found ourselves double dating. After having a drink at a bar, we decided to drive across town to a restaurant which was recommended by our two young ladies. In separate cars we raced to the restaurant. When my date and I arrived, we were pleased to have won the race.

About thirty minutes later we received a call from Chuck's date. The news was not good. Chuck had been stopped for speeding. When he opened the glove compartment to retrieve the car registration, the cops noticed a pistol. Chuck was spread eagled on the hood. When the policemen realized that Chuck did not have a gun permit, off to jail he went.

My task was clear that Friday night - bail a classmate out of jail once again. It was near midnight when I approached the desk sergeant in the large Las Vegas jail. When I explained my mission, I was told, in no uncertain terms, that Chuck was going to stay in jail until the following Monday. I explained to the desk sergeant that his prisoner, Lieutenant Chuck Young, was a fine citizen, a West Point graduate and an Air Force pilot. I said I would be pleased to vouch for his outstanding character.

When the desk sergeant learned of the West Point connection, he asked, "Do you know my cousin, Gayle Linkenhoger?" I replied that I knew him well. The desk sergeant asked me to describe him. I said that Gayle was from Texas, was tall, had dark hair, was a lacrosse player, and graduated in my class - the class of 1956. Happily, my description did the trick. Chuck would be released.

I followed a policeman deep into the jail. We went through three iron doors. When I reached the large cell which had housed Chuck for the past couple of hours, he was off in a far corner. The cell was full of some of the toughest looking characters I had ever seen. I was pleased to see Chuck. He was even more delighted to see me. A fine friendship between Chuck Young and me was reinforced that night. Within a couple of months, I served as best man in Chuck's wedding to Cole Brown.

The Many Challenges of Winter Survival School

As freshly minted fighter pilots our next stop was Stead Air Force Base which was located outside of Reno, Nevada. We were to attend the Air Force Winter Survival School which ran for about three weeks. There were about two hundred men in our class. Most were officers. Our first challenge was a nighttime assault on a simulated enemy base. Our entire class was captured; we became "prisoners of war." We were placed into large, underground, unheated bunkers. We were not fed; it was bitterly cold and we slept on rough gravel floors.

During the first full day of captivity we were taken to a building to be interrogated. Forced to kneel on a concrete floor, I was grilled for about an hour. I was told that America was an imperial power which had stolen much of Mexico, destroyed many Indian tribes and denied freedom to millions of Filipinos. America was accused of being the worst imperial power in human history.

I was told I would be treated much better if I would just admit to this reality. When I tried to counter the arguments, I was shouted down. There was no torture and no waterboarding. However, my bony knees became very painful. The next stop was even less enjoyable. I was placed inside a black box which was smaller than a coffin.

Placed vertically, I could not stand up straight in the box - I was too tall. The door was slammed shut and I was locked in. The first 30 minutes or so were not too bad. After that I began to slip slowly to a crouched position in the bottom of the box. Over time my legs and knees began to hurt. I desperately wanted to stand up again. Try as I might, I could not push myself up.

Because of small cracks around the door, I could survey the inside of the box. On the floor, I found a piece of string about two feet long. I noticed a nail high above my head. After many attempts, I lassoed the string around the nail. My plan was to use the string to pull myself up to a vertical position. I was very careful since I did not want the string to break or the nail to come loose. Long story short, my scheme worked. I would stand up for a while, then slide down and then haul myself back up. This went on for a couple of hours. When I was released the guards were surprised that I was vertical and relatively pain free.

SURVIVAL SCHOOL: DEAD MAN NUMBER ONE

My favorite story from Winter Survival School starts with my escape. Somehow we learned that escape attempts were permitted. If we reached a spot about one half of a mile away, we were to be given our freedom. Together with a few fellow prisoners we planned an escape. We volunteered to go on a work party to collect wood outside the walls of the compound. We snuck away from our guards, split up, and raced toward freedom. I got close but failed to reach the goal.

I was captured and taken back to the compound. I was then told that I would be shot by a firing squad. My task was made quite clear by a senior guard. I was to make my death seem very realistic. He told me how to fall down when the blanks were fired.

The entire group of POWs were ordered out of their bunkers and assembled so they could watch my demise. They were located far enough away that they could not observe me closely. The firing squad of six guards lined up. I was offered a final cigarette which I declined, since I had not smoked since I was five years old. I was then blind folded and my hands were tied behind my back. When the rifles fired in unison, I fell down and did not move. One of the riflemen then did something I did not expect. He shot me up close. I bounced a little and then lay still.

I was then hauled off by four guards. My hands were untied and I was given some hot soup. The guards told me I had done a good job. The next step soon followed: Using a string, they then hung a sign around my neck which stated in bold letters. DEAD MAN NUMBER ONE. It turned out to be quite a nice title, for I got to eat meals and to stay warm. I did not have to return to the frigid bunker.

Of all the ranks, positions, titles, and nicknames received in my 86 years, "Dead Man Number One" was the most special. Upon hearing this story recently, a friend suggested that DEAD MAN NUMBER ONE would look good on my tombstone.

The next challenge of Winter Survival School would be quite a test. Seven days of simulated escape and evasion in the High Sierra Mountains of eastern California.

Each of us constructed our own snowshoes using stiff branches and parachute cord and off we went for a long distance trek. It was late April; the ground was covered with snow on the north side of every hill. The temperature was below freezing each night but above freezing during the day. The three biggest tests we faced were lack of food, the cold temperatures at night and the fast moving Little Truckee Creek. Having nothing but two high energy bars to eat for four days while we expended great amounts of energy climbing up and down steep hills made us experience real hunger.

We were not permitted to hunt or fish with one exception. The porcupine was fair game. Our groups consisted of nine officers. We were accompanied by an enlisted man who was a survival expert. He served as a safety observer in case any of us were severely injured. He stayed out of our sight but on one occasion he was very helpful. He spotted a porcupine. This athletic young man climbed high up a tree. He knocked the large porcupine to the ground. My classmate, Lee Denson, chased after it and, with great determination, killed it.

I was chosen to be the butcher. Using my survival knife, it was very tough going. I cut the porcupine meat into nine portions. In the meantime, others dug a pit, lined it with rocks and built a roaring fire. Once the rocks became very hot the fire was scooped out. The butchered porcupine meat was placed in shallow water in two large cans. The rocks were piled around the top and the sides of the cans. The rock oven did its work for twelve hours. The result was surprisingly tender meat which tasted a bit like sweet pork - one of the finest, one course meals I had ever enjoyed.

The next challenge was crossing the creek. The spring runoff had turned the Little Truckee Creek into a raging river. We took off our snowshoes. Facing the oncoming river and using our snowshoes to break the force of the rushing water, we slowly sidestepped our way across. At the deepest, the river was waist high but its power was impressive. Also, the water was really cold. After I made it across, I watched my teammates closely as they fought their way across.

One teammate, Stu Bowen, was swept away by the raging water. I ran along the bank, got a bit ahead of him, and waded out into knee deep water. I was able to reach out to him with my snowshoe. He grabbed it and, soaking wet, he made it to the shore. I think he would have made it on his own, but he appreciated my help.

The final few hours were a test of our stamina. Three West Point classmates, Lee Denson, Stu Bowen and I, trudged for mile after mile in frigid weather. The crusty snow conditions didn't work for snow shoes. However, our boots often punched through the ice-covered snow. Progress was painfully slow. Stu struggled to keep up. For the last mile or two, the three of us walked side by side with Stu in the middle leaning on my left shoulder and leaning on Lee's right.

In order to avoid going through the entire school again, we had to reach our goal by a certain time. The three of us made it with less than an hour to spare. All of us lost weight, the skin on our hands was cracked and bleeding and our hunger was quite profound. I started the school at a slender 175 pounds. I finished at 161. Most lost more weight than me. A 30-pound loss was not unusual. The expression, "death warmed over" was used to describe us as we finished the survival school.

Upon graduation, Chuck Young, Lee Denson and I drove to Phoenix to attend a special event. The handsome Chuck Young married the lovely, charming, southern lady, Ellen "Cole" Brown. I served as best man and Lee was ring bearer. Chuck and I were company mates at West Point and had been roommates on two occasions during our flying school days. He eventually left the military and became a very successful dental surgeon. Cole was from Florida. She had been an airline hostess stationed at Love Field in Dallas when Chuck met her. Of all the lovely ladies in Dallas, Cole was the most attractive of them all.

Chuck and Cole had two daughters. Laura first and Lissa next. Laura has worked for many years as a land easement specialist at the Virginia Outdoors Foundation. Her passion is preserving greenspace throughout the State of Virginia. Lissa graduated from West Point in 1986. During her senior year she was the deputy brigade commander - the second highest cadet leadership position. Since 2014 she has served as an assistant professor in the Department of Behavioral Science and Leadership at West Point. Starting in 2014, Lissa has served as a good contact for the class of 1956 at West Point.

Chapter Four:

FIRST OPERATIONAL ASSIGNMENTS
AND CONNOR DYESS, 1958

MY NEXT ASSIGNMENT was at an airbase in eastern France. I arrived at my new base in early June, 1958. I was stationed at Toul Rosiere Air Base. My squadron was the 10th Tactical Fighter Squadron which was part of the 50th Tactical Fighter Wing. The Wing consisted of three squadrons, with 25 aircraft per squadron. All of the pilots in each squadron flew the single seat, supersonic F-100D - the Supersabre. Our mission was to deliver, when ordered to do so, nuclear weapons on military targets on the nations of the Warsaw Pact (the Soviet Union and its allies). Most of our targets were enemy airfields in Czechoslovakia.

The weather was bad throughout all of northern Europe during the winter months so getting gunnery practice was very difficult. In order to get gunnery and bombing practice in better weather, fighter pilots, on occasion, would deploy to Wheelus Air Base in Libya, North Africa. The United States had a good relationship with Libya in the 1950s largely as a result of a large annual grant. The flying weather there was excellent most of the year and the bombing range gave us the opportunity to practice weapon deliveries, using dummy bombs, of course. In the summer, temperatures often reached above one hundred degrees. When the wind blew from south to north, the heat was quite intense.

On one occasion, I was taxiing out to the runway when I got a radio call from the control tower. I was ordered to return to the aircraft parking area. When I asked why, the response was quite simple - the runway was melting. The wind was blowing from off the Sahara Desert and the temperature was 117 degrees.

We were housed in open bay barracks which were not air

conditioned. We found the best way to stay cool enough to get some sleep was to drape damp, cool towels over our naked bodies. Some pilots tried sleeping on the roof. Bad idea. Biting flies would chew them up all night long.

As young carefree pilots, we were full of crazy ideas about how to harass each other. This is how we dealt with pilots who had too much to drink at the Officer's club. There were a few young pilots who could not control their drinking. If they were not on the flying schedule the next day, they felt free to have a few extra drinks. Before a pilot returned to the barracks, we would take his bunk, hide it outside, and rearrange the bunks. When the inebriated pilot returned, he could not find his bunk. As he stumbled around in great frustration, we watched with great glee. But alas, I am getting ahead of myself.

CONNOR DYESS CAPTURES MY HEART

During my gunnery school period in Arizona (in the fall of 1957) I had a decision to make which would turn out to be life changing. I had been asked to participate in two weddings during the Christmas period of 1957. My roommate at West Point, Don Holleder, who was a first lieutenant in the Army, asked me to be his best man. The wedding was to be held in Arlington, Virginia. At about the same time, Pete Verfurth asked me to be an usher at his wedding, which was to be held in Phoenix. The weddings were to be held on the same day, December 28, 1957.

Pete Verfurth was marrying Anne Miller, a University of Arizona Kappa Alpha Theta. Anne was from one of the founding families of Phoenix. Pete had met Anne while we were in flying school near Tucson. I had been around Pete and Anne for much of their courtship. Although Pete and Anne had become good friends, Don Holleder was an even closer friend, having been my roommate at West Point for three years.

I had to make a choice, and, thank goodness, I made the right decision. It was a decision that impacted my life most profoundly in a number of interesting ways. As fate would have it, Pete and Anne Verfurth's second son, Robert, would, many years later, become a member of our family. Robert Verfurth married our daughter, Serena in 1990.

I flew from Phoenix to Northern Virginia to be the best man in the wedding of Holly. Don was marrying Caroline Pierce from Alexandria, Virginia. Caroline's father was a well-respected banker and community leader in Northern Virginia. I had dated Caroline a couple of times when I was a cadet so I was pleased that Holly had chosen her as his bride.

A couple of days before the wedding of Donald Walter Holleder to Caroline Pierce, Holly told me that I must <u>marry</u> the maid of honor, Connor Cleckley Dyess from Augusta, Georgia. I was quite surprised by this advice. You see, I was enjoying bachelorhood and had not yet met Connor. I asked Holly why I should get married and why I should choose Connor as my wife. He said that Connor was beautiful, a red-head, a southern belle and an Episcopalian.

At this time in my life I had an attractive girl friend named Wendy Capitka. She was from Steubenville, Ohio and was an airline hostess for Braniff Airlines. She was stationed at Love Field in Dallas. In short, it was not love at first sight with Connor. My first impressions of Connor were favorable. Holly was correct in his description of her.

However, she smoked cigarettes, I thought her hair was too curly and she kept staring at me. On the night of the wedding I had a bit too much to drink as I escorted Connor to the after the wedding party at the officer's Club at Bolling Air Force Base, in Washington, DC. On a lark I traded her for a bass fiddle. The bass player danced with Connor and I fiddled.

When I returned to Arizona, I wrote to Connor to apologize for getting smashed the night of the wedding. This led to a series of letters between Connor and me. I soon realized that she was someone I wanted to spend time with. It was five months later, in May of 1958, that we were able to meet again. Connor visited me briefly in Hampton, Virginia just before I flew off to France for my first operational assignment in the military.

My mother was living in Hampton at the time. After my sister's marriage and my graduation from West Point, Meps Smith decided to leave New York where the winters were so harsh. She picked Hampton because she had many friends there and because the climate was much warmer.

During Connor's visit to Hampton in May, 1958, a magic moment occurred. In the backyard of our family's dear friends, the "Empy" Potts, a game of croquet was underway. Connor and I were a team. She was trying so hard but she kept falling behind. As her partner, I would send my ball in her direction to try to help her through the course. There was something about her that afternoon that I found endearing. Helping her was a joy.

During that same visit, Connor and I went out to dinner at the Officer's Club at historic Fort Monroe, Virginia. As we walked into the large dining area, I noticed that everyone was looking at Connor. She was absolutely gorgeous. With her striking red hair and her stately posture, she drew the attention of men and women alike. Never before had I dated a young lady who drew so many glances of admiration.

By the end of her visit to Hampton, I realized how special she was. For the next seven months ours was a romance of correspondence since I was living in France and she was in Augusta. Her letters were very special. As she described her life in Augusta, I became more and more impressed with her intellect, her character and her willingness to share her feelings with me.

My first operational assignment in France had many ups and downs. One of the big downers was dealing with the wing commander of the 50th Tactical Fighter Wing, Colonel Henry Newcomer. He was a West Point graduate; smart, fluent in French and a fine tennis player (I played as his partner quite often). He had one major fault - hyper ambition. He wanted to outperform the other Wing Commanders in Europe by flying more sorties per month. He accomplished this goal by ordering us to fly when the weather was below landing minimums (200-foot ceilings and ½ mile visibility).

This led to exciting, yet dangerous situations. I remember one time, I had just landed in "below minimum" conditions. Fortunately, I broke out just in time to find the runway and land safely. I was back at the squadron area and hanging up my flying gear when traipsing by were three grim faced officers, First Lieutenant Ray Karam, my squadron commander and our wing operations officer.

Ray had landed safely but he landed on the taxiway and not on the runway. The ground control radar operators had lined him up incorrectly. At the exact moment of his touchdown, Lee Denson was taxing his aircraft up the taxiway. Seeing Ray's aircraft coming at him at a high speed, Lee quickly turned off the taxiway as Ray raced on by.

A few months later, Colonel Henry Newcomer was promoted to the rank of brigadier general and reassigned to Turkey. We were pleased to see him go. At his departure party a group of fighter pilots, led by Dick Kuiper, sang, parodying Gilbert and Sullivan's HMS Pinafore, "He polished up the apple so carefully that now he is a general in old Turkey." General Newcomer seemed to enjoy the gentle ribbing he received that evening.

In January, 1959, Connor flew into Paris for a two-week visit. Such a visit was not something to take lightly back then. In those days, it could be seen as inappropriate for a woman to travel so far to see a man she was not married or even engaged to. During an international phone call on Connor's birthday I asked her to come to France for a visit. That call was followed by a letter where I made the case that since we loved each other, we should find a way to be together.

At that time, a good friend, Charlie Hamm, was a squadron mate with me. Charlie, his young wife, Jane, and their infant child, Jose, lived in a small apartment in the City of Nancy, France. When I told Jane that I was not sure Connor would come, Jane was kind enough to write to Connor and ask her to stay with them during her visit. This letter was greatly appreciated by Connor and her parents.

Connor and I had a delightful time together in Paris, Nancy, France and Garmisch, Germany. It soon became clear that Connor was smart, quick witted and had a fine sense of humor. All the people she met enjoyed her company. During this visit, we spent a few days skiing in Germany. Connor's skiing skills were non-existent, but everyone in our skiing group was impressed by how hard she tried.

There was something mysterious and magical about Connor. My previous girlfriends had all been outgoing and self-confident. Connor was shy and did not enjoy talking about herself. I slowly came to the conclusion that I wanted to spend my life with her. I felt that if I did not propose marriage Connor would return to Augusta, get married to someone else and I would lose her forever. I just could not let that happen.

At this time, I knew that Connor's father had been killed in World War II and that her mother had married an Army Air Corps officer, Charlie Goodrich, after the war. I also knew that Colonel Goodrich had been a prisoner of war in Germany. I was aware that Connor had moved around often as a child and had lived in Northern Virginia for a while.

But there was much I did not know when I proposed marriage. For instance, I did not know Connor's father, Jimmie Dyess, was a recipient of the Medal of Honor and the Carnegie Medal (the only person in history to be awarded both), that her uncle, Hervey Cleckley, was a renowned psychiatrist, or that Charlie Goodrich had been the senior American officer in the huge German prisoner of war camp, Stalag Luft III. I also did not know that Connor was a talented lyric soprano who had had solo singing and acting roles in numerous musical productions.

In late January, 1959, in the home of our friends Charlie and Jane Hamm, I proposed to Connor Cleckley Dyess. Her answer was "When?" I was delighted. It was thirteen months after we had first met but we had been together a total of 22 days. It had been a romance and love story nurtured by letter writing. Long distance phone calls, particularly international ones, were expensive back then. There was no Facetime, texting or email. The best way for us to connect was with letters.

Before flying back to the United States for our wedding in May, 1959, one event of note took place at Toul Rosiere Air Base. I was driving on the perimeter road just inside the fence that circled the base. It was a Sunday so there was very little flying that day. I was paralleling the runway when I heard a loud and unfamiliar sound. To my right was an F-100 flying at a high speed about five hundred feet above the ground. The airplane was doing distortions like I had never seen before. Clearly, the airplane was out of control. Within about ten seconds I saw a pilot eject; a few seconds later a second pilot ejected. Thankfully both parachutes deployed. The airplane leveled off and flew a couple of miles before it crashed.

A few weeks later, the accident investigation team called me to testify. With the exception of the two pilots in the out-of-control aircraft,

I was the only fighter pilot who had witnessed the event. I used a model of an F-100 to demonstrate the flight of the aircraft. After I explained what happened I was challenged by one of the team members. He told me that there was no way an airplane could have gone through the extreme gyrations which I described.

I was very firm in my response to his comments. I told him and the whole investigation team that although I never imagined an aircraft could have done what it did, I was absolutely sure that my description was correct. My certainty seemed to convince the board. This experience in dealing with an aircraft accident investigation team was helpful to me many years later when I served as a fighter wing commander and had to deal with five aircraft crashes.

Six days before the wedding, I flew back to the States. When I arrived in Augusta, Connor met me at the airport. Up to that time, I had not met her parents or anyone else in Augusta. I was a brash fighter pilot and a Yankee. My mission was to spirit the lovely Connor Cleckley Dyess away from Augusta. Happily, I was greeted warmly by Connor's family and friends.

Three days before the wedding I met with the Reverend Charles Schilling, the rector of Saint Paul's Church. Schilling had become an Episcopal priest prior to World War II. During the war he served as an Army chaplain. After landing at Normandy, he was wounded three times. One of the most decorated Army chaplains in World War II, he received two awards for heroism, the Silver Star and the Bronze Star.

At Saint Paul's church, Charles Schilling greeted me warmly but he quickly got very serious. As I remember his words, Father Schilling said to me in a very strong voice, "Lieutenant, I want you to listen to me very carefully. You are about to marry the most wonderous woman you will ever know. You must treat her with great love and respect for the rest of your life, DO YOU UNDERSTAND ME?" My answer was "Yes Sir." He was absolutely correct about Connor. For more than 61 years I have tried to follow his charge.

Connor and I married in historic Saint Paul's Church in downtown Augusta. My best man was Al Renshaw, a West Point classmate who became a good friend during flying school in Arizona. The ushers included West Point graduates Mario Nicholas, George Lawton, Tom

*Perry and Connor Smith at Wedding Reception in
Old Government House, Augusta, May, 1959.*

Ross and John Snodgrass and my sister's husband, Rocky Barber. With
the exception of Al Renshaw, members of the Big Five from flying
school were not able to attend.

The maid of honor was Muggs Cole, Connor's step-sister. The
bridesmaids were childhood friends, Martha Carpenter, Karine
Wooten, and Sue McMurray. Other bridesmaids included Connor's
cousin, Mary Dolan, Connor's college friend, Robie Strickland, and
my sister, George Anne Barber. The junior bridesmaid was first cousin,
Greer Ewing.

On the late afternoon of May 9th, 1959, the skies opened up and dumped a great deal of rain on Augusta. The east parking lot of the church had more than 8 inches of standing water. The radio advised people to avoid downtown Augusta. Al Renshaw and I took off our shoes and socks, rolled up our trousers and waded to a side entrance of the church. Despite the flood, the turnout was good and the ceremony commenced only about 15 minutes late.

The wedding reception was held at Old Government House on Telfair street. By the time the wedding was over, the rains had stopped. Thirty-one years later, our daughter, Serena, was married at Saint Paul's. Rob and Serena Verfurth had their wedding reception at Old Government House. Serena wore Connor's wedding dress. The daughters of Greer Ewing Brannon would be in their wedding.

Three days before our wedding, Connor's uncle, the noted Augusta psychiatrist, Hervey Cleckley, presented me with a certified check for $100. He suggested that when we stayed in his favorite city, Paris, we dine at the two best restaurants in the City of Lights. We dined elegantly at Tour D'Argent and at an elegant restaurant in the Bois de Boulogne. One hundred dollars covered the cost of both meals with wine. One hundred dollars in 1959 was comparable to one thousand dollars in 2020 currency.

The day after our wedding, Connor and I flew off for our honeymoon in Europe. Our first stop was on the beautiful, unspoiled island of Majorca in the Mediterranean Sea. We rented a Vespa motor scooter. My checkout did not impress Connor. She watched her fighter pilot husband drive the Vespa into a wall outside our hotel. It took me a while to master the motor-scooter skills.

On this scooter, we toured the island for about ten days. The next stop on our honeymoon was Paris where we stayed for three nights at the small, quaint, Hotel Celtic. Located near the Champs Elysees, it was the perfect spot from which to enjoy Paris in the springtime.

We then drove four hours east to the lovely city of Nancy in the Province of Lorraine. Connor and I loved France, the people, the language, the cuisine and the culture. We lived in a tiny rental apartment on the outskirts of Nancy. No one in our neighborhood spoke English so we had lots of opportunities to practice our French. It was helpful that Connor had studied French in grammar school, high school and college and I had studied it at West Point. In addition, Connor had (and has) an impressive ear for languages.

From France to Germany, 1959

Sadly, in the fall of 1959 our fighter wing was ordered out of France by President Charles De Gaulle. Off to Hahn Air Base in Germany we went. Located in the Hunsruck area of West Germany, Hahn was south of the German city of Koblenz and quite close to both the Rhine and Mosel rivers. Hahn Air Base had the worst flying weather of any Air Force Base in the world. Hence all of the fighter pilots learned to take off, to fly and to land in very bad weather. Fog, low ceilings and poor visibility was the name of the game, especially during the fall and winter months.

At Hahn Flugplatz, we lived in a small apartment which was on base. We made many good friends, partied as only fighter pilots can party, and enjoyed short vacations in Austria, Paris, Oslo, and Copenhagen. In the spring of 1960, in Oslo, Norway we purchased a brand-new Mercedes Benz 190 SL. After we received a NATO discount, this fine sports car cost us $3600. This classic convertible had a soft top and a separate hard top. We kept it for fourteen years. It was not a practical car as our family grew since the back seat was tiny. When we finally sold it, Connor could not watch as it was driven away - it was so hard to give up. In 2020, if it was in mint condition, our 1960 Mercedes would be worth $180,000.

Flying Story: Stuck Throttle

I was flying over Germany in my F-100, a single seat and single engine fighter aircraft. I was in the holding pattern waiting for my opportunity to descend and land. The weather at my home base (Hahn Flugplatz) was terrible. The ceiling was 200 feet and visibility was 6/10th of a mile (barely above minimums for landing). As you came down the final approach you had to pick up the runway visibly if you were going to land safely. Advanced instrument landing systems were not available in 1960.

On the ground were highly skilled radar operators who would guide the pilot down using rapid radio calls. If the weather got

below a 200-foot ceiling or a visibility of less than one half of a mile, a pilot would be ordered to divert to another base where the weather was better.

Just before it was time to begin my descent, I realized that my throttle was frozen. I could not move it forward or backward. This was quite a problem. On my descent, I had planned to reduce the throttle setting to 80% of power - but it was stuck at 93%.

If the weather had been clear, this would not have been much of a problem. I could have put the speed brake down, put the aircraft into a tight turn and pulled back hard on the stick. This maneuver would have slowed the aircraft so I could have lowered the landing gear and flaps. I still would have come down final approach fast, but I could have shut down the engine with the fuel shut off switch in the cockpit just before crossing the runway threshold.

But accomplishing that tight, high g-force maneuver in the heavy clouds would have been hard and dangerous. I declared an emergency and told the agency, which controlled all flight operations in the area, of my problem. I then put both feet up on the sides of the instrument panel. Using as much leverage as I could, I pulled hard on the throttle with both hands. The throttle started to bend - I thought it was about to break off. My thoughts at the time - if I have to punch out, I will want to show the accident investigation team the remainder of a throttle.

In the meantime, I was running low on fuel. I started my descent while still pulling really hard on the throttle. Just as I entered the low hanging clouds, the throttle became unstuck. With a huge sigh of relief, I called off the emergency and made a normal landing.

By the summer of 1960 I found myself working in Wing headquarters as a staff officer. I continued to fly on a regular basis with the 10th Tactical Fighter Squadron. One day I was called into the office of Colonel Levi Chase, the operations officer for the 50th Tactical Fighter Wing. A gruff sourpuss, Chase explained that Hahn Air Base would soon host an airshow. To my surprise, I was given the responsibility, along with my fellow fighter pilot, Von Christiansen, of organizing and conducting this show. Both of us were first lieutenants at the time.

Included in the show would be acrobatic teams from a number of nations. Working out the timing was a major challenge since some of the teams flew fast jets, while others flew slow moving propeller driven aircraft. Also, some teams were scheduled to put on a full show while others just flew by in close formation. The morning of the show, I briefed all of the participants in English and in my halting French.

Unfortunately, there were broken clouds so some teams could not perform their full show. Handling the timing from high up in the base tower in a couple of different languages was just part of the challenge. Some teams failed to follow my directions. The large crowd seem to enjoy the flybys and the acrobatic team performances but there were a couple unfortunate gaps when timing broke down.

The air show probably ranked as a B but it was a great learning experience for Von and me. Our bosses trusted us and did not second guess our many decisions. Many organizations on base followed our directions even though we were just two first lieutenants. What a treasured moment it was to have been given this responsibility and allowed to carry it out as we thought best.

Back to the United States, 1961

In the summer of 1961, Connor and I were off to England Air Force Base near Alexandria, Louisiana. A small city of about 70,000, Alexandria was a three hour drive northwest of New Orleans. Connor had disliked the dreary weather in Germany and was delighted that we were headed to a base in the South. We loved Alexandria and made many friends including Jerry and Arden Gentry who were our neighbors. Jerry, a fellow fighter pilot, later became a renowned test pilot. During his brilliant Air Force career, Jerry received three major aviation awards, the Harmon, Kincheloe and Chanute Awards.

In Alexandria, Connor received many invitations to sing. Our son, McCoy, arrived on schedule in the summer of 1962. From the moment of his birth McCoy has been a delight, always loving, kind and considerate. I spent much of the time overseas on long deployments while Connor stayed busy with her singing and acting gigs and raising McCoy.

During the two and a half years, while I was stationed at England

Captain Perry Smith with F-100D in the background, 1963.

Air Force Base in Louisiana, I deployed to Turkey on three occasions. The length of these deployments was four months each. The following are two stories from my tours in Turkey which are worth highlighting

Along with another fighter pilot, I took a trip by train from Cigli Air Base near Izmir to Istanbul for a four day visit to that fascinating city. It was the fall of 1963. When visiting a large bazaar, I entered a shop. The shop owner spoke good English. Once he determined that I was an American, he inquired about the Birmingham church bombing that had occurred a few days earlier. I was totally at a loss with a reply. I had not heard of the bombing which had killed four little black girls. The Turkish shopkeeper was incensed about both the event and that I knew nothing about it.

At that moment, I realized how much the world was paying attention to events in America. On many occasions in the past sixty years, I have been reminded how often the actions of Americans and the rhetoric of our leaders send messages, both good and bad, to billions of people in more than 200 nations. Sometimes we fall well short of being a shining city on the hill.

THE DRUNKEN FIGHTER PILOT CRAWLS HOME

When my fighter squadron deployed to Turkey, our job was to pull nuclear alert. Our targets were military bases located in the Soviet Union. During each four-month deployment our squadron would host a "dining in." As opposed to a "dining out" where spouses/dates were included, a "dining in" included only officers. On our temporary duty deployments to Turkey, family members did not come along.

The routine at the dining-in was well established. There would be an hour-long cocktail hour followed by a formal dinner and a guest speaker. On my first deployment all went well until the speaker, the head of the Peace Corps for Turkey, rose to speak. He was a poor speaker and we quickly labeled him an over-educated wimp.

Each of us had a hard roll on our bread plate. About five minutes into the speech, the first roll was thrown at the speaker. Within seconds many more were headed his way. I will always remember his expression as he ducked under the table to miss the onslaught. I learned that day an important lesson. Don't serve hard rolls at "dining ins." The lesson served me well when I was a wing commander sixteen years later.

The next "dining in" was even more memorable. For some unknown reason, the dinner arrived an hour late. Hence the one-hour cocktail hour stretched into two. At that time, my drink of choice was Beefeaters Gin. That evening I had at least four of these powerful drinks.

When I realized I was drunk, I tried to walk back to our barracks, which was only one block away. Walking did not work that evening. On my hands and knees, I crawled back to my barracks bed. The next day I had a classic hangover. It lasted more than 24 hours. It was much worse than the bad hangover I had after my high school graduation. This was a humiliating situation for me, a married father and a captain responsible for multimillion-dollar aircraft and nuclear weapons. I learned an important lesson that day in 1962. From that time forward, I swore to myself never to get drunk again. This pledge has lasted until this day.

TOUR OF THE MIDDLE EAST: AN OSKAR SCHINDLER MOMENT

In 1962, when deployed to Incirlik Air Base in southern Turkey, a fellow fighter pilot, Ian Little, and I took a ten-day trip through the Middle East. We visited Lebanon, Syria, Jordan, Israel and Cyprus. The most memorable moment occurred at the Tel Aviv Airport (now called the David Ben Gurion airport). A Lufthansa airliner had just landed. Down the stairs came a tall, elderly gentleman. He appeared to be a

German. As he reached the bottom of the stairs he was greeted by a rush of men and women. They hugged him, kissed him on his cheeks and on his hands and wept. Ian and I were amazed. We had no idea what was going on.

Years later, I had the answer. When I watched Stephen Spielberg's Academy Award winning movie, *Schindler's List*. I asked myself a question. Could that have been Oskar Schindler who was greeted with such joy those many years ago? In fact, after I did my research, it was indeed Schindler. He was making a visit to Israel to receive a major award from the government of Israel. The realization that I had observed, first hand, a historic moment still gives me goosebumps.

FLYING STORY: LANDING IN THREE SHIP FORMATION

One of the great challenges of flying fighter aircraft is having responsibility for every airplane in your formation, or "flight." Much of my flying was in formations of two, three or four aircraft. If I was the flight leader and any of the aircraft had an emergency, I had the duty to assist. This included making calculations about fuel, landing options and emergency procedures. Sometimes these decisions needed to be made quickly and with limited information. The following is one example; I was a flight leader flying out of an airbase in North Carolina.

The year was 1963. I had been flying fighters for five years. I had more than 1000 hours in the F-100 aircraft and was an instructor pilot and a qualified four-ship flight leader. Flying in an air-to-ground exercise over North Carolina, there were three F-100s in my flight. The weather was deteriorating rapidly and all the airbases on the East Coast would soon go below landing minimums (200-foot ceilings and ½ mile visibility). In bad weather, it was normal that each aircraft would come down final approach and land individually. It soon became clear that if all of the aircraft in the air that day were to land safely this procedure would take too much time.

I called the control agency and stated that all three of us would land at the same time. This pleased the controllers and helped them get other aircraft down more quickly. However, it surprised my wingmen. Neither one of them had ever landed in a three-ship formation - nor had I.

I did not have to tell my wingmen to fly very close to me. If they had not done so they would have missed the runway and crash landed in the turf on each side of the runway. Happily, we touched down simultaneously and safely in close formation at Seymour Johnson Air Force Base.

One of my wingmen was our squadron commander. He tended to be hypercritical of any of his pilots who deviated from normal procedures. During the flight debriefing, I expected that he would be harshly critical of my snap decision. I anticipated him saying the following: "Smith, you made a horrible decision. You didn't check with me before you made your decision. None of us has ever made a three-ship landing. What we did was very risky. Captain Smith, you are grounded."

What he said was something like, "Smith, in my twenty years of flying fighters, I never thought of landing in a three ship formation - good job."

OFF TO JUMP SCHOOL AT FORT BENNING

There was an emphasis in the early 1960s on the Air Force having a close relationship with the Army. Fighter pilots were encouraged to attend the Army jump school at Fort Benning, Georgia. I volunteered, so I was off to Fort Benning for the three-week course and the five parachute jumps. Fort Benning has been an important Army installation for many decades. Since 1909 it has been the home of the infantry, the most important branch of the United States Army. It was at Fort Benning in the 1920s and 1930s where the Army trained most of the great leaders of World War II.

Named after a confederate Civil War general who was a strong supporter of slavery, Fort Benning will likely find another name soon. Fort Benning was the home of the largest parachute training school in the Army. This school trained professionals from all of the military services. After earning my jump wings in the fall of 1962, I received the official designation as a "jump qualified forward air controller."

In the 1950s and early 1960s, there was a requirement for properly trained Air Force fighter pilots to be assigned to every Army division. These pilots did not need to be jump qualified if they were assigned to most Army divisions. However, the two Army Airborne Divisions (the 82nd and the 101st) needed jump qualified Air Force fighter pilots who could jump into the combat zone with the Army parachutists.

To maintain our jump qualification the pilots in my squadron with jump wings continued to jump every three months. As a bonus we received jump pay each month. For about a year, I received both flight pay and jump pay. The nearest base where we could practice our parachute skills was at a Louisiana National Guard base near Breaux Bridge, Louisiana. This was deep in the heart of Cajun country. The jump master briefed us in the French language. We jumped into a large field - the biggest challenge was missing the cows.

I continued to make a parachute jump every three months until I left for graduate school in January, 1964. Altogether I made a total of eight day jumps and one night jump. If I ever had to eject from a jet aircraft, I would know how to steer a parachute and make a decent parachute landing fall. That never happened. As a pilot, the number of my landings and takeoffs were the same - the goal of all pilots.

THE DEATH OF A YOUNG FIGHTER PILOT

A major failure on my part occurred in 1963 when I was stationed at England Air Force Base. I was serving as the weapons and tactics officer of the 615ᵗʰ Tactical Fighter Squadron. In this position I was responsible for working with each pilot on various skills. For example, every six months each pilot had to qualify in skip bombing, dive bombing, and the delivery of dummy weapons which simulated nuclear weapons.

As pilots, we flew the single seat F-100D aircraft. One of the young pilots in my squadron was having difficulty qualifying on the nearby gunnery range. When he dropped his small dummy bombs on dive bomb runs he would not come close to hitting the target.

The rules were quite simple. Any pilot who could not come within 140 feet of a target on a regular basis could not qualify as a mission ready combat pilot. This would mean he could no longer

fly fighter aircraft. He would continue to keep his pilot wings, but he would never again fly high-performance fighter aircraft. He would end up flying in large aircraft where he would have assistance from another pilot.

This pilot in our squadron, who badly wanted to gain his fighter pilot qualification, approached me for assistance. I explained, in detail, the technique that most of us used on the bombing range. We would roll in a little bit steeper than recommended in the tactics manual and would release our practice bomb slightly lower than recommended. This technique would lead to greater bombing accuracy.

I will always remember with sadness the day that this young pilot drove his aircraft into the ground. I was the leader of a four-ship flight. The pilot who was having bomb delivery difficulties was flying in the number two position. I was the first to roll in on the target. My bombing pass was routine and my practice bomb landed within about 40 feet of the target.

As I pulled up to the downwind leg, I observed the number two pilot roll in. His dive angle looked about right but he was slow to pull up. Before I could shout at him, he began his pullout at a very low altitude. The nose of his aircraft was slightly above the horizon when he hit the ground. The aircraft exploded into thousands of pieces and the pilot died instantly.

That same day I decided to change my whole approach to leadership and to teaching. Whenever I encounter someone who is incompetent and is putting himself, herself or others in danger, I feel obliged to take action. If I am in an organization which is being damaged by someone's incompetence, I am committed to taking steps to resolve the problem. This usually means removing the individual from his or her job. Part of my responsibility is finding a position where competency can be gained and maintained. In the case of the young pilot, I should have recommended to my bosses that he no longer fly fighter aircraft.

Enjoying vacations while living in Louisiana.

During our two-and-a-half years in Alexandria, Louisiana, Connor and I would take short vacations to New Orleans and to the Caribbean.

In the 1960s there were two performers of note in the French Quarter of the great city of New Orleans. We had the joy of enjoying the musical talents of Pete Fountain and Al Hirt.

On a ten-day trip to Jamaica we stayed at Montego Bay and at Ocho Rios. Beautiful beaches at both spots. There was a grand waterfall near Ocho Rios which provided us with climbing and frolicking experiences.

Perry and Connor Smith enjoying a waterfall in Jamaica, 1963.

Chapter Five:

COLUMBIA UNIVERSITY AND THE AIR FORCE ACADEMY: 1964 - 1968

IN JANUARY, 1964, we were off again - this time to the cold and unfriendly town of Teaneck, New Jersey. We were used to the warm hospitality of Alexandria. The transition was quite a shock. In Teaneck, most of our neighbors showed us no warmth at all. In the aftermath of a major snowstorm in the northeast, I entered graduate school at Columbia University. Two years earlier I had decided that teaching at the Air Force Academy would be a grand way to expand my horizons. I also felt living in Colorado for a few years would be great for our expanding family. Since I had greatly enjoyed my courses at West Point in the social sciences, I had approached the Department of Political Science at the Air Force Academy. For graduate school, I was turned down by Harvard and Princeton but was accepted at Columbia University.

This historic university had a reputation of being friendly toward military scholars. In the 1960s, many Columbia University professors had served in the federal government during World War II. These professors especially enjoyed teaching students who had some real life experiences. I fit the bill with my years in Europe, both as a child and as an Air Force officer. I chose the field of international relations rather than international organization, international law or American government. Since I had travelled so widely, I thought I would be most comfortable in this field. This turned out to be a fine choice.

On my modest pay as an Air Force captain, I could not afford to live in Manhattan so we lived near the railroad tracks in Teaneck. Connor felt like an outsider in this town. January 1964 to June 1966 were a hard two and half years, especially for Connor. Graduate school was really tough. With the arrival of our daughter, Serena, Connor had the full responsibility of raising and caring for two tiny kids. Born in the summer of 1964 at Holy Name Hospital in Teaneck, Serena weighed nine pounds, three ounces. In the hospital, while Serena was nearby, a candy striper came into Connor's room and said, "Have you seen that GIANT baby?" Connor replied, "Yes, she is mine." The candy striper quickly replied, "She's adorable."

Although Connor did not enjoy much of our life in drab, un-friendly, Teaneck, she did have an occasional opportunity to perform on stage. She had solo roles in the performances of the Junior League Follies in Englewood, New Jersey. Mabel Allen, who had attended Randolph Macon Woman's College with Connor, was also in the productions. They had not been friends in college; however, a friend-ship quickly followed. Gus and Mabel Allen became lifelong friends. We skied with them in Lake Placid, New York and, five years later, in Snowmass, Colorado.

I was originally scheduled by the Air Force to spend two years to earn a master's degree. However, my mentor at Columbia University recommended that I skip the master's degree and go straight for the Ph.D. To my surprise and to the surprise of the Air Force, skipping the master's degree was quite common at Columbia University. At first the Air Force did not approve my request but thanks to a kind general in the Pentagon, an exception was made to policy. I was able to save much time by not having to write a masters essay.

READ A THOUSAND BOOKS IN YOUR FIELD

When I asked my mentor, Professor W. T. R. Fox, how I would know when I was ready for the written and oral examinations for the Ph.D., he was quite frank. He said, "Captain Smith, complete all of your courses, get your two languages out of the way and read a thou-sand books in your field." He was serious! At the rate I was reading, it would take another ten years before I could complete the Ph.D. There was no way the Air Force would support me for a twelve-year graduate program.

In desperation, I decided that I needed to learn how to read ex-tremely fast. It took me about three months to gain the skill of speed reading. This skill has served me well for more than fifty years. Books used to be my enemies. Starting in 1965 they became my dear friends. I continue to speed read and I read about five books each month, even now in my 80s.

At Columbia University, the written examination for the Ph.D. lasted for six hours and included many multiple-choice questions plus a couple of essays. The oral examination took place a few months after the written exam had been successfully accomplished. During the "orals", five distinguished professors asked me tough questions for two hours. Fifty-five years later I can still remember the highlights of this oral examination.

A retired professor from Princeton University, who was in his late 70s, asked me this question. "Could I cite a book on the theory of International Relations which was published prior to World War II?" I highlighted a book written by professor Russell. Little did I know that Professor Russell, who had been dead for many years, had been the best friend of the professor who asked me the question. He was absolutely delighted with my answer. His dear friend was remembered and respected for his contributions to the field of International Relations.

Another question and answer led to a good laugh from the five-man panel. Asked if I could name a book written in the 1890s on the German Communist party, I mentioned a book by Bernstein. The follow-up question was, "please tell us a little about this book." I said, "It had a green cover and had about ten chapters. That is all I can remember." My answer was really weak but got some good laughs.

After the orals, I sat outside the exam room to wait for the answer - had I passed or had I failed? Twenty minutes later, the team emerged. Each professor shook my hand and congratulated me. One of the professors, Juan Linz, walked with me across the campus of Columbia University. He told me that I won the retired professor to my side with my answer to the professor Russell question. He also told me that I received good marks for my honesty when I answered the Bernstein question.

Once I had passed the written and oral exams, I was ready to research and write my dissertation. When I approached Warner Schilling, the professor who would be my dissertation advisor, something unexpected happened. I gave him five ideas on what I thought would be good topics for a dissertation. He rejected them all in short order.

Professor Schilling then told me that he wanted me to write on the following topic: How did Air Force planners during World War II chart the future (for when the war would be over)? He told me to make the dissertation short (no more than 250 pages), to do some original research and to get the dissertation done quickly. I learned that researching and writing on a topic that really interested a mentor was a good way to get the task done in a reasonably short period of time. Warner Schilling, a very kind man, was excited about the topic and gave me lots of help.

The dissertation title was: *Wartime Planning for Postwar Contingencies: The Army Air Force Example, 1943-1945*. Professor Schilling was a tough taskmaster but his questions, criticisms and suggestions were very helpful. When it was time to defend the dissertation, one professor gave me a bad time. Bruce Smith was at Columbia University on loan from the Rand Corporation. However, another professor, a sociologist, was quite complimentary. I remember him saying something like, "Captain Smith, I am not sure you realize it, but your analysis confirms an important hypothesis about organizational behavior."

Passing the dissertation hurdle meant that I now had an earned PhD. Later in this memoir you will see how this dissertation, in book form, got me in big trouble.

THE HALCYON YEARS IN COLORADO

Our next stop was Colorado and the Air Force Academy. Teaching in the Department of Political Science was a real pleasure. I taught courses in American Government and International Relations. Also, I served as the assistant lacrosse coach and maintained my pilot skills by flying cadets for orientation rides in the T-33 trainer.

The Political Science Department was loaded with talented Air Force officers as well as an Army officer, a foreign service officer from the State Department and an officer from Britain's Royal Air Force. These faculty members held masters or doctorate degrees from some of the best Universities in America and Europe: Princeton, Harvard,

Columbia, Oxford, Stanford, the University of Paris, etc.

Many of these officers moved on to high ranks in the military while three became university presidents. A few had been Rhodes or Olmsted scholars. In addition, many had solid operational experiences. At no other time in my life was I surrounded by so much intellectual power.

Our department offered two majors: Political Science and International Relations. Both of our majors were popular with cadets and we attracted many of the most outstanding cadets to our department. The most impressive was cadet Frank Klotz from the Air Force Academy class of 1973. Frank would reach the rank of lieutenant general before he retired from the Air Force. During his military career he was both a Rhodes Scholar and a White House Fellow.

During the years from 1966 to 1973, I would serve three tours at the Air Force Academy, one tour in combat and one tour as a faculty member at the National War College. Hence, lots of moves for the family.

Soon after moving into our small house on the grounds of the Air Force Academy, Connor and I decided that living off base and building our own home would be best for our whole family. McCoy and Serena would have their own rooms; there would be a nice size master bedroom as well as a guest room. Also, we wanted a fireplace. Our architect was Henry Lacey who was from Denver. Connor and I soon became good friends with Henry and Jadeen Lacey.

We chose as a location for our new home, Woodmoor, a large subdivision which was ten miles to the north of the Air Force Academy. This brand-new development would eventually include golf, tennis, swimming and a nice clubhouse. Woodmoor was located on the outskirts of the small Colorado town of Monument. As it turned out, our family would live in our home just off of Woodmoor Drive on three separate occasions from 1967 through 1973.

Our years in Colorado were splendid in many ways. Connor's talents as a singer and actress were appreciated by many. She had lead roles in productions of *Hansel and Gretel, Susannah, Oliver,* and *Showboat.* She was a soloist in our church as well as in Junior League Follies. McCoy joined Connor on stage for *Oliver.* He played the role of a pickpocket; he was ten years old at the time.

The ski slopes of Colorado beckoned. On weekends our family would often go skiing at Vail, Breckenridge, Monarch, or Winter Park. Our kids learned to ski at a very young age. The ski conditions in the high country of Colorado were splendid from mid-November through late April.

My Criticism of Vietnam Policy Gets Destroyed

In the summer of 1967, I inadvertently caused quite a bit of controversy. As a faculty member at the Air Force Academy, I had the opportunity to spend six weeks in the summer at a military headquarters. I had the good fortune to be assigned to Hawaii where I served on the intelligence staff of the top headquarters in Hawaii. The general in charge of intelligence did not know how to use me and asked for my thoughts. I told him that I wished to serve on the North Vietnamese desk, a busy place in the summer of 1967. The air campaign over North Vietnam was well underway. Using fighter bombers (F-100s, F-105s, F-4s, A-6s, etc.) from the Air Force, Navy and Marine Corps, American airpower hit strategic targets throughout North Vietnam. Lots of our airplanes were being shot down, many by surface-to-air missiles.

The colonel in charge of publishing the *Weekly Intelligence Digest* for the headquarters asked me to write an article for him. He seemed quite desperate to have articles written each week. I did as he requested but produced an article much longer than the norm. The colonel was delighted. He decided my article could fill up an entire issue. Little did he know that this article would blow up in his face (and a bit in mine). This is a tale worth telling.

Having just finished research and writing a PhD dissertation on airpower during World War II, I felt ready to examine what was happening in the skies over North Vietnam. I composed a thirty-page analysis of the American air campaign. This campaign was given the label: Rolling Thunder.

My article was titled, "Rolling Thunder from a Political Perspective." The analysis was quite critical of the bombing campaign. It stated that with the many restrictions on targets, this campaign was unlikely to be successful. The *Weekly Intelligence Digest* was reproduced in about two thousand copies and sent out to units and headquarters throughout the Pacific. In addition, numerous copies were sent to the Pentagon. About a week later, I received surprising news. All copies were to be destroyed immediately. I had overestimated the willingness of senior officials to accept criticism.

Ironically, when the word got out that this issue of the *Weekly Intelligence Digest* was controversial, it became quite popular. Many folks who would not have bothered to read it picked it up and read it thoroughly before they destroyed it. Two years later, while I was flying combat missions over North Vietnam and Laos, this lesson in generating both controversy and attention was put to the test. But alas, I am getting ahead of myself.

Chapter Six:

OFF TO COMBAT WITH THE TRIPLE NICKEL FIGHTER SQUADRON, 1968

IN JANUARY, 1968, our small family headed to Homestead Air Force Base in southern Florida. I was going to fight in the Vietnam conflict and had a six-month combat training assignment before I left. We rented out our Colorado home and headed from the crisp, clear air of Colorado to the humid heat of southern Florida. Our kids were quite small. Our son, McCoy, was five and our daughter, Serena, was three. Checking out in the F-4 aircraft was a joy. There were about 40 pilots in our class, twenty who would fly the front seat and twenty who would fly in the back. The backseaters were all young pilots, while the front seaters were captains and majors with lots of flying time. I was an Air Force major at this time. I was teamed up with First Lieutenant Ron Hintze; we had a grand personal relationship which continued when we were sent to the combat zone.

Connor and I rented a home in Perrine, Florida, which was located about eight miles north of Homestead Air Force Base. Our small home had a screened-in swimming pool; soon our tiny kids became fine swimmers. Before her fourth birthday, Serena would dive off a diving board, swim underwater the length of the pool and pop up with a triumphant smile on her face.

The flying and academic schedule at the base was light. This allowed for lots of family time during this six-month training program. Since we were all headed for a year in combat, the Air Force leaders were thoughtful in ensuring that family time got a high priority.

In July, 1968 we drove back to Colorado. Connor and kids would spend a year there while I was in Southeast Asia.

Good News from the American
Political Science Association

Three days before leaving for Thailand, I received a phone call from Evron Kirkpatrick, long-time director of the American Political Science Association. He gave me hearty congratulations. When I asked him, "Congratulations for what?" he told me I had been chosen to receive the 1968 Helen Dwight Reid Award from the American Political Science Association. This award designates the best dissertation in the fields of International Relations, Organization and Law.

This news was a complete surprise. I did not know that I had been nominated for an award. The news, coming as it did just before I was to leave my family for a year, was quite uplifting. I later learned that Dr. Kirkpatrick had served in the OSS during World War II and was the husband of the distinguished diplomat, Jeane Kirkpatrick. Many years later, I was able to tell this story to Jeane when she visited the National War College.

Flying a Fighter across the Pacific:
Thirty Air-to-Air Refuelings

With so many F-4s being shot down, there was a constant need to fly more aircraft to the combat zone. I volunteered to ferry an F-4 from an air base in Utah to South Vietnam. My request was initially turned down since I had so little flying time in the F-4 and had so few refueling training missions in that fighter. However, since I had flown "across the pond" in F-100s on many occasions, permission was finally granted. A few weeks after graduating from the F-4 school, I left the family in Colorado and headed off for a year of combat.

Ron Hintze and I met at Hill Air Force Base which was located near Ogden, Utah. We picked up an F-4 and flew it all the way to Da Nang Air Base in South Vietnam. We stopped in Hawaii, Guam and the Philippines along the way so the trip took us about a week. On that trip we learned how wide the Pacific Ocean is. We refueled using large Air Force refueling aircraft (KC-135s). We hooked up to get fuel at least 30 times. We kept topping off our fuel tanks to be sure that if the tanker had to abort, we would have enough fuel to make it to Midway, Kwajalein or some other island along the way.

After dropping off the F-4 at Da Nang Air Base in South Vietnam, Ron and I were off to Udorn Air Base in Thailand. I would fly with the 555th Tactical Fighter Squadron for 180 combat missions from August, 1968 to August, 1969. The nickname for this squadron was "triple nickel" but we usually just used the word, "nickel." I was in the theater for exactly one year. Before we started to fly combat missions, Ron Hintze and I had to fly from Thailand back to the Philippines to attend Jungle Survival School. We spent three days in the rainforest of the Philippines.

Back at Udorn it was time to start flying over enemy territory. On my first combat mission, an instructor pilot flew in the back seat and we hit an undefended target in Laos. The "dollar ride" was a piece of cake. Most of my combat missions were over Laos. Somehow the United States government was able to restrict press coverage of combat activities in Laos.

For the first month, Ron and I flew on the wing of more experienced aircrews. We had to gain experience before we could become a flight lead crew. This process usually took two or three months and around thirty combat missions.

About five weeks into our tour, Ron and I were scheduled for a combat mission. Our squadron commander, Lieutenant Colonel George Hupp, was scheduled to lead a four-ship flight. I was scheduled to be the element leader (number 3 in a flight of 4).

Combat Fighter Pilots Perry Smith and Ron Hintze at Udorn Air Base in Northern Thailand, 1968.

Colonel Hupp failed to show up for the intelligence and weather briefings, so I started to brief the flight. Hupp arrived, announced that I was to be the leader, and that he would become my wingman. At the time, I had only about a dozen combat missions under my belt, but off we went.

We received heavy ground fire and I became very direct with my radio calls. I warned the others in the flight about the ground fire and told them to break off their attack if it got too intense. We all got home safely.

After the debriefing, Hupp called me aside and told me that, as of today, I was a four-ship flight leader. It was a compliment to be so trusted by my big boss. He gave me an important responsibility early in my combat tour. Gruff and dour, George Hupp was a great commander who we all loved and respected.

Please remember, many of the missions were quite routine and not dangerous. Of the 180 combat missions, my backseater and I were shot at on no more than 50 of these missions. Flying over North Vietnam and Laos in 1968 and 1969 was nothing like flying over Germany in World War II.

On all my missions, I was never shot at by a surface-to-air missile or by a MIG fighter. What we faced was old fashioned anti-aircraft fire from 85, 57 and 37-millimeter guns (these guns were not much different than the guns my dad commanded in 1944). The biggest threat was from the modern, Soviet designed, ZSU-23 rapid fire guns. These would fire four rounds simultaneously.

The F-4 aircraft flew very fast. If we saw the gunfire headed our way, I could quickly yank the airplane and cause the bullets to miss. If the tracers were coming right towards us, that was the time to move quickly. My back seater (Ron Hintze for the first half of my combat tour and Mike Heenan on the second) would often tell me "pull right" or "pull left." Having a backseater on combat missions turned out to be a big plus.

Flying Story: Bullpup Blowup

As an experienced combat pilot, I was, on occasion, chosen to fly some especially interesting missions. Firing the bullpup missile

was a good example of an unusual and exciting mission. In Laos, the enemy often kept military supplies in caves. Gravity bombs could not do the job. They could strike the entrance to a cave but could not enter the cave. Hence finding a weapon that could enter a cave and blow up inside was essential to a successful interdiction campaign in Laos. The bullpup missile had the potential to do just that. The first time I fired a bullpup is still seared in my memory.

This large missile was designed to be launched from a fighter. It would proceed at high speed horizontality in the direction of the target. The pilot would steer the missile with a small joystick in the cockpit. He could make the missile take gentle turns to the right and left and up and down. On my first Bullpup mission, I lined up with a cave which was about four miles to my front. I launched the missile. Less that a second later the missile blew up right in front of me. I yanked on the stick to miss the blast area and shouted out a bad word or two.

Upon landing I met with a number of munitions officers and non-commissioned officers. After explaining exactly what happened, they told me rather firmly, "Sir, that could not have happened." It was not the reply I was looking for.

After returning to the squadron area, a fellow fighter pilot suggested I get copies of the strike camera pictures. I received the pictures the next day. Sure enough, there was a clear picture of an explosion directly in front of me.

After running off a number of copies of the picture, I visited with the munitions folks. When I showed them the film, I got the following reactions. "Wow, that is not supposed to happen." "Sir, you sure were right." "How did you miss flying through the debris?" That experience taught me an important lesson. To convince the skeptics, it is helpful to have solid documentation. This lesson would serve me well on many future occasions.

One of the techniques that served me well as far as documentation is concerned was creating "Memos for the Record." Once I started to work in the Pentagon, as soon as I returned from an important meeting, I would dictate to my secretary the highlights of the meeting. Since I took notes in these meetings it was easy to

rattle off the important points, especially the decisions that were made.

ADMIRAL JOHN McCAIN DROPS BY OUR SQUADRON

One of the most memorable events which took place during my combat tour was when the Commander-in-Chief of the Pacific Command, Admiral John McCain, visited our squadron. It was early in my combat tour. A four-star admiral, McCain was especially interested in the air campaign since his son, naval aviator John McCain, was a prisoner of war in Hanoi. After being freed from captivity in 1973, the younger John McCain became a Republican Senator from Arizona. When he ran for the American presidency in 2008, he lost to Barack Obama.

A small man with a pleasant and open demeanor, Admiral McCain was interested in talking to the fighter pilots in the 555th Tactical Fighter Squadron. He asked that only those who flew regularly over North Vietnam remain in the room. The visit took place in the autumn of 1968. I had been flying combat for just a couple of months.

After all of the support personnel had left the room, Admiral McCain was ready to talk turkey with the combat jocks. He asked us to be completely candid and to tell him how best to carry out the air campaign over North Vietnam. The aircrews from my squadron really unloaded on him. They told him that there were too many constraints and the campaign could never succeed under the present limitations. These outspoken pilots gave Admiral McCain many specific suggestions. For instance, we told him that we should be allowed to hit the military airfields and the port facilities throughout North Vietnam,

Admiral McCain listened intently. We had high hopes that some of our recommendations would be accepted and implemented. Sadly, none of them were. Admiral McCain had to deal with Secretary of Defense Robert McNamara and President Lyndon Johnson. I have often thought how troubling it must have been for Admiral McCain to know that he could do nothing to accelerate the end of the war and to get his son home.

The date was 22 February, 1969. I was about halfway through my yearlong combat tour. By this time, I was an instructor pilot with about 80 combat missions under my belt. I was in the process of checking out Captain Wayne Pearson as a flight leader. Hence, I was flying on his wing. Wayne's backseater was Lieutenant Mike Heenan, a navigator and an Air Force Academy graduate. Lieutenant Ron Hintze was, as usual, in my backseat. As a reminder, Ron was my backseater during the checkout in the F-4 at Homestead Air Force Base and had flown in my back seat when we ferried an F-4 across the Pacific Ocean from Utah to Da Nang Air Base in South Vietnam.

Wayne made radio contact with the forward air controller (FAC), a "Raven." Raven FACs flew light airplanes. Their job was to find targets and identify them by hitting them with smoke rockets. The Raven told us by radio that there was a target in the Plain of Jars area in central Laos. The Plain of Jars was one of the few places in Laos where there were very few trees - it was perhaps thirty miles by thirty miles of open country. The FAC rolled in on the target and marked it with a white phosphorus rocket. Wayne then rolled in on this target. He started his bombing run from about 15,000 feet above the ground, established a dive angle of about 45 degree (nose down) and rolled his wings level.

Ron Hintze was the first to notice that there was a problem. He shouted to me on the intercom, "Holy Smoke, Lead is on Fire." I yanked my head around to take a look. All I could see was a ball of fire and lots of smoke headed toward the ground at a high rate of speed. I shouted on the radio, "LEAD, YOU ARE ON FIRE, EJECT, EJECT, EJECT!" Receiving no response, I kept shouting out his call sign followed by "EJECT, EJECT, EJECT!"

Ron and I were hoping to see two parachutes which would indicate that both Wayne and Mike had successfully ejected. Just before the aircraft impacted the ground, we saw one parachute. Our hearts sank. This meant that it was very likely that one of the two had not been able to eject successfully.

Within about three seconds of the crash, I asked Ron to switch our radio to "Guard" channel. This is the emergency radio channel which all aircraft monitor. I did not want to look inside the cockpit since I wanted to keep the crash site in view. Once the channel changed, I called "CROWN, CROWN, WE HAVE AN AIRCRAFT DOWN IN THE PLAIN OF JARS, PLEASE INITIATE A RESCUE MISSION."

A C-130 aircraft with the call sign of "Crown" had the important role of supervising rescue operations for anyone down in Laos or in North Vietnam. Crown answered my call immediately and asked me a bunch of questions: What is the location? How many crew members were on the aircraft? What was my fuel state? How long could I remain in the vicinity of the downed aircrew? Would I need tanker support? etc. etc.

As I circled at high altitude (about 20,000 feet), I kept calling on the Guard channel trying to make contact with the downed crewman. Ron and I were certain that one had made it out of the fireball but we had no idea what his condition might be. After about fifteen minutes of calling and calling, Mike Heenan called on his survival radio (each of us carried in our survival vests two small two-way radios as well as extra batteries).

Mike sounded quite shaken. When I asked what his condition was, he told us that it was "not good" and that he was "afraid of the tigers." I did not know what he was talking about so I queried Ron Hintze using our aircraft intercom system. Ron told me that Mike had been reading a book on Laos and had learned about the tigers in Northern Laos.

I called Mike on the radio and told him that there were no tigers in his area. I directed him to move away from the place he had landed and find a place to hide. I also told him that a rescue team was on the way and that he would soon be rescued. I asked him again how he was doing. "Not good" was his distressed response. This was the second time Mike had used the phrase "not good."

Mike told me that he was bleeding badly. I then directed him to take off his T-shirt, to twist it tightly and use it as a tourniquet. Mike quickly replied, "I can't do that." He told me that he was bleeding from the head. (Later I learned that when he ejected at high speed from his aircraft, his helmet flew off and his parachute did not fully deploy. He crashed into a tree and his head split open). I then directed him to take off his T-shirt, roll it into a tight ball and with both hands press it tightly to his head and hold it there with continuous pressure.

Over the course of the next hour and a half, Mike called me often. He kept asking where the helicopters were. I kept telling him that they were airborne and were flying as fast as they could. In the meantime, many fighter aircraft checked in on the radio with me. So many pilots wanted to help that I had to tell most of them to stay clear.

The first really helpful aircraft to arrive were two A-1 prop-driven aircraft. The Raven Forward Air Controller helped them find the location of our downed airman and they started laying down smoke. The purpose of the smoke was to make it difficult for enemy soldiers on the ground to find Mike.

When the large Jolly Green helicopters came into sight, I was able to tell Mike that he could expect to be picked up very soon. One of the helicopters flew in low and the other held high. The low helicopter hovered about one hundred feet in the air. From the helicopter a sergeant went down on a steel cable. His job was to find Mike, carry him to the cable and place him on the three-pronged seat which was attached at the bottom of the cable. The next step was to have the cable winched up to the helicopter with both Mike and the sergeant at the same time.

Once Mike and the Sergeant had reached the helicopter, the helicopter pilot sent out a message by radio that the rescue was a success. What a relief it was. Tears came to my eyes. It was a moment of great joy and of great sadness. Mike was safe but Wayne was lost. Ron and I flew back to Udorn quickly. We wanted to be on the ground in time to greet the Jolly Green helicopter when it landed at Udorn. Upon landing and taxiing to the aircraft parking area, I climbed down from the cockpit of my F-4 and quickly debriefed a number of people.

A poignant moment came when the crew chief of Wayne's aircraft asked me if his plane was really gone. A crew chief had the important job of taking care of a single airplane. These dedicated sergeants would do much of the maintenance work. Also, they would supervise specialists who would come out to the flight line when needed.

Crew chiefs loved their airplanes and this sergeant had just lost his. His sadness was profound. He felt that he had failed at his job. I told him it was in no way his fault. Try as I might, I was not able to console this deeply saddened Air Force sergeant.

Ron and I then jumped into a vehicle and raced down to the ramp where the rescue helicopter would land. Many officers and enlisted personnel were there. Mike was hustled off the helicopter; I had no chance to talk to him. Soon thereafter, Mike was airlifted to Clark Air Base in the Philippines for surgical repair of his head. It would be three months before I saw him again.

I did get a chance to speak to the man who had rescued him. He was a tall, handsome and very muscular sergeant. When I asked him how the rescue went, he said, "Not good." That was the third time I had heard the phrase, "not good." The sergeant then explained, "Sir, I almost dropped him on the way up the cable." He explained that Mike was so covered in blood that he was like a greased pig - very slippery.

The respect I had for these brave Air Force men was always high. It went up another notch when I realized how dedicated that entire helicopter crew was to a single mission: saving the lives of downed airmen.

About three months later, Mike Heenan returned to Udorn and asked to be my backseater. I readily agreed since Ron Hintze had left the squadron and I needed a new backseater. Mike was given the option of returning home but he volunteered to return to Udorn to complete his combat tour.

COLONEL WENDELL BEVAN: LESSONS IN INTEGRITY

In the spring of 1969, at Udorn Air Base in Thailand, a worldwide tactics conference was held. The topic of the conference was "The Air Interdiction Campaign over Laos." Representatives from every major

American military command were in attendance. There were participants from the Pentagon, the headquarters in Hawaii and Saigon as well as from every fighter, reconnaissance, and special operations unit throughout Southeast Asia.

Panels were established and each panel submitted a report the night before the end of the conference. During the conference, I was flying combat missions with the Triple Nickel Squadron so I did not attend any of the sessions.

In charge of the conference was Major Richard Dowell, an F-4D fighter pilot from the 555th Fighter Squadron. On the last afternoon of the conference, Dowell, who was a good friend, asked me to help draft the executive summary for the conference report. Dick also asked for my assistance with the cover letter which was to be signed by our wing commander, Colonel Wendell Bevan. Colonel Bevan had been the commander of the 432nd Reconnaissance/Fighter Wing since the summer of 1968.

The first sentence of the executive summary of the conference report stated that the interdiction campaign over Laos was a failure. The same point was included in the draft of Colonel Bevan's cover letter. Major Dowell and I went to see Colonel Bevan to ask him to sign the letter. We warned him that this letter was likely to get him into trouble.

Colonel Bevan asked if we agreed with the conclusions of the report. When we told him we did, he said, "Well then, I will sign the letter." And he did!

I walked out the door with the highest possible admiration for this fine man. He trusted us and he was willing to tell, in writing, the unvarnished truth. I should point out that at this time, Colonel Bevan was on the promotion list for brigadier general - he had not yet pinned on his star.

A month later, Colonel Bevan called me to his office. He told me he had been on the phone for thirty minutes talking to the two-star general who was the operations officer for the Seventh Air Force. Colonel Bevan told me all he did was say "Yes, Sir," "No Sir" and "No excuse, sir" as he was chewed out by the general over the phone.

When I tried to apologize for getting Colonel Bevan into trouble, he cut me short. He said that he did the right thing by signing that letter. Sadly, Colonel Bevan was not promoted beyond the brigadier general level. He paid a price for being willing to tell the story honestly, candidly and completely. Sadly, this was a period in the history of the military when criticism was not welcome. Fortunately, this was not always the case.

Tossing our Wing Commander Over the Bar

I have another story about our wing commander Colonel Wendell Bevan. During the Vietnam War there was a well-established tradition at Udorn Air Base. Whenever a fighter aviator completed a combat tour, he would be hosed down by the fire department after he climbed from the cockpit of his F-4.

After changing into a dry flying suit, the happy warrior would go to the bar at the officer's club. While standing at the bar, the fighter jock would be tossed into the air - over the bar he would go. The bartenders would catch him; the aviator would return to the front of the bar. He would then purchase a round of drinks for everyone in the bar area.

After Colonel Bevan flew his last combat mission in the spring of 1969, I saw him standing alone at the bar. It is important to point out that Bevan was a reconnaissance pilot. He flew more than one hundred missions in the RF-4C. However, Bevan flew a few fighter missions in the F-4D during his combat tour.

I approached him and quietly asked. "Sir, have you been tossed over the bar?" He replied, "No." I then asked, "Would you like to be thrown over?" With a smile, he said, "Yes, I would."

I ask a couple of fellow fighter pilots to help. Over the top went the soon-to-be-promoted general officer, the wing commander of the 432nd Fighter/Reconnaissance Wing, Colonel Wendall Bevan. What was crystal clear to me that day was that Bevan wanted to be recognized as a combat fighter pilot. The toss over the bar did the trick.

Flying Story: Escorting Gunships Over Laos

Another combat mission of note took place towards the end of my tour of duty. By the summer of 1969, C-130 gunships were

operating over Laos at night. These aircraft had the call sign of "Spectre." They were very effective in locating truck convoys and attacking them with their cannon. However, there was a problem. These slow-moving aircraft received a great deal of anti-aircraft fire from the ground.

Our job as fighter aircrews was to protect these vulnerable gunships. We would fly high above the C-130. When the gunship would begin to receive ground fire, we would roll in on the enemy anti-aircraft guns. We would drop canisters which held dozens of small bomblets. Most of these bomblets were designed to explode on contact with the ground. Some had delay fuses that would cause the bomblets to explode a few minutes after landing on the ground. These delayed munitions discouraged the gun crews from manning their guns and also reduced the accuracy of the guns.

I can remember on a number of occasions as I rolled in on the guns, seeing tracer rounds from five or six guns headed towards me. There were a few times when I was sure I would be hit - but it never happened.

We carried eleven of the canisters which held the bomblets. We would drop our canisters one at a time. This meant that eleven times, we would roll in on the guns in the black of night, with tracers flying up at us from a number of gun positions. This also meant that we had to refuel a couple of times and then return to our position of escort and support. An F-4 aircraft with a load of munitions could remain with the gunships for about an hour before fuel would run short. The KC-135 tankers could not fly over Laos. It was a thirty-minute trip from the gunship to the tanker and back. Plus getting fuel took another fifteen minutes. These missions lasted about four hours - some of the longest of my 180 combat missions.

One of the most dramatic missions was when the C-130 I was escorting was receiving a great deal of gunfire from various positions. The tracers were arching up from the ground and coming very close to hitting the gunship. I called the C-130 pilot on my radio and told him to go home. He was reluctant but when I insisted that he was soon to be shot down, he left the scene. His gunfire had already hit the first and the last truck in the convoy as well as a couple of other trucks in between. I told him that we had plenty of ordnance and could take care of hitting the rest of the trucks in the convoy.

These truck convoys consisted of about twenty trucks. Since they were carrying ordnance, they would explode and burn when they were hit by gunfire or bombs. The explosions were quite spectacular. Also, the trucks would burn after they exploded. Since the trucks were on a narrow road, they could not escape once the first truck and last truck were struck. It was our understanding that the drivers had holes to dive into along the side of all of these roads.

BRIEFING SOME BIG SHOTS: THE SECRETARY AND THE CHIEF OF STAFF OF THE AIR FORCE

In the summer of 1969, I was asked to brief the Chief of Staff of the Air Force, General Jack Ryan and, a few weeks later, the Secretary of the Air Force, Bob Seamans. By this time, I was one of the most experienced fighter pilots in our squadron. I knew the squadron commander of the Triple Nickel Fighter Squadron, Colonel Bob Taylor, well. He had flown on my wing on a number of occasions. Also, for many months, he had given me the responsibility of writing drafts of letters he would send to families of lost aviators.

Taylor felt an experienced "line pilot" who was flying missions on a regular basis would have the most credibility with the two top officials in the United States Air Force. He chose me to give the briefing and did not require that he approve it ahead of time. There was mutual trust and respect between us.

I briefed the two top Air Force officials on our fighters performing the gunship escort mission. During my briefing, I played an audio tape of one of the more exciting missions. The tape was unedited. As we were getting shot at over Laos, my voice rose and my commands to my wingman became very direct.

The briefing went well with the Chief of Staff, but not so well with the Secretary. When Secretary Seamans asked if we had everything we needed, I said "no sir." I followed up by stating that we did not have any "Rockeye" (Rockeye is an armor piercing bomblet).

Just after the Secretary departed the briefing room, a major general, clearly unhappy with my answer, confronted me. He asked, "Major, why don't you have Rockeye?" I told him I did not know. He then stated in strong terms, "Well you get some!"

My thought at the time (and I still think) - what a dumb interaction. He had to know that as a line fighter pilot, I did not have the power to obtain a munition. I guessed that the general wanted the Secretary of the Air Force to be protected from bad news. At that time in 1969, in the squadron operations building at Udorn Thailand, I told myself that I would never, ever, play that game.

On reflection, of all the briefings and speeches which I gave in my life, those two presentations were special. Standing in my flying suit in the combat zone and having flown combat only two days before, I had strong credibility with the audience. That is the good news. The bad news was the wisdom from the field did not impact the decision making of the high level officials in Saigon, the Pentagon or the White House.

In contrast to the Vietnam conflict, I reflect on the wonderful story of Colonel George Marshall "telling it like it is" during World War I. Marshall strongly criticized General "Black Jack" Pershing. Pershing, the top American commander in France, welcomed Marshall's criticism. Soon thereafter, he placed Marshall into a vital position on his staff. Years later, in a 1939 meeting in the Oval Office, Marshall criticized President Roosevelt and said that "he did not agree with him at all." A few months later, Roosevelt selected Marshall to be the Chief of Staff of the Army.

During my year with the Triple Nickel, I became friends with more than one hundred aviators. Most were pilots but a few were navigators. Throughout the squadron there was a culture of profound trust. If your wingman shouted out, "Break Right," you did exactly what he said. If someone in your flight needed gas badly, you would move aside and give him first priority on the tanker. If a fellow aviator got "gassed" at the bar, you would escort him back to his hootch and get him safely into bed.

There were no women in our squadron but there were nurses in the hospital, red cross workers, and a few administrative officers who were women. Whenever we had a squadron party we would invite a few women to join us. Our parties were held about once a month. They were designed to say farewell to those who had completed their year in combat and to welcome new arrivals.

I would be remiss if I did not highlight a few of the fighter jocks who became close friends. Bob Taylor, Richard Dowell, Harry Spannaus, Goldie Goldfein, Ray Grazier, Don Burch, Nick Kehoe, Doug Melson, Ron Hintze, Mike Heenan, Firecan Dan Walsh, George Hupp, J.R. Alley, Hark Harcrow, Norm Smedes, and Greg Boyington. During my year with the Triple Nickel, the squadron had three commanders: George Hupp, Bob Taylor and Norm Smedes. All were fine commanders, leaders and fighter pilots.

Bob Taylor deserves special mention. When the Vietnam War ended, the Air Force leadership decided to close down permanently a number of squadrons. The 555th Tactical Fighter Squadron was on the chopping block. Bob Taylor was a general officer in the Pentagon at the time. He worked closely with the Air Force programmers and saved the squadron. The 555th Fighter Squadron is alive and well. It is stationed at Aviano, Italy. During two successful air campaigns, Bosnia, 1995, and Serbia/Kosovo, 1999, this iconic squadron played an important role. As of 2021, the 555th was assigned late model F-16s. In the future, it is likely that it will transition into F-35s.

Chapter Seven:

~~~

HOME FROM WAR, 1969

WITH THE COMPLETION of my combat tour in late August, 1969, I returned to my family and to the Air Force Academy. Being back home was special. It was a magic moment for all of us. It is hard to explain the joy that a family feels when a loved one returns from combat - safe and sound. Every day is a blessing. Yet looming on the horizon was an event that reminded us about the fragility of life.

In the fall of 1969, Connor and I were having dinner in Denver with two friends, Henry and Jedean Lacey. Henry had been the architect for our house which was built in 1967 in Woodmoor. Over time the Laceys had become good friends. The dinner was at the Palace Arms restaurant in the historic Brown Palace Hotel. We were celebrating my safe return from Thailand. I was sitting next to Henry. Connor and Jedean were sitting side-by-side directly across from Henry and me. We were enjoying cocktails. Our meals had not yet been served.

All of a sudden, Henry gasped loudly, threw up all over the table and collapsed against my right shoulder. I shouted out his name but got no response. With some assistance from a waiter, I placed him face up on the floor of the restaurant. I commenced to give him mouth to mouth resuscitation. A man came to assist and began pushing on Henry's chest. An emergency call was made and within about fifteen minutes, an EMT team showed up. In the ambulance and at the hospital the EMT worked hard on Henry but to no avail.

About a week later, Henry's brother, a medical doctor, called me. He told me that an autopsy showed that Henry had not had a heart attack. Hence there was no reason for him to die. Henry's brother asked me to explain exactly what happened that evening. He seemed to feel that it was my fault that Henry had not been revived.

He may have been correct. If I had gone for the heart and had been very aggressive in pounding on his chest, Henry might have lived until the EMT folks arrived. The lesson I learned that evening was as follows. If someone has no pulse, top priority must be on the heart and not on mouth-to-mouth support.

PUBLISH AND PERISH?

By the time the spring of 1970 rolled around, I found myself in professional trouble again. After my dissertation had earned the award from the American Political Science Association, the Johns Hopkins Press approached me about publishing it. I was thrilled. Soon after the book hit the street, it was reviewed in the Washington Post. Does that sound like good news? Nope. The book review, written by Bernard Nossiter, was quite positive. The problem was - Nossiter had a well-deserved reputation of being a harsh critic of the military. The title of the published book was *The Air Force Plans for Peace: 1943-1945*. Although the book praised the Army Air Corps for its planning efforts during the Second World War, it criticized a number of aspects of this postwar planning effort. Bernard Nossiter highlighted these criticisms.

There is an expression in the academic world "publish or perish." Professors in colleges and universities who do not have their work published are often denied a tenure position. Without tenure, the future of professors is quite limited. My situation highlighted the flip side of the publish or perish truism. In my case, I came very close to creating a "publish AND perish" category.

The phone call for me came from the top lawyer in the Air Force. When he got me on the phone, he identified himself and said. "Major, you are in serious trouble." When I asked why, he told me that I should have received clearance from the Air Staff to have my manuscript published. In as calm a voice as I could muster, I explained that it had been cleared by the Air Staff. I also told him that it had been cleared by the Office of the Secretary of Defense and the State Department. He was quite surprised and asked me to send him documentation - which I did. Was that the end of my troubles? Oh No - it was just the beginning.

Retired Air Force Lieutenant General Ira Eaker read the Washington Post book review. After reading my book, Eaker wrote a long letter to the Chief of Staff of the Air Force, General Jack Ryan. General Eaker accused me of being disloyal. He recommended that I be removed from my faculty position at the Air Force Academy and that I never be promoted again.

This letter from one of America's aviation pioneers put General Ryan in an awkward position. An "action" was started in the Air Staff. Major Bob Springer, whom I had never met, became the action officer. The guidance Springer received from his immediate superior was clear - hang the bastard. After reading the book and checking out my background, Springer decided to create not one but two decision papers. One was to destroy my career, the other was to save it.

The final decision was made by General Ryan. He asked Major Springer, whom he knew well, what he should do. Bob Springer, God love him, said, "Sir, I suggest you save him." Also in support was the Superintendent at the Air Force Academy, Lieutenant General Tom Moorman. He intervened on my behalf and on behalf of the Air Force Academy. Others who helped were Ray Coble, Lee Butler, Glenn Kent and Russell Dougherty. The fact that I had recently returned from a combat tour in Southeast Asia may have been a factor in my favor.

The lessons which I learned from this experience were as follows. First, certain retired officials retain considerable influence and are willing to put pressure on the top active duty leaders. Second, most leaders of government institutions, and large organizations in general, do not welcome strong criticism - especially from an insider. Third, to avoid big trouble, a critic needs to follow the rules on the publication of criticism. Finally, it is helpful if the critic has allies who are willing to support him.

CHASING DOWN A RUNAWAY CAR

The first sign of trouble was a moving cloud of dust on a hill to my right front. An old car was kicking up the dust as it rolled down a hill towards Academy Boulevard. Something seemed strange about this car.

It was rolling backwards. In the front seat of this car, two small heads were bobbing in and out of sight.

I was stopped at a traffic light, just returning from flying a mission out of Peterson Air Force Base near Colorado Springs, Colorado. The year was 1970. The runaway car was headed in the direction of the four lane boulevard. I threw my car into park, jumped out and raced toward the runaway car. I had recently returned from a combat tour in Southeast Asia and was in good physical shape. Also, I was used to making quick decisions. My hastily developed plan was to catch the car before it reached the highway, yank open the front door and grab the emergency brake.

I failed in all my goals. I did not stop the runaway car. Also, the car got about halfway across the highway before it stopped. But there was much good news. The backward-moving car had slowed down as it rolled through a shallow ditch on the edge of the highway. By the time it entered the highway, the car had slowed to about four miles per hour. Just before I reached the car in my high-speed chase, a woman beat me to the car. She popped open a front door, dived in and grabbed the emergency brake. The car came to an abrupt stop.

Within a few seconds, others arrived on the scene. A group of us pushed the car off to the side of the highway. We parked it there. The heroic lady told me that she was late to an appointment. She asked me to take care of the kids; both were crying. I took one, who was about four years old, by the hand and carried the younger one in my other arm. Up the hill we went. I asked the oldest boy where his mother was and he pointed to a nearby townhome.

As the three of us entered the living room, we observed the mother smoking a cigarette and chatting with some friends. As soon as she saw the three of us, she started to berate her kids. After I briefly explained what had happened, her diatribe became more focused, "I told you to never play in the car!!" Please remember - these were very young children who had been left outside with no supervision.

I expected that she would thank me. However, the haranguing of the weeping children continued. The "thank you" did not come. I told her where the car was located, shrugged, and walked back to my car and drove home. My adrenaline continued to pump for quite a while.

My only regret was not getting the name of the lady who beat me to the car. I would have loved to acknowledge and thank her for a fast and successful act.

On the National War College Faculty

After a full academic year (1969-1970) at the Air Force Academy, I was off to Washington, DC for an assignment as a faculty member at the National War College. The National War College is the most prestigious of the professional schools for senior military officers, foreign service officers and civil servants. In the 1970s there were five American war colleges: The Naval War College, Army War College, Air War College, National War College, and the Industrial College of the Armed Forces. Each college had about two hundred students. Being a graduate of any of the war colleges was special for a military officer or a senior civil servant. It was an indicator that your career was in fine shape. In the 1970s students at the National War College had an option of doing extra work and taking extra courses at night. By doing so they could earn a Master's Degree from George Washington University.

Although I was a faculty member, I was given a diploma with the class of 1971. Many years later, I served as the Commandant of the National War College. Hence, I got to know, quite well, the classes of 1971, 1984, 1985, 1986 - a total of about 800 outstanding individuals as well as about 80 highly competent faculty members.

As a junior faculty member in the autumn of 1970, I hosted the Distinguished Visitor Program. Renowned individuals would visit the college for late afternoon sessions. Attendance by students and faculty was voluntary. Usually about fifty would show up. Cyrus Vance, David Lawrence, and General Buzz Wheeler all gave fine talks. They also engaged in robust question and answer sessions following their talks. As the official escort, I would meet the visitor at the airport and would chat with them on the way to the college.

Three chats were memorable. The year was 1971. Cyrus Vance had served as Secretary of the Army and Deputy Secretary of Defense in the 1960s. He was not yet the Secretary of State (he served as Secretary of State from 1977 to 1980 during the administration of President Jimmy Carter). In the car on the way to the College, Vance told me that he was opposed to any attempt to rescue our POWs. I cautioned him that many of the students had friends in Hanoi - these students would not be pleased with his position. When the subject came up, Vance handled the question well - explaining that there were good arguments on both sides of the issue.

With retired four-star General Buzz Wheeler, our discussion in the car was not a pleasant one. Wheeler had served as the top military officer in the United States for the longest period in history - six years. From 1964 to 1970, he served as Chairman of the Joint Chiefs of Staff. Unlike other members of the Joint Chiefs of Staff, Wheeler had little combat experience. He was a brilliant staff officer but he was generally not respected by the rank and file of the military.

I asked General Wheeler if he ever considered resigning from his position as the Chairman of the Joint Chiefs of Staff. He said he did but he felt that he could be more effective serving in the government than on the outside. My follow-up question did not go well. Politely, I asked him if he still felt that way. General Wheeler went cold silent. Clearly, he thought this brash Air Force lieutenant colonel had gone too far with his questions.

A third distinguished speaker was also memorable. David Lawrence was well known for having created the magazine, *US News and World Report* in the 1920s. Eighty-two-year-old Lawrence told of his interviews with President Woodrow Wilson in Paris in 1919. He was a young reporter at the time. For those of us in the room who loved history, this was a special moment.

RETURN TO THE AIR FORCE ACADEMY
AND MORE CONTROVERSY

By the time I returned to the Air Force Academy in 1971, I was a lieutenant colonel. I was appointed as deputy head of the Political Science Department. Colonel Richard Rosser, who had replaced Wes Posvar as the head of the department, was my boss. Soon after my return, Rosser's secretary, whose time I would also share, told me she had a problem. She was losing her skill of dictation and asked me for help. I had never given dictation before but she soon taught me. I have always loved to talk and was not a proficient typist. So dictating letters and memos soon became a big part of my life. She was happy and so was I. Having someone with dictation skills turned out to be very helpful as I moved into many future jobs.

Under the leadership of Colonel Rosser, the Department of Political Science undertook some exciting projects. Because there were so many creative officers in the department, some of these projects got Rosser into big trouble. The department had written and published a book on Defense Policy (*American Defense Policy*). Since this book was being used in so many war and staff colleges and in various universities, our department received sizable royalty checks each year. With these funds in hand, someone came up with the idea of hosting an annual Interservice Conference on Defense Policy.

We invited the very best young minds in the military (from captain to colonel) to visit the Air Force Academy for three days. In order to receive an official invitation, the officer had to agree to produce a paper on an issue relating to national defense. This officer also had to agree to make a short presentation on his or her paper. No participant would receive an honorarium but all of the expenses would be paid for out of our department's Defense Policy Fund. Because we would not use any government funds, we felt that we did not have to go through the long process of coordination and approval. That turned out to be a mistake.

We were looking for creativity and, by golly, we got it! Super-smart officers who served in the White House, in the Pentagon and in the field quickly signed up. One of the officers we invited to the conference was Colonel Bob Taylor. Bob had been my squadron commander in the 555th Fighter Squadron during my year of combat flying. When he received his invitation, Colonel Taylor was serving as a military assistant to the Secretary of Defense. The invitation to Taylor led to a major controversy. Bob told the Secretary of Defense, Elliot Richardson, about the conference. Richardson was intrigued and asked to be invited. He volunteered to make a presentation to the conferees. We were thrilled at first but this excitement soon turned into dread.

The senior leaders in the Air Force had not been informed about our conference. They had assumed that we had invited Secretary Richardson without informing them - a big no, no. But that was not the worst of it. A top Air Force officer in the Pentagon asked his staff to look over the papers which would be presented.

Lieutenant General Bob Dixon, who was in charge of all personnel and manpower issues, blew his top. He had just read a paper which sharply criticized the personnel policy of the Air Force. All of a sudden, the Department of Political Science at the Air Force Academy gained the reputation as being subversive and unprofessional.

Colonel Rosser and the Department of Political Science survived the onslaught from the Pentagon. But within a year, the Department would face its greatest crisis.

THE DESTRUCTION OF AN ACADEMIC DEPARTMENT

In 1973, a decision was made to disestablish the Political Science Department at the Air Force Academy. This department had been created from whole cloth in 1955 by Colonel Wes Posvar, a West Point graduate and Rhodes scholar. Posvar had recruited talented young officers and arranged for them to complete graduate work at the best universities in America and abroad.

When Posvar retired from the Air Force and became President of Pittsburgh University, he was replaced by Colonel Richard Rosser. Rosser continued to attract fine faculty members. When Rosser retired, the Dean of Faculty at the Air Force Academy decided to combine the large Political Science Department with the small Philosophy and Fine Arts Department. I was teaching at the Air Force Academy at the time and I thought this was a really bad idea.

Since I was not able to convince the Dean, I decided to take the issue to the very top - to the Superintendent of the Air Force Academy, Lieutenant General "Bub" Clark. I had known General Clark rather well. He and my father-in-law, Charlie Goodrich, had been in Stalag Luft III together during World War II. Bub Clark had great respect for Charlie Goodrich and the leadership he had displayed in the German prisoner of war camp and during the march to freedom in 1945. Whenever Lieutenant General Clark saw me he had always recognized me and greeted me in a friendly way.

But the day I walked into his office, General Clark treated me with disdain. I pointed out politely but firmly that of the more than 2400 four-year colleges and universities throughout America, none of them had such a department. I felt the reputation of the Air Force Academy would be damaged when the word got out about such a kludge. I failed in my appeal.

There is a bit of good news. Three years later when I visited the Air Force Academy, I was granted a meeting with the new Superintendent, Lieutenant General Jim Allen. He seemed pleased to have a visit with me. At the time, I was a colonel and was serving as a military assistant to the Deputy Secretary of Defense. General Allen, who had held a number of key positions in the Pentagon, asked me lots of questions about Pentagon activities. He was interested in the current Pentagon issues and personalities.

At the end of our meeting, he asked me if he could do anything for me. I smiled and told him - please reestablish an independent Political Science Department. I then told him the sad story. He said he would do as I asked and he did.

In the spring of 1973, I was given a marvelous opportunity - to be the head of this wonderful, if controversial, academic department. After serious consideration, I decided to return to the operational Air Force, accept a Pentagon assignment, and leave Colorado. At the Air Force Academy I had taught a course on defense policy. I had become fascinated with the policy and decision making in the Pentagon. Also, I had been encouraged by my friends to serve a tour in the Pentagon as a way to broaden my career horizons. Finally, a successful staff tour in the Pentagon often led to a top level assignment back into the operational Air Force.

Since earning my wings as an Air Force pilot, I had always hoped to be a wing commander of a fighter wing. It was a dream job. My thought was that after three years in the Pentagon, I would likely get an assignment which would be the steppingstone to a wing commander's position. As it turned out, that plan worked out well - but it was a very bumpy road along the way.

Chapter Eight:

THE PENTAGON, THE FIRST TIME, 1973

IN THE SUMMER of 1973, I was off to the Pentagon and three years of staff work, the first two years in the Air Staff followed by a year in the office of the Secretary of Defense. For two reasons Connor and I chose to look for houses in McLean, Virginia. First, this area had the best public schools in Northern Virginia at the time. Second, the commute from McLean to the Pentagon down the George Washington Parkway was relatively easy. Folks told me that if I left my home by 6:45 AM, I could reach the Pentagon parking lot in 30 minutes or less. We purchased a house in McLean - the cost was $90,000. Quite high, since in those days four-bedroom houses in Northern Virginia cost on average about $60,000. But it was a good house, in a fine neighborhood, near top public schools and Saint John's Episcopal Church.

THE MANY CHALLENGES OF THE PUZZLE PALACE

To many people, the Pentagon is a strange and forbidding place. It is one of the most complex bureaucracies in the world, yet it operates quite well when the leadership is first rate. How decisions are made and then carried out is worth explaining. Here are a few takeaways.

1. Most decisions made by the Department of Defense require the support (or, at a minimum, the acquiescence) of each of the military services.
2. In the twentieth century the coordination process was very slow. An "action officer" would take a decision package from office to office to get approvals. By the time the package reached top officials it usually had at least 30 signatures of support. In the past twenty years, this coordination exercise has been accomplished electronically - a much faster process.
3. Most of the issues are routine and not controversial.

4. As you might expect there are competitions and rivalries among and between the military services. These rivalries are related to budgets and missions. For instance, should the Army or the Air Force have the mission of close air support of ground troops. However, since each of the services has to rely on the other services for support, the rivalries are usually not very intense. As an example, the Army must rely on the Air Force for airlift support (to haul troops, weapons, supplies, etc.) and the Navy for ship support to carry heavy equipment to overseas locations. The Navy relies on the Air Force for air refueling support while the Air Force relies on the Navy for shipping support - especially for heavy weapons like bombs and missiles.

5. The level of talent at the Pentagon is quite high. Generals, Admirals and senior civil servants recruit the smartest officers and non-commissioned officers from around the world. For instance, when I was the Air Force planner, I would contact the commandants of the various war and staff colleges in the early spring of each year. I wanted to find out which students were the best thinkers and writers. I also was interested in those who had the highest career potential. With the help of my friends in the Air Force personnel office most of these recruits would be assigned to the Air Staff the following summer.

During the period from the summer of 1973 to the summer of 1976, I held five separate jobs in the five sided "fudge factory". I was a junior colonel when I arrived. I had hoped to serve in Air Force Plans and my wish was fulfilled. During the first two years, I served as a branch chief (with six officers and two secretaries working for me), as a deputy division chief, as a division chief and as a joint planner. From 1975 to 1976, I served as a military assistant in the Office of the Secretary of Defense.

PENTAGON STORY: HOW TO GET THINGS DONE FAST

A few months after arriving in the Pentagon in 1973 as an Air Force planner, I was walking down the hall along the outer ring (E ring). Out into the hall jumps an Air Force three-star general, Dutch Huyser. He was my boss at three levels above me. He stopped

me, looked me in the eye and said, "Colonel, I want you to send a full squadron of our best F-4 aircraft to Israel and get them in the air within twenty-four hours. I just promised Henry [Kissinger]." Doctor Kissinger was the National Security Advisor to President Nixon at this time. His influence was enormous.

The Middle East War of October, 1973 was underway and the Israeli Air Force badly needed F-4s and Maverick missiles. I reminded General Huyser that the Air Force did not own these aircraft. These aircraft were under the command of a Joint Commander who was stationed in Florida. Huyser said, very firmly, "I know that Colonel. You get those fighters in the air now. Be aware, you are going to get in lots of trouble and so am I."

Many phone calls later, bureaucratic barriers were knocked down and 24 F-4Es from Seymour Johnson Air Force Base in North Carolina were launched. With full airborne tanker support (KC-135 aircraft), they flew directly from North Carolina to Israel. The four-star Army general who owned the aircraft was really angry when he learned that he had permanently lost a full squadron of his best aircraft. No one had asked his permission. I am sure General Dutch Huyser got in trouble - I never did. I learned a valuable lesson. Bureaucratic barriers can be overturned when the cause is right and key folks are willing to take risks.

My most interesting challenge during my first year in the Pentagon was authoring an analysis of Air Force actions during the Middle East War of 1973.

The top Air Force planner, Major General George Loving, wanted the report to be completed shortly after the end of this short war. I was asked to prepare the report. I assembled a small team of officers. These team members did most of the research. My job was to consolidate their analysis and insights and produce the report. Using a couple of first-rate secretaries, I dictated the report. Within three weeks our team had produced a 100-page analysis. Having authored a two-hundred page dissertation on Air Force planning seven years earlier, I found the task pretty easy. In this case I had plenty of first-class help.

General Loving seemed pleased with the report but he felt something important was not included. He stressed that a crisis often provides opportunities to accomplish things that cannot be done during normal times. He felt the Air Force dropped the ball by not being very creative during this crisis. Prior to this time, I had never really considered the concept of "opportunity planning."

PENTAGON STORY: BEING TOSSED OUT OF CONGRESS

In 1975, the highly admired Senator Scoop Jackson was holding hearings on Capitol Hill on the issue of nuclear arms control. The Secretary of Defense, James Schlesinger, was scheduled to testify. I was told to sit in on the hearings, to take notes and to report back to the Chief of Staff of the Air Force, General David Jones. Jones and the other chiefs were scheduled to testify the next day before the same committee. They wanted to be sure to stay on the same page as the Secretary of Defense.

When the hearings commenced, I was sitting in a corner of the hearing room along with my colleagues from the other services. Just before the hearings commenced, I saw Richard Perle, a close advisor to Senator Jackson, whispering into the Senator's ear while looking over at us. I had a sense that we were in trouble. When Jackson kicked off the hearings, he highlighted how important and how sensitive these hearings were. He then welcomed Dr Schlesinger and asked him to introduce those who were accompanying him.

Schlesinger then introduced his military assistant and his assistant for arms control. Jackson then looked over at us and asked who we were. None of my colleagues spoke up so I jumped to my feet, introduced myself and said I was here to represent the Chief of Staff of the Air Force. My colleagues followed me by introducing themselves. Jackson then said in a polite but firm voice that it was best if we would depart (I cannot remember his exact words).

I returned to the Pentagon and reported immediately to General Jones. I explained that I thought it was Richard Perle who got us tossed out. General Jones smiled, agreed with me and told me that he thought Perle wanted to drive a wedge between the Secretary of Defense and the service chiefs on the issue of arms control.

As I walked up and down the corridors of the Pentagon over

the course of the next few days, lots of friends congratulated me for getting thrown out of a Congressional hearing. Also, they wanted to know the details. Incidentally, Richard Perle had a nickname - "The Prince of Darkness." He had a reputation of being someone who was very clever and always trying to outsmart people. Victory was always his goal. The best way I can describe Perle is by comparing him to Roy Cohn. Cohn was a close advisor to Senator Joe McCarthy and later to Donald Trump. Perle, like Roy Cohn, was very smart, clever and manipulative. However, Perle, unlike Cohn, had a moral compass.

One of the very best jobs in the Pentagon for a colonel was that of a "joint planner." I was honored to be chosen for that position in the summer of 1974. There were four of us in a small, windowless office. All of us were Air Force colonels. In the 1970s many of the most important actions in the Pentagon took place in conjunction with the other military services and the joint staff. Our job as joint planners was to negotiate on behalf of the Air Force. When I walked downstairs to the offices of the Joint Staff, I had to be well prepared. I needed to have a "going in" position as well as "fall back" positions. My task was to represent the Air Force in the best possible way.

The biggest advantage I had in these meetings was a reasonably solid depth of knowledge. My combat experience, my years of duty in France, Germany, Turkey and Thailand, and my teaching of defense policy at the Air Force Academy and at the National War College all helped.

My speed-reading skills were also very valuable. I had, in most cases, read more deeply than had negotiators from the other services and the joint staff. Hence, I tended to have a deeper understanding of the issues than my colleagues. Knowledge was power in the halls of the Pentagon. I loved the job of joint planner and had hoped I could stay in that position until I finished my three-year Pentagon tour in 1976. But alas that was not going to be.

PENTAGON STORY: JOB INTERVIEW
WITH THE SECRETARY OF DEFENSE

In 1974, after serving on the Air Staff for over a year, I was nominated to be a military assistant to the Secretary of Defense.

The interview took place in the impressive office of the Secretary. Jim Schlesinger asked me a bunch of questions - mostly about my evaluation of various senior active duty Air Force generals. When he asked me if I had any points to raise, I suggested that he not hire me for the job. He seemed quite surprised and asked why. I told him that I was a controversial person within the Air Force. I explained that I had received a great deal of criticism about a book I had published only four years earlier. He asked for a copy, which I had with me, and sent me on my way.

I was not hired - which pleased me. I had some specific reasons why I found the job unattractive. First, I never wanted to be someone's flunky. Second, if I was given this job, I would likely have to stay in the Pentagon for an extended period of time. That would probably mean that I would never obtain the dream job of a fighter wing commander. Third, Schlesinger had the reputation as someone who was difficult to work with. Finally, I really liked the job I was holding at the time, and the fine people I was working with.

A few months later, in the summer of 1975, I was hired as a military assistant to the Deputy Secretary of Defense, Bill Clements. I did not want this job either but I had no choice. Clements was a wealthy oil man from Texas. For many years he had been active in the Republican party. After I worked for him and Jimmy Carter was elected to the Presidency, Clements returned to Texas and served two terms as the Governor of Texas. Working for Bill Clements, a tough, hard bitten oil man from East Texas, was quite a challenge.

Mr. William Clements had high regard for Navy, Army and Marine officers - but he had less respect for those of us who wore blue uniforms. Clements and the Chief of Staff of the Air Force, General David Jones, had a toxic relationship. On one occasion, I observed, with considerable embarrassment, Clements harshly criticize General Jones.

In the fall of 1975, I sat in on a meeting with Secretary of Defense Jim Schlesinger and Bill Clements. At that meeting, Clements was very frank. As I best remember his words they were. "Jim, if you keep treating the President like the village idiot you are going to get your ass fired." Sure enough, a couple of weeks later, President Ford fired Schlesinger. Donald Rumsfeld replaced him as Secretary of Defense.

In those days, Rumsfeld was a very impressive young man. Decisive and humorous, he had great relationships with the White House and the Congress. Hence, I was deeply disappointed in Rumsfeld when he served for the second time as Secretary of Defense. The invasion of Iraq in 2003 and the total lack of planning for the postwar period were mistakes of the first order. Incidentally, I wrote Rumsfeld a few months before the invasion urging him to fire General Tommy Franks. His reply to me by note was brief - "Franks will work out OK." He did not. Franks had no plan for dealing with Iraq after the war - a fatal mistake. This oversight cost more than five thousand American lives and tens of thousands lives of innocent Iraqi citizens. Recent rankings of American generals list him as one of the worst generals in American history.

PENTAGON STORY: GETTING FIRED

Nine months after assuming the position as a military assistant to Mr. William Clements, I got a phone call from a friend, Colonel Sam McClure. Sam was serving in the personnel office of the Air Staff. Sam told me to pack my bags - I was being assigned as a maintenance officer in a fighter wing in Germany. This was quite unexpected news.

I reminded Sam that I was in a two-year assignment and had been in the job only nine months. He said, "Perry, you don't have that job any longer." I asked, "Sam what is going on?" He was very frank, "Perry you have been fired, you are history, you are toast." He then went on to explain that I would be the chief of maintenance of the 50th Tactical Fighter Wing at Hahn Air Base. It was not a flying assignment, so a less appealing job in my mind. Although I worked directly for Clements, he did not fire me personally. Clements handed off that job to an Air Force colonel he did not even know.

The next day, I asked Mr. Clements, "Sir, I understand I am headed to Europe?" He replied, "Oh, Perry, I forgot to tell you, the Air Force wants you back flying airplanes and I am willing to let you go." The real story has two parts. First, Clements did not have the gumption to fire me himself. Second, when I asked him the key question, he lied to me.

This event was a major milestone in my career and my life. After a military career of twenty years, I had had one minor setback (my book which was critical of Army Air Force leaders during World War II). Being fired by the Deputy Secretary of Defense was a major setback. My "golden" career had just come crashing down.

Bill Clements never told me why he wanted me gone but I think there were three reasons. He did not respect fighter pilots, he thought I was serving as a spy for General David Jones, the Chief of Staff of the Air Force, and he had little respect for anyone associated with an Ivy League university.

There were some important lessons learned as well as an unforeseen outcome. First and foremost, it was a lesson in humility. I had failed in my job. Second, I learned how not to fire people - a valuable lesson.

This event led to a blessing in disguise. I was getting back to the operational Air Force. I was about to go to work for a wonderful man, Colonel Paul Albritton, the wing commander of the 50th Tactical Fighter Wing at Hahn Air Base in Germany.

On reflection, the lessons learned from this failure helped me in the following years. As I moved into command positions, I had to "drop the hammer" on a number of people. If that person worked directly for me, I gave him or her the news directly. I felt it was wrong to ask a personnel officer, an assistant or anyone else to give the person the bad news. I told them honestly why they had to move on.

One sidebar to this story is what happened while I was checking out of the Pentagon. Friends would see me in the hall. Some would say, "Way to go Perry." I reminded them that I had just been fired. The reply would be, "I know that Perry; but if you got fired by Bill Clements you must have been doing something right."

As far as my family was concerned, my wife, Connor, was angry that I had been fired. McCoy and Serena were excited that they would live in Europe for a few years. They had grown up listening to stories of my childhood in Italy and my family's travels in Greece and Switzerland soon after the end of World War II.

They thought it was completely normal to spend some time living in Europe as kids and were excited about the possibilities. Connor was less excited about returning to dreary, cloudy Hahn. She remembered being a newlywed living in a tiny apartment on the fourth floor of a walk up concrete block apartment. She did not look forward to living once again deep in the German forest, away from any German villages or culture. As it turned out, our second tour at Hahn Air Base turned out to be a delight.

Chapter Nine:

FOUR AND A HALF YEARS
IN EUROPE: 1976 - 1981

THE SUMMER OF 1976 in Washington was a time of great celebration. The war in Vietnam was finally over and our POWs had returned from the horror of the Hanoi Hilton. A tragically flawed president, Richard Nixon, had left office. America had a president who they trusted, Gerry Ford, and the United States was celebrating its 200th birthday. The fireworks display on the National Mall was the most spectacular in history; more than five million flag-waving Americans observed the display from Washington and from Northern Virginia.

In mid-July, 1976, our family, plus two cats and a dog, flew from Dulles Airport to Frankfurt International Airport to begin an adventure that would take us to two American bases and one British base in what was then West Germany.

HAHN AIR BASE: THE SECOND TIME

My job at Hahn Air Base as Chief of Maintenance was a very challenging one. Sixteen hundred professionals worked for me. Most were enlisted troops, about twenty were officers and another sixty were German nationals. The eighty F-4 aircraft which were assigned to the 50th Tactical Fighter Wing were old and beat up. Many had flown in the Vietnam War just a few years previously. A fighter plane that goes into combat nearly every day is placed under a great deal of strain. When being shot at, the pilots yank the airplanes around to avoid the gunfire. Some of our F-4s had been hit by enemy gunfire and most had been "bent" - having pulled too many G forces on too many occasions.

While I was Chief of Maintenance at Hahn Air Base, I dressed each day in a fatigue uniform rather than in a flying suit or in a blue uniform. I wanted to relate as closely as possible with my troops who all wore fatigues. It was also important for me to spend most of my time on the flightline, in the maintenance shops, the munitions storage areas, etc.

Handling the paperwork in my office was a breeze. My secretary was very proficient in taking dictation and in keeping my desk in good shape. I had hired her soon after I arrived at Hahn. She was clearly the most qualified of the candidates. When I went home the evening I hired her, I told Connor I had some good news and some bad news. The good news was I had just hired a first-rate secretary. Connor immediately said, "I bet the bad news is that she is gorgeous." As usual, Connor nailed it.

When I asked someone to come to see me, no one seemed to object. The troops of all ranks loved to visit my office just to have a chance to gaze at her (Cindy was married to a fighter pilot; she soon became pregnant so their interest was platonic). I had learned in the Pentagon that having a welcoming front office is something every leader should strive for.

I decided the only way I could do my job was to trust those who worked for me and to spend lots of time on the flight line and in the various maintenance shops. Fortunately, I knew the F-4 and its systems well from a pilot's perspective. My 180 combat missions in the same model aircraft, the F-4D, gave me some credibility with the maintenance troops and with the pilots in the 50th Tactical Fighter Wing.

During the year I served in aircraft maintenance at Hahn Air Base, I worked closely with my deputy, Lieutenant Colonel Jim Beard. He was a terrific officer whom I leaned on and trusted. He understood maintenance well and gave me candid advice. Jim Beard was a fine athlete, having been a star baseball player at Virginia Tech. We became tennis partners and we won a club championship, playing against German competitors. In my seventy years of playing tennis, it was the only tennis championship I would ever win - so it was quite special.

I had been in the Air Force for more than twenty years but had had very little contact with men and women in the enlisted ranks. That all changed at Hahn Air Base. I gained great respect for the dedication, hard work and talent of the airmen and sergeants who worked in air-craft maintenance. What I also appreciated was their candor. When I asked a question, I got an honest and forthright answer.

Besides Jim Beard, another officer at Hahn Air Base comes to mind. Captain John Desiderio was a young maintenance officer with a great attitude and fine work ethic. Many years later John rose to the rank of colonel and became the chief of maintenance at another Air Force wing. For those Air Force officers who specialize in aircraft main-tenance, reaching the rank of full colonel is not easy. Also, being given the job of chief of maintenance of an operational wing is the pinnacle of success.

The commander of the 50th Tactical Fighter Wing at Hahn Air Base was Colonel Paul Albritton. As the chief of maintenance, I worked directly for him. He was a superb commander and he soon became my role model. His wife, Pat, was a warm and talented southern lady. She was the ideal commander's wife. Connor and Pat soon became fast friends. Two of the Albritton children were very kind to McCoy and Serena. They made them feel welcome on our arrival at Hahn. Although we were at Hahn for less than a year, we became fast friends with the Albrittons. In 2020, Paul celebrated his 90th birthday. The covid-19 crisis caused the planned celebration to be cancelled but good wishes poured in from all over.

Once a month, Paul and I would drive down to Ramstein Air Base, the home of the commander of all of the Air Force units throughout Europe. We reported on the monthly results of a maintenance test pro-gram that the 50th Wing was conducting. On these trips, Paul and I got a chance to get to know each other well. He had a first-class analytical mind and a fine sense of humor. Soon there was a feeling of mutual trust and respect. There may be a lesson here: senior leaders who spend substantive one-on-one time with each other are likely to find working together easier.

No More False Reports

One story from our year (1976-1977) at Hahn Air Base is worth telling. On many evenings I would drop by "Maintenance Control" to see whether we would have enough "operationally

ready" airplanes to meet the flying schedule for the next day. I had been in my job for about six weeks when I looked up at all the aircraft status boards to see mostly red "Xs." In other words, most of the F-4s were out of commission - they were not in flying condition.

At 4 AM each morning the sergeant in charge of Maintenance Control would submit a report to higher headquarters. In order to receive the highest rating, 70% of the aircraft had to be "operationally ready." That evening I asked the sergeant if we would make the 70% figure within the next few hours. He smiled and said "Yes, sir." But then he said something that got my full attention. He said, "We always report 70%."

When I asked him the key question, "Even if we don't have 70% ready?" He said, "Oh yes sir, but by the time we start the morning flying schedule we usually are in good shape." I then asked, "but what if we went to war at 4 AM?" He said quite frankly, "We would be short." As politely but as firmly as I could, I asked him if he was comfortable falsifying an official report almost every night. He said, "No sir," He then explained that he had been told by the previous Chief of Maintenance to always report C-1, no matter what. (C-1 was the rating which indicated that seventy percent of our aircraft were fully capable).

I then asked him how he would feel if he started to report honestly. He said that he would feel much better. The next morning I got on the schedule of the wing commander. I was very frank. I told Colonel Albritton that we were falsifying the 0400-maintenance report almost every morning. He was both surprised and concerned. He asked me what I thought we should do. I told him, "We should start reporting honestly and we should start doing so right away." Happily, he told me to start reporting honestly each night and continue to do so.

Before I left his office, I suggested that he should alert his various commanders that the 50th Tactical Fighter Wing was about to go from C-1 to C-4 (from the top rating to the lowest rating). This report went all of the way to the top officials in the Pentagon so the reaction was likely to be very strong.

Within a few days, we started getting the help that we needed (mostly more spare parts and more maintenance personnel) to be able to maintain a C-1 rating. We also received permission to get spare parts from the nearby German fighter units. I have wondered, on occasion, if Paul and I taking a strong stance for honesty led to our both being promoted to general officer.

BACK TO FLYING AT BITBURG AIR BASE: 1977

As the spring of 1977 rolled around, I got the totally unexpected news that I would soon move to Bitburg, Germany and would become the vice wing commander of the 36th Tactical Fighter Wing. Even more exciting - I would soon check out in the F-15, the newest and best fighter aircraft in the world at this time. Having been fired from a key job in the Pentagon less than a year earlier, this news was way above wonderful.

The family loved Hahn Air Base, the high school was brand new and we had all made many friends. Everyone in the family and many at the base understood that going to Bitburg was a huge opportunity for me professionally. A few close friends told me that this would lead, within the next year, to my dream job, being named the wing commander of the 36th Tactical Fighter Wing.

FLYING STORY: FLIGHT CHECK IN THE F-15

Soon after arriving at Bitburg I flew an airliner back to the United States. At Langley Air Force Base, Virginia, I received my checkout in the brand-new F-15 fighter. I had not flown a fighter aircraft since my combat tour eight years earlier. Hence, I had a bit of trepidation as I climbed up the ladder that day in the summer of 1977. The F-15 turned out to be a much easier aircraft to fly than the F-4 or the F-100. The Eagle was especially easy to land - it would touch down onto the runway sweetly.

It was a treat not only to fly the world's best aircraft but also to visit with my mother, sister and nephews who lived in nearby Hampton, Virginia. After about ten sorties in the F-15, it was back to Bitburg. The job of vice wing commander was easy compared to being chief of maintenance at Hahn Air Base. After flying a few more missions, it was time for me to receive my standardization/

evaluation check ride. If I was to be rated as a fully qualified combat fighter pilot, I had to pass this check ride.

In most aircraft, an instructor pilot climbs in your aircraft and gives you a full checkout. But when an aircraft has only one seat, the instructor pilot flies in a separate aircraft and flies on your wing throughout the flight. The instructor pilot that day was Lieutenant Colonel Ron Fogleman. All went well on the evaluation mission until it was time to land at Ramstein Air Base. As we entered the clouds, Ron was flying close formation on my left wing. There was moderate snowfall throughout the entire area. About six miles short of touchdown, we received some bad news from the controlling agency. Weather throughout central Germany had deteriorated and Ramstein was "below minimums." Hence we could not land there.

I quickly asked "which nearby base is open." The answer from the control agency, "Zweibrucken." I asked for directions to nearby Zweibrucken Air Base. Soon we were on final approach to that base, Ron hung closely on my wing and we landed safely. The snow continued but the base stayed above flight minimums. Since I had so little experience piloting the F-15, I thought Ron might take the lead. He did not. Trust was the name of the game that day.

Incidentally, the talented and charismatic Ron Fogleman received many promotions in the upcoming years. By 1992, he reached the rank of four-star general. Two years later he became the Chief of Staff of the Air Force. He was the first graduate of the United States Air Force Academy to become the Air Force Chief of Staff.

The wing commander at Bitburg, Brigadier General Fred Kyler, was quite a character. He did not look like a typical fighter pilot. He was short, plump and dumpy. In fact, he looked like the goofy cartoon character, Mr. Magoo. When our family arrived at Bitburg, Fred had been the wing commander for three years. He would stay for one more year. Fred Kyler holds the record for being the only Air Force fighter wing commander with four years in command of the same unit.

General Kyler hated doing paperwork. He was delighted when I volunteered to write drafts for most of his correspondence, including officer effectiveness reports and endorsements to these reports. He

*Two F-15 Fighter Aircraft in
formation over Germany, 1977.*

spent much of his time flying F-15s, jogging around the base and visiting folks at the bar at the Officer's Club or the Non-commissioned Officer's Club.

After we got to know each other well, I asked him what the secret to his success as a commander was. His answer was quite simple. "Every morning I thank some people, at noon I thank others and before I go home at night, I thank some more people." His folks really liked him - he was a plain looking, plain speaking man who just loved his job. Also, he was willing to trust people - he gave power away.

During the period when I was the vice commander of the 36th Tactical Fighter Wing, Connor was placed in a difficult situation. The Wing Commander's wife, Jean Kyler, had a problem with booze. By noon, she was often quite tipsy. Jean was unwilling to serve in the informal, but important, role of "wing commander's wife."

Connor found herself having to fill in for Jean at various meetings and functions. Fortunately, Connor received lots of support from the wife of my boss's boss, Major General Dan Druen. Audree Druen knew Jean Kyler well. She understood the awkward situation that Connor faced. Connor was deeply appreciative of the advice and support she received from the caring Audree Druen, a lovely lady.

General Druen was the commander of the 17th Air Force. He was stationed at Sembach, Air Base in Germany. Under his command were a number of fighter wings throughout Germany. He loved to come to Bitburg where he got a chance to fly the F-15. As a result of these visits Connor and I got to know the Druens quite well.

DREAM JOB: WING COMMANDER

In the late spring of 1978, a magic event took place at Bitburg Air Base. I was told that I would soon be given command of the 36th Tactical Fighter Wing. What an honor! I was a 43-year-old Air Force colonel. I had been fired from a key position in the Pentagon just two years earlier. Of all the jobs in the United States Air Force, this one ranked at the top, in my opinion. This fighter wing with its brand-new F-15s was the show unit for the United States Air Force in Europe. This marvelous new airplane and the 36th Tactical Fighter Wing received lots of attention.

The top Air Force commander in Europe, General Bill Evans, a four-star general, sent high-level visitors to Bitburg in remarkable numbers. As a result of the extra burden on this fighter wing, I was authorized a protocol officer. An Air Force captain, Carol Parrington, was highly competent and gave me advice and criticism without hesitation.

Having about one hundred fighter pilots under my command was both a joy and a challenge. These were the very best of the best among Air Force pilots. Many had combat experience. Fighter pilots tend to be very self-confident, smart and, most of all, willing to speak their minds. I had no trouble getting unfiltered comments and criticism from these cocky and brash fighter jocks. There was one thing all of the F-15 pilots had in common. They just loved the "Eagle." The only real problem I had with the pilots was they wanted to fly the aircraft more often.

Just before I assumed command of this marvelous unit, I talked on the phone to a West Point classmate and close friend, Charlie Hamm. Charlie was already in command of a fighter wing. When I asked for his advice, he was very frank. He told me to fire somebody and do it soon after I took command. He said that this act would get everyone's attention. He explained that folks would know that I was really in charge and was willing to make tough decisions.

I was very uncomfortable with his advice. Yet less than two weeks after assuming command, I fired the Air Force colonel who was serving as the Bitburg base commander. The story is worth telling.

In the Air Force at the time there was a great deal of emphasis on the issue of fraternization. Having affairs with someone who worked for you was a big no, no. When it was clear that the base commander was in gross violation of this policy, I asked him to tell me what was going on. He told me this relationship was strictly platonic. I had all kinds of information to the contrary.

I called my various bosses and told them of my decision. The Vice Commander of the Air Forces in Europe, Lieutenant General Ben Bellis, asked me to come down to visit him. I told him the story and mentioned that the base commander had told me about the relationship being platonic. Bellis gave me support and told me he would find a job for the departing colonel.

Later that day, I was told to visit General Bill Evans, the top Air Force leader in Europe. When I entered his office, he put me at ease. He asked about the platonic relationship and then said, with a twinkle in his eye, "His play and her tonic."

When I was the commander at Bitburg, I had a marvelous set of leaders at higher headquarters at Sembach (Major General Dan Druen) and Ramstein (Lieutenant General Ben Bellis and Generals Bill Evans and John Pauley). They all firmly believed that their jobs were to support commanders in the field. They did not endorse micromanagement. Hence, except on rare occasions, I did not have to check with my bosses when I made decisions. The feeling of mutual trust was both profound and deeply appreciated.

Through the years, I have stayed in contact with Dan Druen, Sadly, his wife Audree died a few years ago. Dan had a wealth of experience in the fighter business. He understood fighter pilots well. However, his greatest strength was his willingness to trust people. He had many opportunities to second guess me - especially when I made a bad decision.

The respect and affection that all of his wing commanders had for their boss, General Dan Druen, was something to behold and to celebrate. Dan's books, *Sometimes We Flew* and *Sometimes We Flew Too,* tell many of his exploits.

GIVING AN AMBASSADOR A RIDE IN THE F-15

On one occasion during my time as commander of the 36th Tactical Fighter Wing I was put in a very awkward position. Soon I found myself being chewed out by a major general from higher headquarters. Here is the story. The U.S. ambassador to the Soviet Union, Malcolm Toon, visited my base. I showed him around and then took him out to supper in downtown Bitburg. Ambassador Toon had served in the Navy during World War II; he was not an aviator.

On the way back to the base, Ambassador Toon said to me. "Colonel, I want to fly in that airplane you have been raving about, please set up a flight for me in the morning." Of the eighty F-15s at Bitburg, four were two seat versions. These were used to check out new pilots. They were also used, on occasion, to give dignitaries and journalists an opportunity to better understand the capabilities of this marvelous fighter aircraft.

I tried to talk Ambassador Toon out of the idea, telling him about the heavy G forces and the fact that many get airsick when given flights in highly maneuverable fighter aircraft. I was very frank. I told him these F-15s were designed for young people to fly. Born in 1916, Toon was 62 years old when he visited Bitburg.

Ambassador Toon then hit me with a powerful argument. "Colonel, I want to fly in an F-15 so the next time I see Brezhnev (the leader of the Soviet Union at the time), I can tell him I have flown in the world's best airplane." I just loved his rationale and found his argument persuasive. Earlier in the evening, Ambassador Toon told me that he had been a PT boat commander in combat in World War II. He pointed out that, unlike Jack Kennedy, his boat did not get sunk. Ambassador Toon was a tough, no-nonsense, self-confident man. He was not used to having his requests turned down.

On my mobile phone (yes, we had mobile phones in 1978), I called my operations officer. I asked him to call the headquarters in Ramstein to get permission from higher headquarters to fly the ambassador. He did so and received the permission I was seeking. But when he called me back, he told me that I was in big trouble. He predicted that I would get a call from a very angry two-star general who was serving as the operations officer for the US Air Forces in Europe.

Sure enough, the next day Major General Bill Clement called me to chew me out. He was clearly very angry. He accused me of encouraging Ambassador Toon to make the request for the flight in an F-15. I listened politely but then told him in very direct terms that it was not my idea. I then explained how I had tried to talk the ambassador out of taking this flight. General Clement finally calmed down when I quietly but firmly explained that he had a misunderstanding of the situation I had faced. Incidentally, Malcolm Toon enjoyed his flight; I am sure he told the top leaders in the Soviet Union about his great adventure.

A RIDE FOR THE CHIEF
OF STAFF OF THE FRENCH AIR FORCE

Another high-level visitor to Bitburg was the Chief of Staff of the French Air Force. General Maurice Saint-Cricq. He spoke English well, was handsome and charming. He had flown combat in World War II so he was about twelve years older than me. Higher headquarters at Ramstein had given him permission to get a back-seat flight in an F-15B aircraft. Although France was not a member of NATO, the French military and the American military had a warm relationship which dated all the way back to World War I.

Since he was such a high-ranking officer, I decided to climb into the front seat and to be the pilot on this flight. After demonstrating some of the flight characteristics of the F-15, I suggested that he pilot the aircraft himself. He was delighted. He flew the aircraft for almost the entire flight but when it was time to land, I regained the flight controls.

After our F-15 touched down, I held the nose quite high in order to take advantage of aerodynamic braking. This was the standard procedure since it reduced wear and tear on the brakes. After we had landed and had been rolling down the runway for about 2000 feet, I was asked, "Colonel, when are we going to touchdown?" It was one of the nicest compliments I have ever had. The landing was so gentle, that he did not know we had already landed. I should point out that the F-15 was very easy to land and smooth landings were the norm for all of the F-15 pilots.

After climbing down from the cockpit, the French four-star general said to me, "I never thought that I would fly an airplane better than the Spitfire, but I just did." In my weekly column in the base newspaper, I told the story of the French general and the Spitfire.

Avoiding Micromanagement

There was a problem with being the commander of a high-profile unit with a brand-new aircraft. Staff officers at higher headquarters just loved to get involved in our operation. When I first assumed command, the commander of all Air Force units in Europe, General John Pauley, had told me that he wanted me to run the wing and if I needed his help to let him know.

After being in command for about three months, I wrote General Pauley a letter of complaint. I pointed out a number of examples where one of his mid-level staff officers had directed us to take an action that just didn't make sense. For instance, the F-15 landed so gently and at such a low speed that, unlike the F-4, it was not necessary to change tires often. Changing tires on the F-15 after every five landings (the rule for the F-4) made no sense.

Within a week, I was told to report to General Pauley at his base at Ramstein. I flew down in an F-15 and walked into his conference room in my flying suit. In the room was General Pauley and all of his generals - they were wearing their blue uniforms. Pauley welcomed me and reminded everyone that I was the commander at Bitburg. He then did something truly amazing.

General John Pauley, god love him, told everyone in the room that it was unacceptable for staff officers from his headquarters to micromanage the folks at Bitburg. He then asked each general officer what he was going to do to assist Perry Smith. Clearly my letter got results, although there were some general officers in the room who did not care for the brash colonel from Bitburg.

FLYING STORY: SAVING AN AIRLINER, 1978

In 1978, I was flying an F-15 over Germany when I received a call from the controlling agency. An airliner was in trouble - and I was asked if I could help. The controller explained that the pilot's airspeed indicator was reading zero. This meant he had no way of knowing how fast he was going. This would be a problem on his descent and landing.

I located the airliner and joined up on his wing. After making radio contact, I suggested to the pilot that he fly on my wing all the way to touchdown at the Frankfurt airport. He said, "I can't do that." He explained that he did not know how to fly in formation with another aircraft. I then suggested plan B, that I fly on his wing and read off my airspeed every second or two. Since we would be flying together, we would be flying at the same speed. The airline pilot liked the idea so we headed to the airport. I asked him what speed he wanted to maintain at each phase of the flight.

About every two seconds, I would radio to him our mutual airspeeds. He informed the control agency that we would be coming down together. The airline pilot did all the navigating - all I had to do was fly a few feet off his wing and read off my airspeed.

When we got to the most important part of the flight, the final approach, he lowered his landing gear and flaps. He had told me that he wanted to maintain 125 knots all the way to touchdown. I kept reading off the airspeed. 124...125.... 126...125, etc.

As he began to round out for his touchdown, I moved my throttles forward and flew back to my base at Bitburg, Germany. I have often wondered what the passengers thought when they saw a fighter jet flying off the wing of their airliner. Did the pilot let them know what was going on? If so, did it cause them any concern?

What lessons can be learned from this event.

1. When you are in trouble, ask for help. Too many people try to solve problems by themselves. Ego, insecurity, lack of the ability to trust others or lack of a robust braintrust are just a few reasons why people are unwilling or unable to reach out for assistance.
2. When you are asked to help someone who is in need, drop what you are doing and move quickly to assist.
3. Be creative in looking for a solution to the problem.
4. If your first answer doesn't work, come up with another.

If the airline pilot had tried to land without assistance, he would not have wanted to get too slow. Hence, he would probably have come down the final approach very fast. As he rounded out for a landing, the airliner would have floated way down the runway and landed long. There is a strong likelihood that he would have run off the far end of the runway.

During my time as commander of the 36th Tactical Fighter Wing, four F-15 fighter aircraft crashed. Perhaps the most interesting story among these crashes involved a twelve-year-old German boy.

FLYING STORY: F-15 CRASH

A Bitburg fighter pilot, Gene Santarelli, was flying over northern Germany in December, 1978. He was practicing combat maneuvers by simulating air-to-air combat with two other F-15s. Each pilot was rapidly moving his aircraft in various directions as he tried to outsmart and out maneuver the other pilots. The goal was to get into an advantageous firing position.

Suddenly, something extremely unexpected and frightening happened. Gene's aircraft pitched forward and downward radically. He was thrown to the top of his cockpit and his helmet banged hard against the canopy.

A few seconds later, the fighter aircraft changed directions and pitched up. In both cases, Gene was hit with strong "G" forces. On the pitch down, the negative G forces were so severe that the tiny blood vessels in both his eyes burst.

His cockpit quickly filled with smoke. When he tried to maneuver the aircraft with his stick and rudders there was no response. Gene realized that he had totally lost control of his aircraft.

Gene then made the correct decision and ejected from the aircraft. The ejection sequence was normal with the canopy ejecting first followed quickly by the ejection seat. The parachute opened properly, his ejection seat fell away and he floated down to the ground under a good parachute. He was shaken but his only injuries were to his eyes and a hyperextended leg injury. It took three weeks before his bright purple eyes returned to white again.

The accident investigation team found the crash site but attempts to determine the cause of the accident were going nowhere. On the ground there was a large hole; nothing was left but small bits and pieces of the aircraft and engine. As the wing commander, I was especially interested in why the F-15 had gone totally out of control. Could this happen to other F-15s? Were all the F-15s throughout the world in danger of this happening?

About a week after the crash I asked, at the morning staff meeting at Bitburg, for the latest news on the accident investigation. Someone spoke up and said that the team had interviewed lots of folks on the ground. The results were negative with one exception.

A twelve-year-old German boy, during a school recess, had been watching the maneuvering F-15s. He described what he saw. He had watched one aircraft violently moving. He then saw smoke, and observed the ejection of the pilot. The boy then told the accident investigator, "and then the wing came off."

When this information was relayed to me in my morning meeting, I laughed. How silly, I thought. Wings don't fall off brand new fighter aircraft. These aircraft are so well designed that they can withstand enormous G-forces in every possible direction.

After a pause, someone spoke up. "Why would a young boy lie about something like that?" Someone else chimed in, "Maybe he wasn't lying, perhaps he was telling the truth." BINGO - I finally woke up and started listening.

I recommended that the accident investigation team go back

to the crash area and see if a wing could be found. Sure enough, less than a mile from the crash site, the wing was located. It had floated down like a leaf and was in good shape. By studying the shear points, the team was able to figure out what had happened to that aircraft and why it had gone out of control. Soon thereafter, corrective action was taken on all F-15s throughout the world.

Often, we forget that it is important to listen carefully and to make sure that we hear both the direct message as well as any subtle or hidden points. That day in 1978 when I failed to listen to the message of a young boy was a turning point in my life. I vowed to be a better listener and to really focus and to hear as well as to listen.

WING COMMANDER: IT'S NOT JUST ABOUT FLYING

As Wing Commander at Bitburg Air Base, I had 4000 people working under me, so the job was about much more than flying and maintaining the F-15 fighter jet. The following are some examples.

The day was the second Friday in October, 1978. I was in my office when the phone rang. My secretary had departed so I answered the telephone on its second ring. A sergeant, whom I knew, was calling me. He told me that there was about to be a riot outside the base post office. He suggested that I get there and do so quickly. The problem - the Army troops had not been paid and a long weekend was coming up. The Carter administration had been at loggerheads and the government was shut down for a few days. The Air Force folks had received their pay earlier that day but not the Army troops.

I called my director of finance and asked him how much cash was in his safe. After a slight hesitation he said about $600,000. I then told him that I wanted him to pay about two hundred Army troops. I said I would send them to his office. He gave me lots of reasons why he couldn't do as I asked. Some were excellent reasons. For instance, he did not have access to the pay records of Army soldiers. Also paying troops in cash was strictly forbidden by Department of Defense directives and Air Force and Army regulations.

I then asked him if paying Army troops was illegal or unethical. He said no. I then told him that, as the wing commander, I would waive all directives and regulations. I explained that he could blame me if he got in trouble.

He then said that he needed an hour to call in his troops, get support from the Security Police Squadron and set up the pay tables and pay lines. He also explained that it was best to be done at the non-commissioned officers club since his finance office was too small to handle a large number of Army troops.

I then raced down to the post office. It was snowing quite hard. I told everyone to listen up. I then explained that everyone would be paid this evening in cash. I also explained the amount each would receive would not be exact but it should all be straightened out by the next week. I told everyone to wait an hour and then proceed to the NCO club. They were especially pleased that they would get cash, since the base bank was closed.

For the rest of my tenure as the commander at Bitburg Air Base, my relationship with Army troops was a warm one.

One of the more interesting aspects of being a commander of a large military unit was dealing with the daily police blotter. When I arrived at work around 7 AM each morning, on my desk was a twelve to fourteen-page document. Prepared by the Security Police Squadron, this document listed all of the bad or unusual occurrences of the past twenty-four hours. Much of the information was quite mundane: lights left on in a squadron building, door ajar at another building, flat tire on a police vehicle, etc.

However, some of the reported events were of greater interest and concern. Examples included a sergeant charged with driving under the influence of alcohol or drugs, a fist fight in the non-commissioned-officers club, property missing from the transportation squadron's building, etc. Other reports were even more serious: child abuse, spouse abuse, a weapon missing from the security police armory, a safe containing top secret documents that had been left open.

I soon realized that there were aspects of leadership which are seldom discussed in books on management. I also came to understand that many people who teach leadership have never faced agonizing dilemmas such as dealing with psychopathic, sociopathic or narcissistic people or sending people to jail.

Something to keep in mind about a Wing Commander of an air base outside the U.S., is that you are essentially everyone's boss. You are comparable to the CEO of every business in town, the Mayor, the Superintendent of Schools, the Chief of Police and the head of the Hospital. The behavior of military, civilian and dependents (family members) on and off the job is your responsibility because their behavior reflects upon the relationship of the United States and the host country.

Let me cite one specific example of the kinds of issues a commander faces. One morning I noticed on the police blotter that a sergeant had been picked up at the main gate because he was driving erratically. The security policeman noticed a strong odor of alcohol on the sergeant's breath. The inebriated sergeant was driven to the hospital and ordered to take a blood test. Then the security policeman took the sergeant to his apartment. In the meantime, another security policeman delivered the sergeant's car to his apartment complex.

I kept an eye on the police blotter over the next few days. I was interested in how high the alcohol content in the sergeant's blood would be. To my surprise, the lab result showed him to have zero alcohol in his bloodstream. However, the test showed that his blood was positive for amphetamines. I called in my vice commander and asked him to thoroughly investigate this incident - clearly something was amiss.

The investigation showed that the sergeant with the drinking problem, after being escorted back to his apartment, was deeply distressed. This was the second time he had been caught while driving under the influence of alcohol. He knew that he would lose his driver's license for six months. His wife worked on base but did not know how to drive and he had no way to get to work himself.

That fateful evening, the sergeant shared his distress with a neighbor. This led to a trip back to the hospital. The sergeant and his neighbor convinced a young corpsman at the hospital to take blood from the neighbor and to toss out the blood of the drunken sergeant.

What the neighbor failed to tell his friend was that he was popping pills. What was crystal clear - three of my troops were in trouble (the drunken sergeant, his pill popping friend and the corpsman at the hospital who switched the blood samples). The police blotter and the subsequent investigation helped me understand the whole story.

Leaders who deal with a daily police blotter month after month after month understand the realities of life throughout their entire organization.

A happier example of being a Wing Commander was when there was a heavy snowstorm at Bitburg. McCoy and Serena, who were in high school, knew that I was the one who called off school for a snow day. They lobbied me hard and after talking with my weather experts, I canceled school for the next day. To get the word out to families who lived off base, I had to make a decision by eight PM the night before. They were thrilled to spend the day sledding down the hill behind the Wing Commander's house with their friends and were so proud that their dad had given everyone a snow day!

Promoted for Handling Failure Well

In the summer of 1978, the commander of all of the U.S. Air Force units in Europe visited Bitburg. Connor and I hosted General Bill Evans and his wife for dinner. I quietly expressed to him how pleased I was to be the wing commander of the 36th Tactical Fighter Wing. I asked that he let me stay at Bitburg for four years or more. I would then happily retire as a colonel.

I told General Evans that I was not interested in being promoted to general officer. He agreed with me that I had the best job in the Air Force. He then hinted that, if the Air Force chose to promote me, he could not prevent that from happening.

During our short 21 months at Bitburg, I served as vice commander for a year and as commander for 9 months. The new F-15s had a superb record for the first nine months but then the crashes came. From April, 1978, until December, 1978, five brand new F-15s crashed.

This was a massive failure on the part of the fighter wing and its commander. Two weeks after the fifth aircraft crashed, I was informed that I was on the promotion list for new brigadier generals.

I was really surprised. I was going through a period of massive failure (the aircraft crashes). Also, I had been fired from my Pentagon job just two years earlier.

A few months later I asked General Pauley, who had replaced General Evans as the top Air Force Commander in Europe, how I managed to make the promotion list. His answer was interesting. He told me that I had handled failure well. He explained that each of his wing commanders was failing. One had a drug ring on his base, another, a racial problem, another, a problem of many flunked NATO inspections, etc. etc. General Pauley explained that since I handled failure well, I would probably handle success well. Hence, he put me at the top of his priority list for promotion.

In my leadership workshops, I usually tell this story. I explain that I learned more from my failures than from my successes. I suggest that everyone in the audience is likely to encounter professional failures. These are both humbling and learning experiences. I also make the point that having failed often, I tend to be tolerant of other people's failures.

GETTING HELP FROM THE PENTAGON

One of the advantages which I gained from three years of duty in the Pentagon was learning how to get things done in the huge "Puzzle Palace" bureaucracy. On two occasions, when I was the wing commander at Bitburg, I used that knowledge to get help.

Having received an especially unhelpful message from the Air Staff, I made some phone calls to find out who had written this particular message. When I got that staff officer on the phone, I told him that I was the wing commander at Bitburg and I needed his help. I explained in detail why the message he had written was going to cause us great difficulty.

I then asked him to pull out his pencil. I dictated to him the clarifying message that he needed to send to me. He was reluctant to help. He explained that the original message had been approved and signed out by one of his bosses, a general officer. I asked him, did you compose the message. He said that he did. I then replied, "OK, please give me the general's telephone number. I will be happy to explain to him my problem with your message." The staff officer quickly woke up. He told me he would do as I asked. I did not threaten him but he got my message. The waiver arrived by message the next day.

The second example is more interesting. On my letterhead stationery, I wrote a letter and sent it directly to the Office of the Secretary of Defense. I sent it to Secretary Harold Brown's military assistant, Colonel Bud Coyle, a good friend. I was quite sure Bud would show it to Secretary Brown. Before I sent this letter, I cleared it with my boss, Major General Dan Druen. He told me that he had no objection to the letter; he thought it might do some good.

The letter pointed out a number of areas at Bitburg that needed help. For instance, our aircraft hangars and maintenance shops had roofs that were leaking. These leaks were causing damage to expensive equipment. We had money in our budget for these repairs but we could not use these funds because they were "fenced." In other words, these funds could be used for one specific purpose and could not be transferred to more needed projects. I asked for a waiver and sure enough within a couple of weeks, the waiver came through and the funds became available.

Later I found out that Secretary of Defense Harold Brown loved my letter. It was rare for him to receive critical feedback directly from a commander in the field. Incidentally, Secretary Brown was careful in protecting me from being hammered for going out of channels. In sum, if I had not served in the Pentagon, I doubt if I could have figured out a way to solve some of these thorny problems.

INTERESTING F-15 TACTICS

I would like to conclude this section on the F-15 by telling two more stories. When I was the wing commander at Bitburg, a tactics manual was written by F-15 pilot, John Madden. When he flew with the Triple Nickel Squadron in 1972, Major Madden had three aerial victories over North Vietnam. As a result, John had great credibility among his fellow fighter pilots at Bitburg. Major Madden suggested that the title of the manual should be TWENTY TO ONE.

John felt that for every F-15 we would lose in combat, twenty enemy aircraft would be shot down. I was skeptical. I thought this was too optimistic a goal. However, Major Madden was so persuasive that I agreed with the title. How right he was.

As of 2020, the kill ratio of F-15 versus enemy aircraft is 106 to zero. American, Israeli and Saudi pilots have all had great success. Just think about this for a moment. Not one F-15 has been shot down in air-to-air combat. No fighter in the history of aviation has had that kind of record of success.

My second story relates to air to air combat training in Spain and in England. The best training for fighter pilots, whose mission is to engage the enemy in aerial combat, is "dissimilar" air combat training, for instance when F-15s engage Navy F-14s or Air Force F-5s. Flying over the Mediterranean Sea, I had the chance to take on some hot-shot Navy pilots flying F-14s. My leader was a first-rate F-15 fighter pilot, JJ Winters. Winters had 481 combat sorties in the F-4, the second highest total of the entire Vietnam War. I could not have picked a better leader for this mission against the two Navy F-14s. Since the F-15 was a more maneuverable aircraft than the F-14, JJ and I had an advantage as we entered the engagement.

However, the Navy had a third airplane in the dog fight. This so-called, "wild card," snuck up behind me. His arrival was totally unexpected. Happily, JJ observed my difficulty and engaged the wild card F-14 before it could get into a firing position. Over time JJ became a good friend. Three years later, after a couple of beers, JJ enticed me into running the Marine Marathon with him.

On another occasion, I had the opportunity to take on an aircraft which had dissimilar performance characteristics. Out of Alconbury Air Base in England, I engaged a small Air Force F-5 in simulated combat. I did not do well. The F-5 was so small that I lost sight of it. The skilled, "aggressor" pilot won the contest.

Unlike my successful dogfight against Navy F-14s, the Marine Marathon did not go well. JJ Winters and I ran together for fifteen miles and had a nice visit along the way. As we approached the Lincoln Memorial for the second time, I looked over at him - he looked terrible. It turned out that he had a stress fracture in one of his legs. He slowed to a walk. Since there was nothing I could to assist him, he suggested that I keep running which I did.

Shortly thereafter, I hit the wall. We both limped along for the last seven miles. However, by golly, we finished. We both completed the 26.2 miles in less than four hours. Not bad for someone with a fractured leg and another person who was in his late forties.

Both in dogfighting F-5 aircraft and in long distance running, I gained lessons in humility. I had many others.

Off to Northern Germany for a NATO Assignment, 1979

Soon our family was off to northern Germany to a NATO base at Rheindahlen. Located near Dusseldorf, Germany, this large base was run by the British Army. Our family would live there for two years: from January, 1979 to January, 1981. This assignment turned out to be an opportunity for growth since all of us learned how the British lived, worked and played. We also learned of the social and cultural proclivities of the British, Germans, Dutch and Belgians. The North Atlantic Treaty Organization (NATO) had been created in 1949. By the 1970s it was a fully functional military alliance with a simple mission - to protect the democratic nations of Western Europe from invasion by the Soviet Union and its allies.

In January, 1979, as a brand-new brigadier general, I became the operations officer of the Second Allied Tactical Air Force - a NATO command. Under my supervision were those who would engage in combat. Other generals in this headquarters were responsible for personnel, logistics and planning.

My immediate boss was a German Luftwaffe Major General Paul Monreal. My top boss was a British Air Marshall (3-star officer) Sir John Stacey whose military career was with the Royal Air Force of the United Kingdom. Both officers were delighted that the Americans were now part of their headquarters. We were welcomed with open arms. These leaders were especially pleased that more than one hundred American fighter aircraft were now committed to the defense of the north German plain.

Soon after I checked in, a senior NATO civil servant visited me in my office. In the process of welcoming me, he became quite emotional. Tears appeared in his eyes. He told me that my arrival into this northern German headquarters meant that the Soviets would never invade. He explained that the vulnerable north German plain would now be protected by American airpower.

It was at that moment I fully understood how important the arrival of the Americans into this headquarters was. It sent a strong signal to our allies and to the nations of the Warsaw Pact. As of January, 1979, America was fully committed to defending West Germany from the Baltic Sea to the Austrian border.

Working for me at this NATO base were officers and non-commissioned officers from Belgium, Germany, the Netherlands, the United Kingdom and the United States. It soon became clear that I had two big advantages as the operations officer for this NATO command: my combat experience and the fact that I was "current" in the world's best fighter aircraft, the F-15. I was one of the few people in this headquarters who had combat experience and no one else in the entire headquarters had flown the American F-15.

In 1979, there were about thirty Air Force colonels who were promoted to brigadier general. I was one of the younger ones and would normally have waited at least six months before I assumed the new rank. However, when I arrived at the NATO headquarters, I was a brand-new brigadier general. A few days before I arrived, I had been "frocked." This was quite an unusual event in the United States Air Force. For reasons of protocol, it was important that I arrive at the NATO headquarters as a general officer and not as colonel.

Soon after our family arrived at the base at Rheindahlen, Air Marshal John Stacey, the commander of the Second Allied Tactical Air Force, hosted a formal dinner. "Ladies Guest Nights" included the senior officers and their wives from the five nations in the headquarters. At the dinner John Stacey made a brief talk. He explained how he worked hard together with American general Al Haig to bring the Americans into his headquarters. It was an extremely warm welcome. Al Haig, who was the top general within NATO in 1979, would later become Secretary of State under President Reagan.

Prior to the dinner, British Air Commodore Bob Price, who was responsible for setting up the event, had done his homework. He learned of Connor's singing talent. Connor was asked to be on the program that evening. While she sang three songs, I looked around the audience. It was clear to me that many felt that the reason I had been promoted to general officer was because of my lovely, talented wife. Among the British, Germans, Dutch and Belgians in postwar Europe, the role of the wife was quite important. That Ladies Guest Night in the spring of 1979 was a grand evening from start to finish.

Lingering WWII Memories and Sensitivities

Many of the officials in this headquarters were serious students of warfare. They were especially knowledgeable about World War II in Europe - much more so than I was. All of the generals in the headquarters were older than I was. Some had had combat experience during World War II, while others (the Belgians and the Dutch) had vivid memories of what it was like to live in Europe when the Nazis were in charge. This leads me to the Martin Visser story. Dutch General Visser was a colleague who served as the top plans and program officer for the Second Allied Tactical Air Force. He was about five years older than me.

Martin and I were driving around Germany, Belgium and the Netherlands visiting NATO air bases. Since he was Dutch, I asked him how he felt about the Germans. He was very candid and emotional when he told me his story. He was a teenager living with his family in the Netherlands when, in 1940, the German Army invaded his country. Soon afterwards, the Visser family adopted a young Jewish girl. They falsified her records to remove any indication that she had Jewish parents. However, everyone in Martin's family knew that, if she was discovered, the Jewish girl and the entire Visser family would be sent to a death camp.

Martin explained to me that every time he hears the distinctive sound of a German police siren, it deeply troubles him. He is reminded of the fear he felt when he heard that noise for five long years. He told me frankly that he would never, ever, be comfortable with Germans.

This discomfort factor between the Germans and those from other nations cut many ways. When it was time to give heavy guidance to a Belgian major with serious drinking and absentee problems, I was asked for help by my boss. Since the Belgian major did not work for me, I did not understand why I should be involved.

My boss, who was German, explained that, as an American, I did not carry any negative baggage. It was at that moment when I realized the enormous amount of trust and goodwill we enjoy as Americans. I also realized that my German boss was sensitive to the feelings of other cultures towards a still healing relationship with the Germans.

THE BLACK FOOT STORY, A GERMAN SOLDIER

One of my most delightful friends from our days in Rheindahlen was a German Army major general, Chris Shoeneman. He was the operations officer for the Northern Army Group. Hence, he and I had similar jobs and we worked together quite often. I asked Chris one day where he got the nickname, Black Foot. What follows is his amazing story.

General Shoeneman reminded me that during the 1930s, young Germans boys were great fans of American western movies. Cowboys and Indian "shoot 'em ups" were wildly popular. One of the tribes, the Blackfoot Indians from Montana, was especially well known among young Germans.

When Germany invaded Russia in the summer of 1941, Chris was a brand-new soldier in the infantry. He had been too young to participate in the 1940 German invasion of France, Belgium and the Netherlands. During the summer of 1941, seventeen-year-old Private Shoeneman marched eastward for nearly one thousand miles.

Not once did he get a ride on a truck, tank or any other vehicle. At 5 AM each morning he and his fellow soldiers would be awakened and given some bread and soup. For the next sixteen hours Private Schoeneman would march with his unit across Poland and deep into Russia. Keeping up with the fast-moving German tanks was a real challenge. He did not have to do much fighting since the Russians were in full retreat.

Before the march began on 22 June, 1941, Chris's sergeant told him to never take off his boots. If he did so, his feet would swell and he would not be able to get them back on. Chris followed the order of his sergeant - not once did he take off his boots. After two months of marching, Private Chris Shoeneman was selected for officer candidate school. He got a two week break back home - and finally removed his boots.

His black socks were so embedded in his skin that he could not scrub them off. When he went into the mass shower at officer candidate school, his feet and ankles were still a deep black color. Instantly, he became known as Blackfoot. From 1941 until 1945, he fought on the Russian front.

Early in our friendship, General Shoeneman gave me some great advice. He told me that when you arrive at a new assignment, figure out quickly what section of the organization would likely be a bureaucratic competitor. Get to know the person who is in charge of that section. Spend lots of time, arm and arm, with that person and visit lots of units and sections.

If you show folks in both organizations that you plan to be good friends with your cohort, they are less likely to engage in bureaucratic battles. When I returned to the Pentagon in 1981, I immediately approached the Air Force programmer, General Chuck Cunningham. I told him about Chris Shoeneman's advice. We agreed that we would never bad mouth each other or our respective staff members.

Our Children's Lives in Europe

During our two years in northern Germany, McCoy and Serena attended an international school in the Netherlands. They lived in a dorm from Monday through Friday but returned to our home in Germany for the weekends. In 1980, McCoy graduated from AFCENT (Allied Forces Central Europe) High School. He was the salutatorian in his class and a National Merit Scholar finalist. Soon he was off to Colorado State University in Fort Collins, Colorado.

McCoy had attended three high schools in two different countries. Serena would leave AFCENT in the middle of her junior year and attend one more high school in Northern Virginia. She would have attended four high schools in three different countries. Serena's choice of college was Sewanee, the University of the South, a small liberal arts school on 10,000 acres on the Cumberland plateau in eastern Tennessee. She wanted to explore her southern roots after being raised by a southern mother, but never living in the South. Serena ended up getting a full scholarship to study in Germany her junior year of college, so she wasn't away from Europe for long.

Connor's Musical Talents in Full Bloom

During our two years at Rheindahlen, Connor became deeply involved in an on-base musical company called WRMS (West Rhine Musical Society). This first-rate amateur group, run by the British, produced two musical productions each year. When the leader of WRMS realized that Connor was a fine lyric soprano, she was asked to join the group. Soon she was chosen to be one of WRMS's major performers. I was so proud of Connor. She was superb both as an actor and as a singer. On stage she was striking in her beauty and stage presence.

Actress and Soloist
Connor Dyess Smith, 1981.

Connor had the lead role in Gilbert and Sullivan's *Patience*. The show was performed three times before large audiences. Connor played the role of a 17-year-old milk maid. She was on stage for almost the entire show. My role was quite modest. I played the role of a 70-year-old solicitor (with a top hat). Although we were both in our mid-40s, our friends told us that we were perfectly cast: Connor as a young damsel and me as an old geezer.

I was on stage for about three minutes and did not have a speaking role. For the finale, the entire cast was on stage to sing and dance. The twenty members of the cast lined up. I was at the very far end. I found that I did not have the skills to dance and sing at the same time. So I would dance while mouthing the words of the song.

In another production, Connor played the role of Nettie Fowler in the musical, *Carousel.* Her solos were "June is Busting Out All Over," "It was a Real Nice Clambake," and "You'll Never Walk Alone." The applause after each solo from the standing room only audiences was robust and sustained.

Early in 1981, Connor was excited about her upcoming role in *Fiddler on the Roof.* She was in rehearsal and would play the role of Mama. She was disappointed when she learned that I was to be reassigned. We would have to leave Germany before the dates of the performances. I tried to get my assignment postponed for a few months but to no avail.

Our small family (minus McCoy who was in his freshman year at Colorado State University) returned to the United States in January, 1981. We had been overseas for four and a half years and had been stationed at three bases. Our children had attended three schools, two in Germany and one in the Netherlands. The education that they received was first rate. The Defense Department schools were small and the teachers were well paid and highly motivated. Our travels broadened the horizons of the entire family.

We had tried to maximize the opportunity of living in Europe by taking trips during school breaks and summers. We went to Italy, France, Switzerland, Austria, Belgium, Luxemburg, Spain, the United Kingdom, Denmark, Greece, Turkey, Egypt, Israel, and Jordan. The kids visited some countries without us as part of high school sports or choral groups. Connor was even able to take McCoy and Serena to the Soviet Union with stops in Moscow, Leningrad (now St. Petersburg) and Novgorod. I was not able to attend the Russia trip because of my high-level security clearances.

As a result of these international and educational experiences, our children did well when they returned to the United States for college and graduate school. Every time we moved, our family came together nicely - hence we are blessed with warm and loving relationships among our family members. This warmth continues today - it is one our greatest blessings. We have had many more.

Chapter Ten:

~~~

RETURN TO THE PENTAGON: 1981 - 1983

MY NEXT JOB was back in the Pentagon. This time as a major general and the Air Force planner - a wonderful but very challenging job. Having served in Air Force Plans in the Pentagon six years earlier, I was quite familiar with the various elements of this key office within the Air Staff.

President Reagan had just taken the oath of office. During his 1980 presidential campaign Reagan promised to revitalize the military. Sure enough, he did just that. This rejuvenation of our military was timely since all four branches had been denied essential funds during the Ford and Carter administrations. In the late 1970s, morale was low and pay had been badly undermined by high inflation. Retention of good people within the military had become a major problem.

During the two magic years when I served as the Air Force planner I had 250 officers, non-commissioned officers and Department of Defense civilians working for me. All had sparkling records and high potential. Most of these professionals served as "action officers." Their job was to work through a very complex bureaucracy <u>in order to get things done</u>.

THE ROLE OF TRUST IN THE PUZZLE PALACE

Every morning, I faced an "in-box" which contained about twenty "decision packages." Each package contained a cover letter, an executive summary, a coordination sheet, a decision paper and twenty to forty pages of back-up material. My job was to give my approval on the suggested decision. I would sign the cover letter so the package could go up the chain of command to the two top Air Force leaders, the Secretary and the Chief of Staff of the United States Air Force. If the package received my signature of approval it almost always was signed off by the Secretary of the Air Force and the Air Force Chief of Staff. It would become Air Force policy and, in some cases, national policy.

As I examined a package, the action officer would be in my office to answer any questions or concerns that I had. Since I knew each action officer well, I would often sign the cover letter without reading any of the backup pages.

The unspoken message that was sent and received was important. The action officer was <u>TRUSTED</u>. The young officer would leave my office knowing that he or she had just made Air Force policy. These officers could tell their friends and family that they personally made something important happen in America's most complex bureaucracy. By trusting them, they learned to trust me. The feeling of mutual support and respect was both powerful and profound. In short, my approach was "sign without reading." I did not use this approach for the first couple of months. However, once I got to know my action officers it was easy to move to the "sign without reading" pattern.

A Funding Windfall Arrives in the Pentagon

In the spring of 1981, I was sitting in a meeting of the "Air Force Board" which consisted of a number of two-star general officers. Our job was to give advice to the top leaders in the Air Force. We were working our way through a major budget exercise (planning for the next five years). Funds were, once again, very tight and we were making cuts in important programs. Into the conference room came a very excited Air Force colonel.

He did something quite unusual - in a very strong voice he told the briefer to stop speaking immediately. The visiting colonel then announced, "Gentlemen, I have some very good news. The Air Force will get an extra 10 billion dollars." Someone asked, "for next year?" The colonel replied with a joyous smile on his face, "10 billion for next year and for each of the four years following. Gentleman, $50 billion is headed our way." It was a magical moment that all in that room will always remember.

Soon after President Reagan granted the Air Force the additional funds, an important decision was made by the two top officials in the Air Force: The Secretary (Verne Orr) and the Chief of Staff (General Lew Allen). If the Air Force was going to spend these funds wisely, we needed an up-to-date strategic plan.

As the Air Force planner, my job was to orchestrate this effort. I was delighted. Having the opportunity to chart the future of the Air Force at a time of strong budgetary growth was a dream come true.

This plan was called "Air Force 2000." Building this plan was a major endeavor. About a hundred of the smartest and wisest professionals in the Air Force (both military and civil servants), as well as lots of contractors, spent a year devising a plan that would design the future of the Air Force for the next twenty years.

NEGATIVE CONSEQUENCES OF TRIMMING THE FAT

During this period from 1981 to 1983, I got in trouble with almost every major Air Force commander because of my emphasis on divestiture, or getting rid of obsolete or outdated systems. This included the commanders of the Tactical Air Command, the Strategic Air Command, the Military Airlift Command, and the North American Air Defense Command. All were four-star generals. At that time, I was a junior two star general.

As far as divestiture was concerned, I had learned from my dad that hanging on to an obsolete weapon system made no sense. He and his Coast Artillery colleagues had fought hard to retain a mission (coast artillery) that was clearly outdated by the mid-1930s. I did not want to repeat the 1930s Army error in the Air Force of the 1980s. Here is an example where a lesson from the past applied to the present and beyond. If I had not understood the mistake of the 1930s, I don't think I would have been so aggressive in pushing for a major divestiture effort.

The four-star commander of the Strategic Air Command (General Benjamin Davis) was mad at me. He was not pleased to learn that he must give up all seventy-five of his B-52D bombers if he wanted the Air Force to fund two new bombers, the B-1 and the B-2. Other major commanders were unhappy that they too were told to give up aircraft or missile systems. They got their direction from the Chief of Staff of the Air Force, but they knew that I was the one who pushed hard to "unload the dogs."

Although divestiture was important, a more vital goal of "Air Force 2000" was the establishment of just three priorities: stealth, precision and reliability. My planners and I agreed that a plan with too many priorities made little sense. If everything is a "priority" then nothing is a priority. From all my research on planning I knew that establishing more than three priorities was a major mistake.

These three priorities reinforced each other. If our bombers and fighters could not be picked up by enemy radar their survival rate would be very high (stealth). If the bombs they dropped could hit within a few feet of the target, that target would not need to be hit again (precision). If the aircraft did not need much maintenance on returning from a combat mission, it could launch on its next mission very quickly (reliability). To conduct a successful air campaign would require very few aircraft if each aircraft fit these three requirements.

Nine years after Air Force 2000 was completed I served as a military analyst for CNN. I was pleased to report how well the Air Force performed in Desert Storm (the six weeks war in early 1991 to free Kuwait from Saddam Hussein's grip). The story of my six years working for CNN will be described later in this book.

Pentagon Story: Briefing the Joint Chiefs of Staff

During the early 1980s, the Chairman of the Joint Chiefs of Staff was Air Force General David Jones. He felt strongly that each of the four military services should share with each other details on their programs and budgets. Since I was having many opportunities to work with the senior officers from the Army, Navy and Marine Corps, I was asked to present a twenty-minute briefing on the five-year Air Force Program. I was the guinea pig. This kind of briefing had never before been given to the Chairman of the JCS and the service chiefs. In the weeks following, a planner from the Army, Navy and Marine Corps would make a similar presentation.

In attendance at these high level meetings were the following four-star officers: Air Force General David Jones, who was the Chairman of the Joint Chiefs of Staff, the Chiefs of Staff of the

Air Force and the Army, the Chief of Naval Operations and the Commandant of the Marine Corps. Also in attendance were the Operational Deputies (three star officers) of the four branches, some staff officers from the Joint Staff and a few of my Air Staff colleagues.

Never before had I ever briefed such a high-ranking group. There were about 25 officers in the audience, 20 of them were senior admirals or generals. The room was commonly known as the "Tank." It was, by far, the most important conference room in the entire Department of Defense.

Using overhead slides (these were the days before PowerPoint), I explained what aircraft and munitions the Air Force was purchasing, how much manpower was being added, as well as some other highlights from the Air Force five-year program. When I completed my briefing and before the discussion period began, General Jones said. "I have been seated in the tank for seven years, first for four years as Chief of Staff of the Air Force and three years as Chairman, and that is the worst briefing I have ever heard."

I could not help myself - I could not suppress a smile. Having been in the Tank on many occasions, I knew that my briefing was not that bad. I thought someone would defend me but alas it did not happen. The Air Force Chief, Lew Allen was out of town, so the Vice Chief of Staff, Bob Mathis, was representing the Air Force at the meeting. Mathis could have spoken up on my behalf but he said not a word. The only person who was helpful was the Army Chief of Staff, Shy Meyer, who asked me some good questions in a kindly manner.

So why did General Jones treat me with such disdain? Here is my supposition: Jones wanted to send a strong message to the other services. The message was - as chairman of the Joint Chiefs of Staff, I want more details. General Jones wanted to make something crystal clear. When the Army, Navy and Marine Corps bring their briefings into the Tank, they must not withhold important information as Perry Smith just did.

The following is another recollection from my days serving on the Air Staff Board. To remind, this committee was composed of the top Air Force general in each of the major elements of the Air Staff: Operations, Plans, Programs, Logistics, and Manpower. This key committee also included the head of the Air National Guard and a representative from the office of the Air Force Inspector General. A total of seven general officers served on this committee. We knew each other well and the cooperation was good. The fact that all of us had solid operational experiences and most had served in combat gave us a common understanding - that serving the troops in the field was our most important goal.

This committee met about twice each month. It made recommendations that were usually accepted by the two top leaders in the Air Force. Whenever this group met, there were about thirty staff officers sitting in the rear of the room. These were officers from the rank of captain to colonel. These staff officers were there to answer questions which the "principals" (the general officers) could not answer.

Sometime in the summer of 1982, I learned that my West Point classmate, Major General Don Morelli, would soon give a briefing to the Air Staff Board. Don and I had become good friends at West Point but I had not seen him in twenty-seven years.

I looked forward to his briefing on the new Army doctrine. Little did I know that early in the briefing Major General Morelli would show the silly picture of the two of us, one tall and one small, when we were cadets at West Point (see Chapter 2). I cannot remember the exact words that he used when the picture showed up on the large screen. What I do remember is that the audience broke out into sustained laughter. Don was making fun of the two of us. From that moment on, he had the complete attention of the audience.

Don's briefing was brilliant. I was delighted. Up to that time, my Air Force colleagues tended to view the Army as an institution full of fine professionals, but one that was a bit stodgy and stuck in the past. That day everyone in attendance realized that Don was the probably smartest, most articulate, most forward-thinking person in the room.

Sadly, my dear friend, Don Morelli, died of cancer when he was still on active duty. During his last few months, I visited him in his hospital room at Walter Reed Army Medical Center. We shared many laughs on those visits. Until the very end, Don maintained his keen sense of humor.

PENTAGON STORIES: THE SECRET AIR FORCE SWISS BANK ACCOUNT

Of all my Pentagon stories, this one is the wildest. While serving as the Air Force planner in 1981, I received into my office a major whose specialty was as an auditor. I had had no previous contact with him and did not know why he wanted to meet with me. All I knew was that he had something really important to tell me. The conversation started as follows.

Major: "Sir, I have bad news for you today."

Perry: "I get bad news about every hour, what is yours?"

Major: "I can't tell you what I need to tell you."

Perry: "Why not?"

Major: "Sir, my program is so highly classified that we cannot discuss it in your office."

Perry: "How can you tell me?"

Major: "You must come to my office."

So we went up to the fifth floor. After going through some cyberlock doors we entered into a vault with no windows. On a table was a file which was about two feet tall. Not wishing to read a thousand pages, I asked the major to summarize the issue and he did so.

"Sir, there is trouble with the secret Air Force numbered Swiss bank account."

I replied that I did not know the Air Force had a bank account in Switzerland. The major explained that the account of about 10 million dollars was set up during the Vietnam War. The purpose of the account was to support the CIA in some clandestine operations in Laos. He then explained the account had been dormant for a number of years. An important element of this story was the status of this bank account - it was a non-interest-bearing account. Unlike most dormant bank accounts, the Air Force secret Swiss bank account did not grow in value from year to year.

I asked him who was responsible for this account. He said, "You are sir." He then explained that the general who had previously been responsible for the account had done some bad things. I knew this general and had worked for him briefly. He was not only very smart and clever, but also was very skilled in making things happen in the Pentagon.

Here was the clever plan of the dishonest general (his scheme worked for four consecutive years). Knowing that the account was audited by a staff officer from the Air Staff every July, the general would take the funds (about $10 million) out of the account in August. He would electronically transfer the funds to his private account in the same bank.

This general's personal account was "interest bearing." The following June, he would transfer the ten million dollars back to the Air Force account. He would keep the interest in his account. Over the course of the four years, he profited by at least $500,000. Since the Air Force did not lose any funds in the process, he may have felt he was free and clear of any criticisms even if he had been caught.

A few weeks later, a meeting was held in the office of the Vice Chief of Staff of the Air Force, General Jerry O'Malley. In attendance was O'Malley (4 stars) and three other senior Air Force officers: the Air Force inspector general (3 stars), the top Air Force attorney (2 stars) and me (2 stars). The swiss bank account issue was discussed.

General O'Malley asked - what should the Air Force do? The inspector general and the attorney both recommended that we take the dishonest general to trial. I was the last to make a recommendation. I was very candid. I said, "Let's not do anything. We will never win this case. We will be wasting time and money if we try to send him off to jail." I predicted that the judge would throw the case out when he learned that we were unwilling to open all of the highly classified material. I then predicted that the dishonest general would thumb his nose at us for the rest of his life.

Four-star General Jerry O'Malley said to me, "Perry you are dead wrong. We must go after this general, whether or not we win the case. We need to send a message to our Air Force that we will not tolerate this kind of activity." Of course, General O' Malley was correct and I was wrong. However, the Air Force did lose the case.

LESSONS FROM THE SWISS BANK ACCOUNT CASE

There is a tendency within many organizations to assume that the top leaders are women and men of high integrity. Trust is the coin of the realm. That was certainly my experience until this case surfaced. This case, involving a general officer I knew quite well, set me back on my heels.

Lesson number one: Do regular ethical surveys up and down your organization. Lesson number two: Encourage whistle blowing. The Air Force major blew his whistle the best way - he blew his whistle internally. He might have thought that I would try to cover for the dishonest general and his action might have got him in trouble. However, he blew his whistle regardless of the consequences. Lesson number three: Take legal action against dishonest activity even if the odds of winning the case are small. The very act of the legal action sends a strong message to people inside and outside the organization.

THE ROLE OF POLITICS IN A PENTAGON DECISION: BRIEFING THE DEPUTY SECRETARY OF DEFENSE

In the early 1980s, the Air Force badly needed a new, large cargo aircraft. The airplane of choice was the C-17. This aircraft had gone through the complete research and development process. However, a decision on actual production had not yet been made. The Deputy Secretary of Defense, Frank Carlucci, asked for a briefing on future plans of the Air Force for airlift. I was told that I would give the briefing.

I thought that selecting me, a fighter pilot, to conduct this important briefing was a bad idea. I reminded my boss that I had no background in airlift operations. I recommended another general who had spent this entire professional life dealing with large, cargo-carrying airplanes.

My boss, General Jerry O'Malley told me "airlifters" had a narrow view of the world. He felt I would have greater credibility because I had operational experience in Europe and Asia and was not tainted with the "airlifter syndrome."

I had to scramble for the next few weeks getting smart on airlift in general and more specifically on the C-17. Two superb staff officers helped me build a case for the C-17 over the C-5. In the Secretary of Defense's conference room, I gave my briefing.

I emphasized that I was not an airlifter but did have a rather broad view of the needs of the Air Force and our sister services. I tried to get strong support from the other services - but failed. Why? They feared the wrath of a certain Senator from Georgia, Sam Nunn. Senator Nunn wanted to reopen the production line for the C-5. Why? The new C-5s would be built in Georgia.

A few weeks later I was asked to visit the Secretary of the Air Force, Verne Orr. Mr. Orr was an elderly gentleman who had a close personal relationship with President Reagan. He was very interested in the future of airlift. After a short discussion, Orr told me that he planned to reopen the C-5 production line and cancel the C-17.

I was very frank with him. I told him he should fire the commander of the Military Airlift Command, General Jim Allen. I suggested that cancelling the C-17 would so undercut Allen's credibility that he should be replaced by someone else. I then suggested that rather than cancelling the C-17, he should postpone its production for five years. In that way Sam Nunn would get his C-5s and the C-17 would stay alive. As I walked back to my office that day, I asked myself, did I really hammer the Secretary of the Air Force? If so, was it the right thing to do? Probably. The decision was made to build some C-5s but also to keep the C-17 program alive.

The lesson I relearned that day was that certain Members of Congress have great influence on the programming and budgeting of the military services. All Pentagon planning must take this factor into account. This helps explain why the best decisions are often not made.

Now is the time to return to the subject of long-range planning. Early in my tenure as the Air Force planner, I reflected on the research I had done on my Ph.D. dissertation fifteen years earlier. The Army Air Corps planners during World War II did not have access to professional futurists. By the early 1980s there were a number of brilliant people who spent their lives predicting the future. My thought in 1981 - let's see if these folks could help us.

I asked my long-range planners to contact the best futurists in America and invite them to visit me in the Pentagon. Every person who was invited accepted my invitation including such luminaries as Alvin Toffler (author of two best-selling books: *Future Shock* and *The Third Wave*) and Herman Kahn (author of *On Thermonuclear War, Thinking the Unthinkable,* and *the Coming Boom).*

HERMAN KAHN AND AIR FORCE PLANNING

Kahn's visit to my Pentagon office in 1981 was especially memorable. He was probably the smartest strategic thinker of his generation. I asked him some key questions: What does the long range future hold and how should our military prepare for that future? I asked him to take me out twenty years. He immediately expressed disappointment with my question. He said, "General, that is not a very good question." He wanted to reach out fifty years. After telling him that there was no way I could get the Air Force to plan beyond twenty years, he thought for a few minutes and then gave me his twenty-year prediction.

"General, I have good news and bad news." The good news was that the Soviet Union would collapse sometime within the next decade. Herman Kahn explained that the Soviets were grossly overspending on national defense and had a corrupt political system. He pointed out some other weaknesses. The Soviet Union had a nearly bankrupt economic system, did not encourage innovation, had few reliable allies and were led by old men with little intellectual power. He felt strongly and convincingly that America would soon emerge as the sole superpower with no major enemy for many decades into the future.

Kahn then gave me bad news: With no discernable enemy the military budget of the United States would be drastically reduced. Kahn felt this would be unfortunate since America would still face considerable threats including the rise of terrorism.

Taking his wisdom into account as well as the insights of other futurists, the Air Force in the early 1980s planned for four possible scenarios. 1) A strong or stronger Soviet Union. 2) A rising high-tech threat. 3) A rising threat from terrorism. 4) No major military threat. As far as the last scenario, I reminded my fellow planners that, for more than a century, the United States did not face a major military threat. I suggested to them that it was possible that this situation could occur again if the Soviet Union collapsed.

On reflection, Herman Kahn was correct in almost all aspects of his 1981 forecasts. The one prediction which Kahn got wrong was his expectation that Japan would become a significant military rival.

When the Soviet Union collapsed in 1991, America became the dominant superpower and remained in that position until quite recently. When Reagan was president, the United States was spending 6.4% of its gross domestic product on national defense. By the middle of the Clinton presidency the support had dropped to 2.9%. Kahn was on target with his calculation that support for national defense would diminish with the fall of the Soviet Union. Incidentally, defense spending in the third decade of the 21st century is about 3.2% of our gross domestic product.

Herman Kahn was not the only genius I got to know. John Boyd and John Warden fit into that category. Boyd and Warden both served a full career in the United States Air Force. The John Warden story will be explained later. The John Boyd story follows just below. Other geniuses I had the pleasure of knowing and learning from include Air Force generals, Lee Butler, Frank Klotz and Barry Horton.

THE BRILLIANT JOHN BOYD

Soon after I returned from Europe in 1981, I was told by my staff that I should spend some time with a recently retired Air Force officer, Colonel John Boyd. He had made major contributions in two areas. First of all, in the decision process in both crisis and combat situations. Second, in helping fighter pilots calculate the best airspeed and altitude to enter a dogfight against specific enemy aircraft.

I was told that John Boyd would meet with me but only if I gave him four hours of my time. The meeting was set up on a Saturday morning. In attendance were about a dozen officers from Air Force Plans. When we got started, I thanked Boyd for his willingness to educate me and my team of planners.

I reminded Colonel Boyd that he asked for four hours and told him he would get four hours. I also told him that none of us in the room would interrupt him but would ask some questions when he finished his pitch. Four fascinating hours followed but there was a problem. Boyd had not completed his presentation.

I told Boyd he could have another two hours. After a short break, Boyd continued. Two hours later, I thanked John Boyd and spent the rest of the weekend processing the insights Boyd had shared with us. Anyone interested in studying and understanding the life and legacy of a true genius might wish to read the book *Boyd* by Robert Corum. This is a well written book which captures the personality and contributions of John Boyd rather well. However, Corum has one thing wrong - that all the generals hated Boyd. In fact, some Air Force generals, including me, had great respect for the enigmatic, stubborn, brilliant Colonel John Boyd.

Thirty-four years after retiring from the United States Air Force, I reflect often on which of my jobs was the very best. When I am asked that question, I always answer: being a wing commander and having 4000 handpicked professionals and 80 brand new F-15s under my command. However, my ability to impact the future of the Air Force was the best during the exciting two years from 1981 to 1983 when I served as the Air Force planner.

Cartoon of Major General Perry Smith at his desk in the Pentagon, 1983.

Chapter Eleven:

Commandant, The National War College: 1983-1986

WHEN MY TWO-YEAR tour of duty as the Air Force Planner was drawing to a close, the President of the National Defense University, Lieutenant General John Pustay, requested me. The Commandant of the National War College was retiring and it was the turn of the Air Force to fill that position. With my academic background I was a natural choice.

My three years as Commandant of the National War College was a grand time to spend as my last assignment in the United States military. As soon as I arrived in the summer of 1983, I announced to the faculty and the staff that I planned to teach - both in the core curriculum and in the elective program.

As I explained to the faculty, when I was a wing commander in Europe, it was important that I flew the F-15 on a regular basis. In that way I would have close

National War College Commandant in the Rotunda of Theodore Roosevelt Hall, 1983.

contact with pilots, maintenance personnel and other support officers and non-commissioned officers. I felt the same way about leading an academic organization. If I taught every week, I would get to know the students well. Also, I would interact with the support agencies such as the library, the print plant, the audio-visual team and many others. If they were performing poorly, I was quite likely to notice.

The core curriculum at the National War College included courses in Defense Policy, Foreign Policy, and the US Congress. It also included courses on the major regions of the world including Asia, Europe, the Middle East and the Soviet Union. Every student was required to take these courses. Each afternoon there was a whole range of elective courses. These included courses on the American Presidency, the Intelligence Community, executive leadership, strategic planning and many others. Each student would select two of these elective courses each semester.

Can't Find a Textbook? Write One!

My most rewarding teaching experiences at the National War College were designing and teaching two elective courses. My course on executive leadership attracted a large group of students. Only three students signed up for my course on strategic planning. I think I am the only Commandant at the National War College who designed and taught elective courses. I also taught within the core curriculum.

My students in the leadership course came from the National War College, the Industrial College of the Armed Forces and from among the international students. The Industrial College focused its attention on logistics, transportation, research and development and weapon system acquisition. The international students were assigned to the National Defense University. They were permitted to take elective courses from both colleges with one exception. They were not permitted to take the few elective courses that dealt with highly classified issues.

Unable to find a first-rate book on senior leadership within governmental organizations, I decided to write one myself and to test it out with my students.

Over time this led to my second book, *Taking Charge*. This book, now entitled *Rules and Tools for Leaders,* has stayed in print for more than thirty years. With 350,000 copies in print, it has been translated into five languages. I think the reason the book has done well is because it was designed to be used rather than just to be read. It contains many checklists: how to plan, how to hire, how to fire, how to run a meeting, how to manage your time, how to manage the electronic workplace, how to thank people, etc.

I also involved myself in the National War College intramural sports program. I competed on the faculty softball, volleyball, and track teams. Each spring, all five of the War Colleges would assemble at the Army War College for two days of sports competition. Each year, the National War College came in dead last. Why? We had the smallest student body and our students were a bit older. Having a high percentage of civilian students was another disadvantage. There were few athletes among the civilians. The annual sports competition each spring was an opportunity for me and my National War College students to eat humble pie.

RICHARD NIXON AT THE NATIONAL WAR COLLEGE

One of the most electric moments during my three years as Commandant at the National War College was the morning the students and faculty spent with Richard Nixon, the 37th president of the United States. Nixon had resigned in disgrace in 1974. When he was invited to the National War College, Nixon had been out of office for ten years. As I recall, the National War College was the first academic institution in the federal government to invite the disgraced Nixon to speak. He had been a persona non-grata for a decade. Former President Richard Nixon was delighted to accept our invitation.

Mr. Nixon flew in from one of the New York airports. Because of bad weather he arrived more than an hour late. I met him at the bottom of the stairs of Roosevelt Hall and walked with him towards the auditorium, Arnold Hall. I told him that we planned on a question and answer period after his talk. His reply, "Let the questions roll." The message was clear - Richard Nixon was in no hurry to depart.

Former President Richard Nixon visits the National War College, 1984.

The former president of the United States spoke for forty-five minutes and answered questions for more than thirty minutes. I was sitting next to the secret service agent in charge of Nixon's security detail. He told me. "He is behind schedule; we need to get him out of here." I replied quite firmly, "I am in charge here - there is no way I am going to cut him off."

It was clear to all of us that day that the former President was a brilliant strategist and a fine speaker. Incidentally, without asking them, I trusted my students not to ask embarrassing questions about Watergate - they validated my trust.

When Nixon had completed the question and answer session, he visited with students in the rotunda of Roosevelt Hall for another twenty minutes. One of the National War College faculty members was Army Lieutenant Colonel Jack Jacobs, a Medal of Honor recipient from the Vietnam War. When Nixon saw him, he said, "I know you, don't I?" Jack reminded Nixon that he had presented him with the Medal of Honor in 1969. Then something amazing happened; tears filled Nixon's eyes and he gave Jack an extended hug. A reminder - this was a man who had the reputation of being someone without personal warmth.

SOME SPEAKERS GET ME IN TROUBLE

The list of speakers at the National War College during the 1983 to 1986 period was an impressive one. To name just a few - close advisors to American presidents: Henry Kissinger, Brent Scowcroft, John Ehrlichman, Zbigniew Brzezinski, Ted Sorenson, Dick Cheney, George Reedy and David Gergen. Distinguished journalists: Walter Cronkite, Sam Donaldson and Ted Koppel. Renown academics: Carl Sagan and Jeane Kirkpatrick. Senior generals/admirals: Al Haig, Jim Stockdale and Andy Goodpaster. Foreign political leader: Petra Kelly.

I got in trouble with some officials in the Pentagon when I brought in Erlichman and Petra Kelly. On the other hand, the students and faculty seemed to appreciate the diversity of speakers and viewpoints. They understood and supported my view that the National War College should be a school of education and not of indoctrination.

Each year the National War College would spend an entire day examining the decision-making process in the White House in the area of National Security. We invited former chiefs of staff or national security advisors to every president from Eisenhower to Reagan. One day, I got into big trouble. An outstanding faculty member, David Kozak, invited two people to be panel members. One was the Secretary of the Army, Jack Marsh. Secretary Marsh had served as deputy chief of staff to President Gerald Ford. Another panel member was John Erlichman, who had been a close advisor to President Nixon.

John Erlichman had spent time in a federal prison as a result of his illegal activities in support of the Watergate break-in in 1972 and the subsequent coverup by President Nixon, Bob Halderman, John Erlichman and others.

When Secretary Marsh learned that he was scheduled to be on the same panel with Erlichman, Marsh blew his top. In my office, he told me how stupid I was and that he would not appear with "that crook"

Erlichman. The schedule was quickly adjusted and Secretary Marsh and John Erlichman never saw each other that day.

Even more controversial than having "that crook" as a speaker was the invitation to Petra Kelly. She was in the news at the time since her Green Party in Germany was on the ascendance. She was an elected member of the Bundestag. As the top leader of that party, she was a thorn in the side of the German government. Petra Kelly and her colleagues were in favor of a number of radical initiatives including disbanding the NATO alliance.

When the Defense Minister of Germany, Manfred Werner, learned that Petra Kelly had spoken at the NWC he wrote a letter to his good friend, Caspar Weinberger. Werner's handwritten letter was one of protest. Weinberger was the U.S. Secretary of Defense at the time and my boss about five levels above me. I survived that crisis largely because we had received written permission from the Office of the Secretary of Defense to have Petra Kelly as a speaker.

Ms. Kelly was very articulate as she explained that the Soviet Union was not a threat to West Germany. However, during the question and answer period she did not do well. Here is an example. She was asked what Germans would do if West Germany was invaded - like Hungary had been in 1968. She replied that the Germans would change all the street signs so the Russian Army would get lost in the German cities.

Let me share a few more of my favorite stories from those delightful three years at the National War College.

The faculty and I were quite pleased to learn that Ted Sorenson had agreed to fly down from Boston to participate in a panel discussion on presidential decision making. Sorenson had been President John Kennedy's closest friend for many years before Kennedy became our 35th president. Sorensen had played a role in authoring *Profiles in Courage,* a book which earned Kennedy the Pulitzer Prize in 1957.

When Sorensen visited with me in my office, I gave him his honorarium check. I was surprised when he immediately opened the envelope and took a look at the check. The honorarium was the grand sum of $100; that was all we were authorized to pay.

Ted Sorensen looked at the check, smiled, and said to me, "General,

I am pleased that the National War College still believes in free speech." Everyone in my office that day laughed, including me. I shared this story with faculty and students alike. Incidentally, I failed in my attempts to raise the honorarium.

To gain a sense of the quality of the research and writing of our students, I reached out to the faculty for help. Each fall, I asked to see the first drafts of the best research papers and the worst. With the assistance of the superb dean of faculty, Colonel Roy Stafford, who screened the papers, I read the top ten and bottom ten papers during each of the Christmas holidays in 1983, 1984 and 1985.

One paper, written by Air Force Colonel John Warden, was very impressive. In fact, it was the best research paper I read during my three years as Commandant. In early January, I called Colonel Warden into my office, praised his work and recommended that he expand the paper and publish it as a book. I gave him a few minor suggestions on how it might be improved.

Air Force Colonel John Warden, 1987.

I was so impressed by Warden's analysis and writing style that I mailed drafts of his paper to a number of senior officers in the Air Force. Sometime in the spring of 1986, Colonel Warden became an important resource for me. As you will see, he assisted me on many occasions after I retired from the Air Force.

John Warden's book, *The Air Campaign*, was published in 1988. During the 1991 Gulf War, when I was a military analyst on CNN, I recommended it to a large television audience. Within three days, this breakthrough book sold out all around America.

One of the most important aspects of the curriculum at the National War College was the overseas trips. Each spring, the students and faculty would break into groups and spend two well planned weeks visiting key locations throughout the world. I had the pleasure of leading trips to Eastern Europe (1984), to China (1985) and to India and Pakistan (1986).

Let me share with you just one story. In the 1986 trip our group of about twenty flew from Delhi to Ladakh Province in the Himalaya mountains. This province which borders both Pakistan and China is of strategic importance to India. A full division of Indian troops is stationed there. They are conditioned to operate as high as eighteen thousand feet without oxygen. Within two hours after landing, I became very dizzy. The Indian general who was my host took me immediately to the military hospital, gave me two pills and a bowl of soup and put me to bed. I slept for about three hours. I recovered nicely. When bedtime arrived, I was given a bunny hat and two hot water bottles. None of our rooms were heated and at night the temperature dropped well below freezing.

One Saturday morning, Connor and I joined the students and their family members at a session with Otto Kroeger. One of the most delightful, funny and insightful speakers I have ever heard, Dr. Kroeger introduced us to "Myers Briggs." It was a magic day for our family. We learned that Connor was an introvert. Since Connor was so animated whenever she was on stage, I had assumed that she was an extravert. In fact, in all four categories of Myers Briggs Connor and I were on opposite ends of the spectrum. That may be why we have such a strong marriage. We help each other see a wide segment of reality.

Jimmy Doolittle: A Most Famous Aviator

In 1985, I received a telephone call from a man who helped save my career in 1970, retired General Russ Dougherty. He asked me if Connor would agree to be the soloist at a birthday party for a famous American. Jimmy Doolittle, named by many as the most outstanding aviator of the 20th century, was to celebrate his 90th

birthday in Washington, DC. Connor was delighted to be asked; she accepted the invitation immediately. Incidentally, General James Doolittle is one of the few people to have received both the Medal of Honor and the Congressional Medal of Freedom.

Most people are familiar with the Doolittle raid on Tokyo on 18 April, 1942. That daring raid of B-25 bombers lifted the spirits of Americans. But Doolittle had many other accomplishments. He set speed records and long-distance flight records throughout the 1920s and 1930s. He was the first aviator to fly an aircraft from takeoff to landing without looking outside the cockpit. After the Tokyo raid, General Doolittle commanded the 12th Air Force and the famous 8th Air Force during World War II.

The special birthday party for Doolittle was held on the second floor of the Smithsonian Air and Space Museum on the mall in Washington, D.C. In the audience was Anne Morrow Lindbergh, the widow of Charles Lindbergh, who, in 1927, was the first to fly solo across the Atlantic. Also attending the dinner was Stuart Symington (the first Secretary of the Air Force when that branch was formed in 1947) and Claire Boothe Luce (the famous actress and playwright). Her stage play, *The Women* was not only a hit, it was also the first Broadway play where the cast was all women. Claire Boothe Luce was the most accomplished woman of her generation. She served in the US Congress, was the ambassador to Italy, and received the Presidential Medal of Freedom.

In addition, many of the pioneers of American aviation were in attendance. The tables of the notable aviators were placed directly under the aircraft they had flown on missions of historic importance. The top active duty leaders of the Air Force were also in attendance. If it had not been for Connor's lovely voice, we would not have been invited to attend.

Anne Morrow Lindbergh spoke briefly to the audience. She said that she never attends events like these any more. However, she felt compelled to come to Washington to celebrate the life of her dear friend, Jimmy Doolittle. The aviation pioneers of the 1920s and 1930s knew each other well. They participated in air shows together throughout America. Since Anne flew in the same airplane with her husband, Charles, she was fully a member of the admired group of aviators.

Prior to sitting down for dinner, Connor and I visited briefly with her. At age 80, Anne Morrow Lindbergh was a lovely, gracious lady who was the author of a number of books which Connor loved. She signed and personalized a copy of her book, *Bring Me a Unicorn*. "To Connor Smith, with all good wishes and thanks for her song." Signed, Anne Morrow Lindbergh.

The next day, the National War College hosted General Doolittle and some of his family members. Although Doolittle was not asked to speak, he met with some members of the National War College Class of 1986. Incidentally, Doolittle has been portrayed in a number of Hollywood movies as a large, tough talking Army Air Force pilot. (For example, Spencer Tracy played Doolittle in Mervyn LeRoy's 1944 movie *Thirty Seconds Over Tokyo* and Alec Baldwin played Doolittle in Michael Bay's 2001 movie *Pearl Harbor*.) In

Jimmy Doolittle visits the National War College, 1986.

fact, Jimmy Doolittle was a small, polite, and modest man. Of all the distinguished Americans with whom I had the pleasure of spending time, Doolittle tops the list.

Soon after I retired from the military, I returned to Roosevelt Hall to face a federal judge. For the only time in my life, I was facing a formal charge of sexual discrimination. An incompetent secretary who worked for the Dean of Students at the National War College had been fired a few months previously. She claimed that, at my suggestion, distinguished guests would call her a "pervert" as they passed her desk.

Fortunately, the federal judge was a wise woman. She realized quickly that this secretary had serious mental health problems. The judge dismissed the case. Having the hearing in Roosevelt Hall was probably helpful - a place of great dignity and solemnity.

I should close this section on the National War College on a high note. For the faculty, staff and students this was (and is) a splendid institution. During the 1980s, the National War College had perhaps the best speakers' program of any school in the world.

Close friendships were established; many have lasted a lifetime. A few members of the staff and faculty deserve special mention. They enriched the lives of everyone they encountered. Mary McNabb, Myra Evans, Bard O'Neill, David Kozak, Roy Stafford, Dick Kuiper, Jack Jacobs, Ilana Kass, Al Pierce, Steve Szabo, Fred Coffey, Lynn Davis, Mark Smith, Rat Cooper, George Thibault, Peter Moffatt, Gordon Beyer, and Peter Huhn.

Many of the students moved on to positions of great responsibility in the various branches of the military, the State Department, the CIA, the Secret Service, the Coast Guard and other federal institutions. By the time they graduated they had gained a deep understanding of national security, military strategy, international affairs, and war gaming. After retiring, most continued their lifelong dedication to duty by supporting worthy causes both local and national. I have often thought how wonderful it would be if members of Congress, cabinet officials and even American Presidents and Vice Presidents could spend a year of study at the National War College.

Chapter Twelve:

Civilian Life - Media, Speaker, Teacher, Author, 1986

THE DECISION TO retire from the Air Force was an easy one. I had reached thirty years of service and was at the end of the normal three-year assignment at the National War College. In addition, the Air Force was offering me a backwater job. This was a strong signal that the top leaders no longer had any interest in my continuing service. The retirement ceremony and party were both handled well. At age fifty-one, I was ready to launch into some new adventures. Little did I know at that time how wonderfully rewarding my life would be in the decades ahead. The next thirty-five years could best be described as "one thing leads to another and another and another." Not having regular employment gave me the opportunity to accept enticing invitations of all kinds.

Retirement in the summer of 1986 meant a return to the home we owned in McLean, Virginia. It was the beginning of a new career - as a teacher, an author, and a television commentator. I chose not to look for work with a defense contractor, a university or any other organization, large or small. I wanted to be on my own - with no boss, no bureaucracy and no traffic to fight each day.

Understanding the Heroism of Jimmie Dyess on Roi Namur

As I approached my retirement from the military, I began to focus my attention on Connor's father. I had known for years that he was a Medal of Honor recipient who had been killed by the Japanese when Connor was eight years old, but it was not until the mid-1980s when I realized that Jimmie Dyess was also the recipient of the Carnegie

Medal (the highest award for civilian heroism). I soon came up with the idea of researching his life and perhaps writing his biography. At the 30th reunion of the West Point class of 1956, I suggested to some Army classmates that Connor and I would someday like to visit the Marshall Islands. It was on the island of Roi Namur in the Marshalls that Marine Lieutenant Colonel A. J. Dyess fought and died.

With the assistance of West Point classmates Lieutenant General John Wall and Major General Gene Fox, Connor and I flew to the Central Pacific to visit the Marshall Islands. John and Gene held key positions in the Army at the perfect time for us to make the trip. It was the first time Connor had the opportunity to visit the island where her dad was killed in early February, 1944. The year of our visit was 1986. Eight years later we would visit again. On the second occasion our son, McCoy, accompanied us. We will always be grateful to John Wall who came up with the idea of our visit.

For the people of the Marshall Islands, 1986 was an important year. They were celebrating their independence from the United States. The Marshall Islands had been under the control of the Empire of Japan from 1919 until 1944. Following World War II, a United Nations Trusteeship gave the United States control. On October 21, 1986 a "Compact of Free Association" gave the 58,000 Marshall Islanders their freedom.

At a ceremony on the small island of Roi Namur, Connor was asked to speak. She expressed her gratitude to those who had so carefully preserved the battlefield where her father and his fellow Marines had fought so bravely in January and February, 1944.

Unlike Guadalcanal, Tarawa, Iwo Jima and Okinawa, the Marshall Islands campaign is largely forgotten, even by students of World War II. Yet the invasion of the Marshalls was a vitally important and highly successful part of Admiral Nimitz's strategic campaign to defeat the Japanese Empire. The Fourth Marine Division with strong support from the US Navy captured the heavily defended island of Roi Namur in less than a week. For their acts of heroism in late January and early February, 1944, four Marines received the Medal of Honor including Lieutenant Colonel Aquilla James Dyess, Connor's father.

Connor and I flew into Roi Namur from the larger island of

Kwajalein. These two islands play an important role in support of both NASA and the Department of Defense. The military commander of these islands is a US Army colonel but most of the Americans who work on these islands are contractors. In addition to the Americans, native Marshall Islanders play an important role in supporting the mission. For instance, a team of eight Marshall Islanders is responsible for the preservation of the battlefields on both Roi Namur and Kwajalein.

Roi Namur Island in the Marshall Islands, 1986.

TEACHING LEADERSHIP FOR GWU, THE FBI AND IBM

Soon after retirement from the Air Force, one of my colleagues at the National War College suggested to a business professor at George Washington University that I be invited to speak to his students. Soon thereafter, I became a regular speaker at George Washington University. Located in Washington DC, GWU was a short drive from my home in McLean, Virginia.

My topics were executive leadership and strategic planning. Each audience was composed of middle managers from throughout the Washington, DC area. A student in one of my teaching sessions was a mid-level FBI agent. He arranged for me to speak at the FBI Academy at Quantico, Virginia.

That FBI audience was an especially good one. About fifty "Special Agents in Charge" were at the Academy for a week's training. These were the men (in 1986 all of them were men) who were responsible for the FBI's field offices throughout the nation. As a guest in the audience that day was a professional educator from IBM. As often happens in my life, one opportunity soon led to another.

Quite soon I was engaged in a long-term relationship with IBM, teaching leadership to middle managers. IBM in 1986 was still a huge and very important company. IBM dominated the world of computing from the 1950s through the 1980s. It was listed, year after year, as one of the top five corporations in the world. Hence, teaching regularly for IBM not only enhanced my resume but also led to other speaking and teaching opportunities.

Every month I would fly from DC to New York to conduct classes at the large IBM education center in Armonk. The pay was good, everyone got a copy of *Taking Charge*, and I had enough free time between my speaking gigs to write my next book, *Assignment Pentagon*. (See Appendix).

THREE YEARS WITH THE KELLOGG FOUNDATION

In the summer of 1986, just before I retired from the Air Force, I was given a marvelous opportunity - to work for the WK Kellogg Foundation. In the early 1980s, The Kellogg Foundation had established an impressive leadership program for mid-career professionals. This program was led by a talented woman, Larraine Matusak. Fellows were selected from all over the United States because of their promise in making the world a better place. Larraine, who had heard me speak at a conference in Washington, felt I could make a contribution to her program.

Larraine asked me to conduct a leadership workshop at the beginning of each class. This was a three-year program which was sponsored and fully funded by the WK Kellogg Foundation of Battle Creek,

Michigan. The fellows were extremely smart and energetic. After a couple of years of making these kick-off presentations, I was asked to join Group Nine as one of the six advisors. The kickoff for Group Nine took place in the summer of 1988 at a lovely convention center in northern Minnesota.

The advisors included a banking executive, a college president, a university professor, a federal civil servant, a consultant on higher education and me. Like the advisors, Kellogg fellows were selected to be as representative and as diverse a group as possible. The fellows ranged in age from their late 20s to their early 40s. The advisors were in their 50s and 60s.

The mix of Kellogg fellows included native Americans, Hispanics, African Americans, Asian Americans and Caucasians. Half of the fellows were women. During each of the three years that Group Nine was together we took weeklong trips in order to gain insights on poverty, healthcare, hunger/food production, teambuilding, etc. Our overseas trip lasted for two weeks. The most interesting places we visited were Detroit, Boston, California, Colorado and Venezuela.

The Detroit visit gave us all a chance to observe the difficult issues facing the underserved people in the low income and crime ridden areas of that city. In Boston we spent a full day at one of the great American hospitals, Massachusetts General. Our tour of the Intensive Care Unit was especially interesting. At each bed the medical doctor, who was the director of this large and busy ICU, explained, in detail, the situation of the patient.

One woman in her early twenties had severe head injuries from a skiing accident. That afternoon, the doctor, who was giving us the morning tour, had scheduled a meeting with the woman's parents. His task was to recommend to them that their daughter, who was brain dead, donate her organs. This deeply experienced doctor explained how hard it was emotionally for the family to accept the fact that their daughter who they loved and cherished would never recover. He told us that he had to do this about once a week, a heavy responsibility that few leaders ever face.

Another patient in the ICU was a homeless man with severe alcoholism. This was the man's fourth visit to the ICU. Because he had no health insurance, his medical care had cost the hospital more than a million dollars. Thanks to the candor of the ICU boss and other medical professionals at "Mass General," the Kellogg fellows and advisors gained an understanding of the many financial, leadership, ethical, and personal challenges of healthcare professionals in America.

In California the forty Kellogg fellows and six advisors from Group Nine spent a week examining agricultural issues. We spent time with strawberry pickers near the town of Watsonville, California. We gained a first-hand understanding of the issues of migrant labor. Watching poorly paid workers, who were primarily Mexican, spending each day in stoop labor was painful to observe. Our guides helped us understand some of the complexities of immigration issues - especially as they relate to farming throughout the western United States.

In 1989 Group Nine participated in a team building week with Colorado Outward Bound. It reminded me of the United States Air Force's Winter Survival School. Each day, we were divided into small groups of about ten. A leader was chosen and tasks were assigned. For a long climb up a high Colorado mountain, I was appointed navigator. I failed miserably in this role, although you would think I would have been a strong navigator of the group because of my many years as a pilot. Not only did I get my small group lost I also managed to get altitude sickness.

There were many lessons learned during our week in Colorado. Most of us learned that we could accomplish difficult tasks we never dreamed that we would face. Others, like me, gained humility when they failed to meet a goal. We all gained insights in leadership since most of the challenges required close cooperation within small groups and someone to give directions for the group to follow. We all learned followership skills. Living in an unheated building, getting up before dawn, facing daunting physical and mental challenges and accomplishing tough goals through cooperation, led to many close friendships.

On our trips, I suggested to Dr. Matusak that, rather than have separate hotel rooms, we double up - as a way to get to know each other better. On the two-week Venezuelan trip I asked to room with a Kellogg fellow rather than with an advisor. I requested Willie Larkin. For the first time in my life, I had a roommate who was African

American. He was a delight - a great sense of humor and smart as a whip. As a fellow, Willie Larkin brought lots to the table. Well educated with a PhD, Willie had a quick mind, a fine sense of humor and a charismatic personality. In the years following the Kellogg leadership program, Doctor Larkin served as Chief of Staff to the President of Morgan State University and later as the President to Grambling State University.

Let me highlight one other Kellogg fellow from Group nine, Kathy Bonk. Just after Kathy was interviewed, Larraine Matusak pointed out that Kathy was so smart and so experienced that she would gain little from the Kellogg program. Larraine suggested that we not select her. Someone on the interview team disagreed. She agreed with Larraine's assessment of Kathy's talents, but recommended that we select her since Kathy could teach us all so much. Happily, Kathy was selected. In August, 2020, as I was conducting research on this book, I talked to Kathy on the telephone. She shared with me her recollections from Colorado Outward Bound, twenty-nine years earlier.

One of our challenges that both advisors and fellows were expected to undertake was to climb a 200-foot vertical wall. This was a challenge that none of us had faced before. To help ensure that each of us made the climb to the top safely we wore a helmet and were strapped on a harness. This harness was attached to a long, sturdy rope.

At the top of the cliff was a "belayer" who was anchored to a tree and was responsible for manning the rope which the climber was attached to. The climber could not use the rope to assist in the climb. As the climber ascended the cliff, the belayer would gently take up the slack on the rope. If climbers fell, they would be saved by the rope and the belayer. Kathy was the very last of our group to climb the cliff.

Earlier that day she observed the belayers and found some of them rather cavalier about their responsibilities. Kathy was worried that her belayer would not save her if she fell. As she neared the top, she saw that I was the belayer. She told me twenty-nine years later how relieved she was when she saw that I was manning her rope.

I should point out another aspect of the Kellogg leadership program. I found that about half of the fellows were humble and did not fully realize how talented they were. I was used to dealing with highly self-confident people, so this was quite a surprise. I found myself helping these fellows identify their talents and assisting them in realizing how much they could contribute to worthy causes.

In 1987, Connor received a letter from Frank Pokrop of Milwaukee, Wisconsin. This letter changed our lives in many wonderful ways. Frank had served with Jimmie Dyess in the 24th Marines. In his letter he explained that he had been trying to find Connor and her mother for more than forty years. When he learned about Connor's visit to Roi Namur, Frank finally found her address.

Frank wanted Connor to know his story. As a Marine corporal, Pokrop had fought in the battle for Roi Namur in late January, 1944. Late on the first day of the battle Frank and four of his battle buddies were caught behind enemy lines. They were receiving fire from three separate Japanese positions. All of the Marines were wounded and darkness was approaching. They felt that they would not survive the night.

Suddenly they realized that a rescue team was headed their way. Led by Lieutenant Colonel Dyess, this team saved all of the Marines that evening. Frank wanted Connor and her mother to know that he owed his life to the heroism of Jimmie Dyess. In 1988, Connor and I visited Frank and his wife Maxine in their home in Milwaukee. Thus commenced a deep friendship.

Jimmie Dyess's Medal of Honor citation was vague as to the reasons he was awarded this prestigious honor. Connor had never quite known why her father had received this honor. Frank solved this mystery and gave her a living example of her father's sacrifices.

Frank Pokrop invited us to attend a reunion of the Fourth Marine Division in Las Vegas. Connor was introduced to the assemblage of hundreds of Marines. As part of the introduction, the audience was reminded that this was the first time they had a chance to acknowledge the heroism of Lieutenant Colonel Dyess. With the exception of Frank Pokrop, none in the audience had had any contact after World War II with any of "Red" Dyess's family members.

Connor received a standing ovation which went on for many minutes. Most of the Marines had tears in their eyes when they remembered the leadership and heroism of Jimmie Dyess. Later that day Connor had a chance to visit with Richard Sorenson. Sorenson, like Connor's father, received the Medal of Honor for heroism during the battle for the Marshalls.

Medal of Honor recipient Richard Sorenson and Connor, 1989.

TEACHING IN ASIA AND SOUTH AMERICA

On a number of occasions, I was invited to present talks to war or defense colleges in China, Japan, Canada, Argentina, Uruguay and Chile. Being a major general and the former Commandant of a prestigious war college, I was an attractive candidate for presentations in other countries. I also spoke to high level corporate executives in Venezuela. Each presentation provided me with interesting insights that may be worth sharing.

In Caracas, I encountered a woman of extraordinary talent. Her job was to provide instantaneous translation from English into Spanish. The audience consisted of about one hundred executives from the Mendoza Group. In the 1990s this was a billion-dollar conglomerate with much of its interests in concrete. The translator was in an enclosed room directly to the rear of the auditorium. Through a glass window, she could see me and I could see her. Before my talk, I gave her my notes so she could anticipate my remarks. As I spoke, I used lots of hand gestures. I noticed that she was using my same hand gestures.

She did a splendid job. I was impressed by how the audience reacted so quickly and so well to my points and to my humorous stories. After the session, I asked her why she used my gestures. Her answer was simple and profound. She told me that she became me during my talk. She told me that she felt comfortable becoming me for about an hour. For years, I had heard the expression "mirroring someone." This was the best example of mirroring I ever encountered. I told her she was the best translator I had ever encountered.

What a talent! I learned that day that instantaneous translation is the best way for people with different languages to communicate with each other. After that talk in Caracas, I always asked for instantaneous translation as I made presentations around the world to people who did not have a firm grasp of English.

The talk to the Japanese Defense College was on strategic planning. Before I mounted the platform to speak, I asked the host if it was OK for me to tell my Pearl Harbor story. The answer was a resounding yes. There is a fascination in Japan about the attack on Pearl Harbor that continues today. The Japanese are especially interested in listening to those who witnessed the attack. I shared with my Japanese hosts my analysis of the tactical, operational and strategic lessons of this historic event. They seemed to grasp my emphasis on strategic analysis during the decision-making process.

My speech in Chile was on civil-military relations. The day before I was scheduled to speak to the students and faculty of the Chilean War College, the talk was cancelled. General Pinochet was still running the country. The military leaders in Chile were not interested in hearing my talk on civil-military relations. My message was essentially: go back to the barracks. It is bad for both a military and for a nation for the military to be in charge of governing a nation. Since I had a long trip to Chile, I was allowed to make my pitch to a small group of faculty members. Happily, soon thereafter, General Pinochet stepped down and civilian rule returned to Chile.

In retirement I received invitations to make presentations to many fine American institutions. I spoke to the three service academies, the Coast Guard Academy, all five war colleges and to a number of inter-mediate professional schools for officers. I especially enjoyed speaking each year to the Air Force Senior Non-Commissioned Officer Academy at Gunter Air Base near Montgomery, Alabama. In order to hold the attention of the audiences, I did not use notes or PowerPoint slides. For many years I conducted leadership workshops for the Secret Service. These mid-level professionals were extremely sharp—they challenged me on many occasions.

AT WEST POINT: THE HOLLEDER CENTER DEDICATION

In 1986, West Point completed the construction of a large indoor athletic center. This center housed both a basketball arena and an ice hockey venue. It was initially named the Multipurpose Athletic Center, with the idea that eventually it would be given a permanent, more meaningful name. The large West Point Society of New York favored naming it after Army's great football coach, Red Blaik. As a member of the board of the West Point Society of Washington, DC, I favored naming the arena after Don Holleder, my beloved roommate who was killed in Vietnam in 1967. The two largest West Point Societies in America were at loggerheads. The new Superintendent, Dave Palmer, decided that all athletic facilities at West Point should be named for graduates who had two characteristics. First, they must have played varsity sports which the venue would highlight. Second, they had to be killed in combat.

Bingo. Holly's selection became a slam dunk. Please remember, Holly was not only an outstanding football player but he also played on the varsity basketball team. On October 1st, 1988, the dedication took place. The front portico of the Holleder Center was the ideal location for the ceremony. More than two hundred people attended the ceremony. They included family members, football and basketball teammates from The Aquinas Institute of Rochester and from West Point, coaches, other West Point graduates, friends from Holly's time as an Army officer, and his battle buddies from Vietnam. This event was a grand celebration of Donald Walter Holleder's life.

For four reasons, I was pleased when I was chosen to be the principal speaker. First, Holly had been a dear friend. Second, it was Holly who introduced me to Connor and told me I should marry her. Third, West Point had been an important part of my life - having been born there, having spent my high school years there and having learned so much as a cadet there for four years. Fourth, it was an honor playing an official role in the dedication of a major facility at an institution for which I have the greatest respect.

Here are a few excerpts from my talk that day.

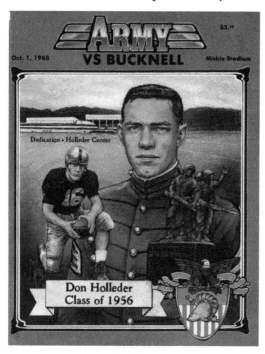

Cover of football program, the day of the Holleder Center dedication, October 1st, 1988.

"In the months since the decision was made, I have thought often of what might be said and what Don might want us to do on this occasion. He would say keep it short, make sure it is done with style and be sure to thank people who I loved and who helped me achieve my goals in life."

Before the Holleder Center dedication, Susie Holleder, Don Holleder's daughter, asked me to tell stories about her dad. Here is one of the stories I told.

"After the Army Navy game when a reporter

asked Don how he felt about the great experiment shifting him from end to quarterback and taking away any chance that he would be a two time All American and a Heisman Trophy candidate, Don answered, 'Last year, I played end and we lost. This year I played quarterback and we won. Do you have any other questions?'"

"Finally, I think Holly would ask us all to do one simple thing - celebrate this day and his life."

OUR LAST MOVE, TO AUGUSTA, GEORGIA, 1990

Connor and I had a major family decision to make in 1989. Since I could do my work from anywhere, I suggested to Connor that we move from our home in McLean, Virginia to Connor's hometown, Augusta, Georgia. Connor had always wanted to "go home" and this seemed like the perfect time. She was so pleased that she broke into tears. This meant that she was going home.

Our new house in Augusta was built by a good friend, Brad Bennett. We moved in on 15 March, 1990. After forty moves Connor and I were finally settled permanently into the home of our dreams. We live in a small subdivision in Richmond County. Every location of interest to us is within a 15-minute drive of our home - including St Paul's Church, the Augusta Regional Airport, the Augusta Museum of History, the Augusta Country Club and our favorite grocery stores. I play tennis three times a week at the Augusta Country Club, except in the extreme heat of summer.

After we settled into our new home, our neighbor, Woody Trulock, invited me to speak to his Cub Scout troop. On the floor in his living room were about 15 scouts, aged 7 through 9. At Woody's suggestion, I wore my flying suit. Woody asked me to speak about the American flag. I discussed the history of the flag and the meaning of the stripes and the stars. After this brief presentation, I told the scouts my Pearl Harbor story - pointing out that I was their age when I watched the Japanese attack on Hawaii on December 7th, 1941.

I then held up the flag and asked them. "How many stars do you reckon were on the American flag in 1941, when I lived in Hawaii?" Some hands shot up. The answer was thirteen. They seemed quite disappointed when I told them the number was 48; that Alaska and

Hawaii had not yet signed up. At my various talks and workshops, I often tell that story - it usually gets a nice laugh. If I had been quick thinking, I would have told the cub scouts about my interview with George Washington.

The next big event in our lives was the marriage of our daughter, Serena, to Rob Verfurth, at Saint Paul's Church in September, 1990. Rob is the son of a great friend and West Point classmate, Pete Verfurth and his dear wife, Anne. The wedding was a particularly special event which ended up being a mini West Point classmate reunion. Serena and Rob mirrored many things from Connor's and my wedding. They were married in the same church, had their reception in the same building, the Old Government House, and Serena even wore Connor's dress and veil. Two of Jimmie Dyess' grandnieces were in the wedding, Sarah and Weesie Brannon, just as his niece, their mother, Greer Ewing, was in ours.

Welcoming Rob into the family was a delight. He has a wonderfully outgoing personality and a great sense of humor. We were sure he would be a great husband and father. Connor and I are so proud of him and are pleased that he has become such an important part of our lives.

CELEBRATING THE LIFE AND LEGACY OF
MARINE LIEUTENANT COLONEL JIMMIE DYESS

In the fall of 1990, after Connor and I were well settled into our new home in Augusta, I commenced research on the story of Jimmie Dyess, Connor's father. The idea was to write and publish a biography on a family member and an American hero. I wondered how many people had been awarded both the Carnegie Medal and the Medal of Honor. One of the first steps I took was to contact the Carnegie Hero Fund Commission, which is located in Pittsburgh, Pennsylvania. My research, prior to my telephone call, showed that the Carnegie Medal was the most prestigious medal of civilian heroism. Carnegie Medals had been awarded ever since 1904. Only the most extraordinary acts of heroism are recognized. Andrew Carnegie, who was a pacifist, made it clear that only civilians were eligible for this award.

My question to the official at the Carnegie Hero Fund

Commission was a simple one. Of the more than nine thousand recipients of the Carnegie Medal, how many had also received the Medal of Honor? The answer I received was: no one, because military men and women are not eligible to receive the Carnegie Medal.

Politely but firmly I replied as follows, "Sir, in my house in Augusta, Georgia I possess both a Medal of Honor and a Carnegie Medal. Both were awarded to the same person, A. J. Dyess of Augusta, Georgia." I explained that as a teenager Jimmie Dyess had earned the Carnegie Medal. Sixteen years later he received the Medal of Honor in combat during World War II. The staff member at the Carnegie Hero Fund Commission was quite surprised. He asked that I send him documentation on the Medal of Honor which I did.

My next telephone call was to the offices of the Congressional Medal of Honor Society. The answer to my question about someone receiving both medals was, "What is the Carnegie Medal?" At that moment I realized that I would have to do the research myself. It took three full days. With both lists in front of me, I searched for the same exact name on each list. With lots of Smiths, Johnsons, Murphy's, Jones's etc., about twenty names were exactly the same. My next step was to determine the date of each heroic act. Someone who earned his Medal of Honor during the Civil War in 1863, could not have earned a Carnegie Medal in 1974. This reduced the number to less than five. Then I checked birthdates and hometowns.

Bingo. The research proved that Jimmie Dyess alone had earned both medals. This realization brought tears to my eyes. I wrote two versions of the book, *Twice a Hero* and *Courage, Compassion, Marine: the Unique Story of Jimmie Dyess*. The second book, which was published in 2015, was needed since the first book left out a number of important aspects of his life and his legacy. In 2016, with the assistance of Mark Albertin, a video, *Twice a Hero: The Unique Story of Jimmie Dyess*, was produced. This video is available on YouTube.

Soon after we moved to Augusta, a highway was dedicated honoring Congressman Doug Barnard. This gave me an idea. How about a road or parkway named for Connor's father, Medal of Honor recipient

Above: Dedication Ceremony for the Jimmie Dyess Parkway in Augusta, Georgia, 1994.

Left: Connor Dyess Smith with the Medal of Honor of her father, 1994.

Jimmie Dyess? Jimmy Lester, who I met when I joined the Kiwanis Club of Augusta, was a member of the Georgia Transportation Board. He grabbed the idea and took it to the Highway Board. Within three weeks, a decision was made. The Jimmie Dyess Parkway was dedicated in 1994 and opened four years later. It links the main gate at Fort Gordon to the major east-west Interstate Highway, I-20. Jimmie's widow, Connor Goodrich, and daughter, Connor, attended both ceremonies. In attendance at the opening ceremony in 1998 was Marine General Ray Davis, a Georgia native and Medal of Honor recipient.

The dedication event in 1994 drew the attention of the local media. Connor was interviewed and a substantive article appeared in the Augusta Chronicle. Through the years, this newspaper has, on many occasions, highlighted the story of Marine Lieutenant Colonel Jimmie Dyess.

ON CAMERA WITH CNN, 1991

The next major event in our lives occurred when I joined CNN as one of two military analysts in January, 1991. I received a phone call from CNN in early January, 1991. The vice president of CNN for guest bookings, Gail Evans, called me. Would I be willing to drive over from Augusta to Atlanta to be interviewed on camera? The topic of the interview would be the likelihood of war with Iraq. Saddam Hussein had invaded Kuwait the previous August and a robust alliance led by the United States was making preparations to retake the country of Kuwait.

After driving the 143 miles from Augusta to the CNN studios in downtown Atlanta, I answered questions on camera for about four minutes. Here is my best recollection of some of the questions I was asked. Question. Did I think war was imminent? Answer. Yes. Question. How soon? Answer. Within the next few days. Question. What weapons would be major factors in the early days of the war? Answer. Aircraft from all four of our military services plus our allies. I was aware of the United States capabilities and potential actions from my time in the Pentagon. Also, I had on the ground knowledge of the U.S. military relationship with many of our allies.

A few minutes after I left the anchor desk, I was asked by a senior

CNN executive if I would be willing to work for CNN. My role - to serve as one of two military analysts for the duration of the war. I asked what the arrangements would be. Where would I stay, what would be the financial arrangements, etc.? The answer I received - CNN would pay for all of my travel and hotel expenses as well as for my meals. I then asked, what about pay for my work? The executive told me that since CNN was going to lose $30 million on this war, I would receive no monetary compensation.

I politely told the executive that these arrangements were not satisfactory. I wished the CNN folks well and drove back to Augusta. On 16 January, 1991, the war commenced. As I watched the coverage on CNN, I had a sudden urge to be involved. I thought it would be a wonderful opportunity to educate a very large number of people throughout the world. My love of teaching led me to ask Connor for her thoughts. She said - if you really want to do it, go for it.

CNN had been founded in the 1980s as the first 24 hour all-news channel in the United States. But it wasn't until the first Persian Gulf War in 1991 that CNN overtook the "Big Three" American networks (ABC, NBC and CBS). This was due to two factors. CNN was the only news outlet that was able to sustain 24-hour coverage. Also, only CNN was able to report from inside Iraq throughout the entire war.

I called CNN and asked if I was still wanted. The answer was a strong yes. So off I went on the two hour and fifteen-minute drive from our home in Augusta to the CNN center. As I drove toward Atlanta, I realized that I needed to gain some insights on the war from someone quite knowledgeable.

I stopped at a motel in Madison, Georgia and telephoned Colonel John Warden. A brilliant student while I was Commandant of the National War College, Warden was the chief architect of the upcoming air campaign over Iraq and Kuwait. I had been in contact with him during the previous few weeks so I knew how to find him. I was sure that he would assist me. As I have described in the National War College chapter, during my 30 years in the Air Force, I had encountered five geniuses. Herman Kahn, John Boyd, Lee Butler, Barry Horton and John Warden. Having Colonel John Warden to assist me during the next six weeks was one of the greatest blessings of my life.

Warden answered a bunch of my questions and told me what I could use and could not use on television. As I continued my drive to Atlanta, I decided to set some goals for myself. First, no secrets for Saddam Hussein. Second, if I got a question for which I did not know the answer, I would say "I don't know." Finally, if CNN did something unethical, I would say farewell, jump into my automobile, and drive back to Augusta.

I arrived at the Omni Hotel in Atlanta at midnight on 16 January, 1991. The Omni Hotel is attached to the CNN Center. You don't even have to walk outside to go from one to the other. The war had been underway for about six hours. As I approached the front desk, the hotel receptionist asked if I was General Smith. When I nodded yes, he said, quite dramatically, "Drop your bags, I will check you in, run to the CNN studios - they are waiting for you."

As I approached the security desk at CNN, someone said, "Follow me." I was rushed to the anchor desk. With no on-the-job training at all, I began to answer questions. The anchor was Patrick Greenlaw. This very first interview during the Gulf War was quite extensive.

As I recall, eleven questions were asked and answered. For the next six weeks, I lived the following pattern of activities. Up at 6 AM, at the CNN studio by 6:30, on the air (off and on) all day long, back to my hotel room by 11 PM. On most days, at mid-afternoon, I went back to my hotel room for a thirty-minute nap.

After about a week, Tom Johnson, the CEO of CNN, invited me to sit in on executive and planning sessions. I expected to sit in the back of the room but I was given a seat at the conference room table. I felt I was a fully-fledged member of the CNN team.

During the first few weeks at CNN headquarters I struggled with the lingo of television journalists. This caused me big problems on one occasion. Let me explain. One week into the war, I asked Bob Furnad, the senior executive producer at CNN, if I could present, on camera, a strategic analysis of the war. I told him I needed four minutes. He agreed.

After I had been speaking directly to the camera for about two minutes, I heard this word in my earpiece. "Wrap." I thought someone

Military Analyst Perry Smith on camera at CNN, 1991.

was saying "Rap," was on the wrong frequency, and was speaking about a rap band. I kept on talking. After I left the anchor desk, Bob told me I had talked for seven minutes. My thought was - good, I got to make many important points including recommending three books (including John Warden's *The Air Campaign*).

Bob Furnad had a totally opposite reaction. He said to me in a strong voice, "Never again." A couple of minutes later I received some more criticism. This time from another senior CNN executive. He pointed at a TV monitor and told me that we don't want the audience to read books, we want them to watch television. Later that day, Tom Johnson, the CEO of CNN told me to disregard the criticism I had received that morning. This was welcome guidance from the top guy at CNN. It was a sign that he trusted me and did not want anyone to second guess me.

In order to keep informed and up to the minute with the combat activities in Kuwait and Iraq, I spent much of my time on the telephone. Fortunately, I had a number of friends who were serving in key positions in the Pentagon. John Warden was helpful but there were others.

Lieutenant Colonel John Barry was serving as a military assistant to the Secretary of Defense. Years earlier I had helped Captain Barry get ready for a number of interviews. He was competing for the prestigious position of a White House Fellow. He was selected for that program. Because of our unique connection and because the powers that be at the Pentagon trusted me to get important information out to the public, I talked to Lt. Col. Barry on the phone every few days to gain an understanding of what was happening at the top levels of the Department of Defense.

The Value of a Braintrust: A Lesson from CNN

During the six weeks I worked for CNN, I gained many insights. For instance, I learned the value of a large and robust "braintrust." Within a few days in January, 1991, I became impressed with how many experts CNN had lined up. I asked Judy Milestone, who was in charge of booking guests, how many names were in the CNN file. In 1991 the number was about 20,000. Examples of these experts included military professionals, professors of history, sociology, psychology, economics, ethics, international relations; also, retired civil servants, politicians, journalists, soldiers, Marines, sailors, bureaucrats, doctors, lawyers, CEOs, etc.

For instance, if there was a major earthquake it usually was a breaking news story. Within a couple of hours, CNN had an expert or two on camera giving commentary. How was CNN able to react so fast? CNN had people located in places all around the world. If the story broke in the middle of the night on the East Coast, an expert living in Delhi, Hong Kong, Tokyo, or Sydney would be awake and quick to answer the call. These experts did not get paid - they were pleased to be asked and to be able to make a contribution. Most would do it because they enjoyed the experience. Others accepted invitations because appearances on CNN enhanced their business interests and their resumes.

I was so inspired by CNN's huge reservoir of support that I decided to build a large personal braintrust of my own. It currently consists of about 600 smart and helpful people. I have their snail mail and email addresses and phone numbers. Inside this list is a smaller list which I call my "ethics braintrust." Members of the group include my family members and long-time friends who have a track record of high integrity.

I had a good relationship with all of the CNN anchors. They were given good questions to ask from the various writers, editors and producers but, on occasion, they relied on me to give them questions to ask.

On my last day at CNN in March, 1991, the anchor, Bob Cain, bid me farewell on camera. He paraphrased Saint Francis with these words, "where there was darkness, you brought us light."

Little did I know that within two years I would be back with CNN. From 1993 until 1998, I served on contract as CNN's military analyst. During my six years working for CNN, a few anchors, reporters, and staff members became good friends. Each had a strong commitment to honest reporting: Jamie McIntyre, John Holliman, Dan Ronan, Judy Woodruff, Bobbie Battista, Natalie Allen, Judy Milestone, Judy Stewart, Ed Turner, Bob Furnad, Sue Bunda, and Tom Johnson. On 13 June, 1998, I resigned from CNN. I will explain that sad story soon.

I enjoyed my years with CNN. I was treated with respect and gained many friends. One of the most memorable experiences was a teaching opportunity at the CNN center in Atlanta in February, 1991. Bob Furnad, a senior executive at CNN, asked me to conduct a workshop on the military. I expected 20 to be in attendance - about 50 showed up. All of these journalists seemed to take genuine interest in my presentation.

After the intense, frenetic and extremely rewarding time as an on-screen military analyst for CNN during the First Gulf War, I drove from the CNN Center in Atlanta to my home in Augusta. For the next week or so, I answered each of the hundreds of letters I had received during my six week stint on CNN.

Soon thereafter, I took on a new project - writing a book about my work for CNN. Getting the book published quickly was a goal. I hired two people who were excellent at taking dictation. By mid-summer, the manuscript was completed and a publisher identified. Connor was a careful editor of both the manuscript and the page proofs. After considering about fifty possible titles, including "How CNN Won the War," the title, *How CNN Fought the War* was selected. The next step was to set up a book party.

The Watergate Hotel in Washington DC was an ideal venue. It was centrally located in downtown Washington and parking was easy Also, ever since the 1972 break-in which led to the resignation of President Nixon, the Watergate was a popular spot for various events. Folks would like to tell their friends - "I have an invitation to an event at the Watergate."

The book celebration was hosted by David Gergen and Newt Gingrich. Both men were well known. David, for his work in the White House, and Gingrich for his very visible activities as a Congressman from Georgia. I got to know them both during my years at the National War College. They were guest speakers each of the three years I was the Commandant. Each time they visited I would have substantive conversations with them in my office.

At the book party the "Capitol Steps" performed a cute sketch. Connor and Serena were in attendance as were nine of my West Point classmates. Also present were Judge William Webster and his new wife, Lynda. Webster had been the Director of the FBI and the head of the CIA. Colonel John Warden, who had been so helpful to me during my six weeks at CNN, attended with his wife, Marjorie. This party was a great way to kick off the publication of *How CNN Fought the War.*

However, not all went well that evening. To my surprise, the publisher was quite critical. He told me at the party that he had just read the book, and it didn't have any "stuff" in it. By "stuff" he meant who was sleeping with whom at CNN, or inside stories about Ted Turner, or salacious commentary on well-known reporters and anchors. He was correct. I had no intention of making this a "tell all" book.

Early in 1992, I was asked to be the graduation speaker at Marietta College in Ohio. At this event I was presented with an honorary degree. My family members from Zanesville would have been pleased

West Point classmates at CNN book celebration
(Alward, Sorley, Renshaw, Stapleton, Crites,
Smith, Verfurth, Amlong, Dowell, Ruffner), 1991.

that a college only seventy miles away had publicly recognized me. I am not sure why I was honored by this college. However, I did know the president quite well and I had been in the news because of my work on CNN the previous year.

EMORY UNIVERSITY AND JEFF ROSENSWEIG

During my early association with CNN, I had the opportunity to meet a young professor from the Goizueta School of Business at Emory University, Jeff Rosensweig. He invited me to be a guest speaker at his MBA class at Emory. From the day of that first workshop in 1992 Jeff and I clicked.

For almost 30 years, Emory University has become an important part of the lives of our family. My connection with Jeff led to both my granddaughters considering Emory for their undergraduate education. We were delighted when both of them moved to Atlanta to enter Emory in 2014 and 2016 respectively. Dyess chose business as her major and soon became a mentee of Jeff. Both Dyess and Porter were members of the Emory cross country and track teams.

At the invitation of Jeff, I conduct a workshop on executive leadership three times each year - for the Executive MBA scholars in the fall and for the MBA and BBA scholars in the spring. Every scholar receives a copy of *Rules and Tools for Leaders*. Starting in 2021, they all will receive copies of *Listen Up,* as well.

Since Jeff and I both feel that education should be fun, I start each workshop at Emory with an apocryphal tale. Here is how it goes. I remind everyone in the audience that my good friend, Professor Rosensweig, is a man of many talents who knows an amazing array of well-known people. With a smile on my face, I mention that Jeff is a world class "Name Dropper." I remind them that Jeff will tell you that he is a friend of Nobel Prize recipients, presidents of the New York Stock Exchange and CEOs of major corporations. Many in the audience smile and nod in agreement. I now have the students all set up for what follows.

With a straight face I tell them a story of an event that never happened. I tell the Emory scholars of a visit Jeff and I made to Rome a few years ago. It was an Easter Sunday so we decided to go to Saint Peters to hear the Pope. The Pope was standing on his balcony while he addressed a large audience.

Jeff whispered in my ear, "Perry, I am a good friend of the Pope." When I voiced some skepticism, Jeff told me he would go through the door where the Swiss guards were standing, go up the stairs and

put his arm around the shoulder of the Pope. Sure enough - a few minutes later there was Jeff. I was so far away that I was not sure that the small man standing next to Jeff was the Pope. So I asked someone standing next to me, "Is that really the Pope?" He answered me with great enthusiasm, "Pope, I don't know, but that is Jeff Rosensweig."

That story gets everyone laughing - they realize, from the very start, that this will not be a

Professor Jeff Rosensweig and his wife, Natalie Allen, 2020.

boring lecture from an old geezer. Incidentally, Jeff was named by the Wall Street Journal as one of the top 12 professors in the world who teach in Executive MBA programs. The students at Emory love and respect him. Jeff and his wife, Natalie, a CNN anchor, have become close friends of our family.

MEETINGS WITH BILL CLINTON IN 1992 AND 1995

In the summer of 1992, I was asked if I would be willing to meet with Governor Clinton to discuss issues relating to defense policy, the military and the Pentagon. Clinton was running for President of the United States against the elder George Bush. I was quite busy at the time. As an admirer of George H. W. Bush, I felt no desire to help his opponent in the upcoming presidential election. However, the person who asked me was a good friend from my days at the Air Force Academy (Dick Klass). He felt that Clinton was likely to be our next President and would value my insights.

I told Klass that I would come to Philadelphia and would not charge for my advice, but I set some requirements.

1. No more than five or six people in the room.
2. Two full hours of discussion.
3. My flight and hotel expenses would be covered.
4. I would have at least fifteen uninterrupted minutes to talk directly to Governor Clinton.

I did not think presidential candidate Clinton would agree to these requirements. Hence, I was surprised when I received a call from Dick to tell me the meeting was on.

In August, 1992, I was off to Philadelphia to meet with Governor Bill Clinton. At that time William Jefferson Clinton was on a high, having been nominated by his party the month before. Also, he was leading in the presidential polls.

In a small hotel conference room were Clinton, Admiral Bill Crowe, Marine Lieutenant General Mick Trainor, Army Lieutenant General Jack Woodmansee and me. I knew Crowe, Trainor and Woodmansee quite well and had great respect for each of them. Clinton was accompanied by a man who was his note taker, Sandy Berger. Of course, Dick Klass, who came up with the idea of this meeting and made all of the arrangements, was also present.

Governor Clinton arrived about twenty minutes late but, for the next two hours, there was a substantive discussion. When it was my turn to speak, I was quite frank with Clinton. I raised four issues with him. First, I strongly suggested that, between the time of his election and his inauguration, he should spend two full days in the Pentagon. He should go through war games all the way to a nuclear decision. I stressed that it was important for him to get to know the members of the Joint Chiefs of Staff and the top intelligence officials at the Pentagon. I knew that Clinton was a great admirer of Jack Kennedy. Hence, I suggested that he did not want to make the mistake of Jack Kennedy which led directly to the Bay of Pigs fiasco.

Second, I suggested that he select, as his national security advisor, someone with a deep understanding of the military - someone like Brent Scowcroft, Colin Powell or Andy Goodpaster. Third, if that was not feasible, then a deputy national security advisor should be selected with a strong military background. Finally, I handed him a personalized copy of my Pentagon book (*Assignment Pentagon*) and suggested that he read it.

Three years later (1995), I was invited to the White House for a luncheon with President Clinton. At the luncheon were about twenty retired generals and admirals - most of whom had endorsed Clinton prior to the 1992 election. At the luncheon, Clinton asked for comments on how he was doing in the National Security arena. During the hour and a half luncheon, no one criticized Clinton. It was the apple polishing of a President which I had read about for years. The praise was glowing until I raised my hand and was recognized. I had not endorsed him in 1992 and felt it was time to be critical.

I reminded Clinton of the August, 1992, meeting in Philadelphia. I then said that at that meeting I had given him four suggestions and, as far as I could tell, he had not followed any of them. President Clinton asked me to remind him of my 1992 suggestions - I did so. As the luncheon broke up, Clinton grabbed me by the arm, wrote down a phone number for his private secretary and asked me to send him the ideas.

He did not approach anyone else. Once again he did not follow any of my suggestions.

My impression of Bill Clinton - very smart, charming, and able to read people extremely well. He works hard to bring his critics to his point of view. Every December, during the eight years of the Clinton administration, we received a White House Christmas card - each one quite tasteful.

CRYSTAL CRUISES: 1992 - 2012

In 1992, my good friend, Jack Weatherford, gave me a suggestion. The idea was for me to serve as an enrichment speaker on Crystal Harmony. Although Crystal Cruises would later commission two more ships, the Crystal Harmony was the only Crystal Cruises ship in 1992. Jack suggested that I join him when the Crystal Harmony sailed across the South Pacific. He told me if I moved fast, he thought I could join the ship in Tahiti. I got to know Jack through the Kellogg leadership program. Like me, he had been an advisor to one of the Kellogg groups. His speaking style was very impressive - lots of humor and no notes.

Thanks to Jack, the invitation from Crystal Cruises came through. Connor and I cleared our schedule and off we flew to the South Pacific. On that twenty-two day voyage from Tahiti to Sydney, I made six talks. The deal was: I would receive no compensation for my presentations. However, Connor and I received a free cruise and Crystal covered my travel expenses from our house to each port and back. Since I love to speak, this was a nice, economical way to travel the world in grand style. On this trip Connor and I first met Dick and Phyliss Corliss, who owned a high-end travel agency. Soon Dick and Phyliss became dear friends.

That first cruise was such a delightful experience that Connor and I decided to sign up for another cruise the next year. Little did we know at the time how many voyages we would enjoy with Crystal Cruises. Jack Weatherford had told us that Crystal Cruises was ranked as the best cruise line in the world. The standard of excellence was really impressive. As a bonus, Connor and I got to meet and visit with many of the passengers. Some had fascinating backgrounds, others were great storytellers and still others gave us good advice on which on-shore excursions were the best.

Jack was a speaker on our first cruise; he showed me the ropes. His rules were as follows: speak no more than 30 minutes, use no notes, look each person in the eye sometime during your presentation, include humor throughout, answer questions for no more than 15 minutes, and end a little early.

I adjusted the topics of my talks based on where we were cruising at the time. Some of my topics included World War II in the Pacific, World War II in Europe, long range thinking, leadership, heroism and dealing with the media. Thanks to our dear friend, Phyliss Corliss, Crystal Cruises upgraded me from an enrichment speaker to a distinguished speaker. This meant that Connor and I enjoyed a suite on the finest cruise ships in the world. Phyliss had a great deal of influence with the various presidents of Crystal Cruises because, as a successful tour agent, she had booked more guests on Crystal than any other travel agent.

We got to know many Crystal Cruise staff members well. Whenever we entered the ship for our next cruise, we were greeted like old friends. The shows which were held each evening were top notch. The speakers and entertainers included Debbie Reynolds, Eddie Fisher, Flip Wilson, and Pierre Salinger. Ms. Reynolds was the star of the number #2 rated movie musical, *Singing in the Rain*. Ed Fisher and Debbie Reynolds were the parents of Carrie Fisher, "Princess Leia" from the blockbuster movie, *Star Wars*.

The top staff members who became good friends included: Captain Reidulf Maalen, Cruise Directors David De Havilland, Gary Hunter, and Paul McFarland. Each voyage was an adventure. We learned so much on each voyage. Of all the organizations I have been affiliated with, Crystal Cruises is ranked at the top in terms of customer satisfaction, sustained excellence and incremental improvement.

For twenty years (1992-2012) we sailed with Crystal Cruises while I served as a speaker. We travelled through Alaska's inward passage (twice), the Panama Canal (twice), Mombasa to Athens, the Black Sea, the Baltic Sea, London to New York, Buenos Aires to Miami, Hong Kong to Tokyo, Miami to Lisbon, Southampton to Rome, and many more.

After having made more than a dozen cruises by 2005, I asked the president of Crystal Cruises if he would host our family on an Alaska cruise. He agreed. What a delightful family vacation we had and the kids and grandkids got the same deal that Connor usually got, so it was a free trip for all.

In addition to these grand cruises, we joined Phyliss and Dick Corliss on two extraordinary adventures. First, a trip which took us to Brazil and Argentina; four years later, a two week Safari in East Africa. In both cases the land trip ended when we joined Crystal, first in Buenos Aires and, a few years later, in Mombasa.

Smith/Verfurth Family on Crystal Harmony, 2005.

The African safari was especially memorable. In the Amboseli Game Preserve, Dick and Phyliss celebrated their 30th wedding anniversary. Connor, with her lovely voice, sang *May You Always* in celebration of such a grand couple.

To spend almost a week in the Serengeti was an experience beyond description. From our Toyota land cruiser, we could see 5,000 animals as our eyes swept the horizon. Our vehicle managed to get flat tires five times as we bumped over and through the rough roads and trails. When the Corliss Group climbed on the ship in Mombasa, we were greeted with joy by passengers and staff alike. We went from rough safari camps to the elegance of the Crystal staterooms, showers, food and drink. It was a memorable transition for all of us.

One voyage was not so pleasant. On a cruise from Southampton to New York City we encountered a major hurricane. For about 24 hours waves of thirty feet broke across the bow of our ship. A few waves reached fifty feet. A marvelous medicine, Transderm Scop, saved me from getting seasick. We were confined to our stateroom for a period of time. The captain was very skilled and we sailed north of Iceland to avoid the worst of the storm. Watching a well-trained crew deal with this storm was a fascinating experience for someone interested in crisis leadership. Safety of passengers was the top priority. The captain received high marks.

BLUE RIDGE CONFERENCE ON LEADERSHIP AND THE SWAG

Starting in 1990 and for more than twenty years, Connor and I would drive up to the Boy Scout retreat in Black Mountain, North Carolina. I would conduct workshops on leadership at The Blue Ridge Conference on Leadership. Since there were more than 400 attendees, I was asked to conduct four workshops at each conference. On occasion, I was a keynote speaker.

One magic day in Augusta in the mid-1990s we learned about a rustic inn which was located at five thousand feet on the edge of the Great Smoky Mountains. Owned and operated by Dan and Deener Matthews, the Swag became our vacation spot every fall. After spending two nights in the austere Boy Scout retreat, we would drive an hour to the west and spend a few nights at the Swag. After I was no longer invited to be a speaker at the Blue Ridge Leadership Conference, we continued to make the Swag our home for five days each fall.

Much like the Crystal ships, the Swag is at the very top in customer care in every way. Located only one hundred feet from the boundary of the Great Smokies, the Swag offers the very best in hiking, views, meals and hospitality. It may be the best rustic inn throughout the Southeast. For many years Connor and I hiked some of the dozens of different trails. In 2019, our family celebrated our 60th wedding anniversary at the Swag.

Dan and Deener Matthews were well into their 80s when they decided to sell the Swag. It must have been a tough decision. A delightful young couple from Knoxville, Annie and David Colquitt, purchased the Swag. They are committed to maintaining the Swag's excellence. In addition, each year they make improvements.

Back on Screen with CNN, 1994 - 1998

By the time of the American incursion into Haiti in 1994 I was back working for CNN. The White House pleaded with CNN not to report that C-130s would soon be launching from North Carolina. The case was made by David Gergen, the White House communications director, that lives would be saved if the arrival American troops in Haiti could be a surprise. Tom Johnson, the CEO of CNN, agreed. This was an example of the media and the US government cooperating on an important issue. After the arrival of American troops, CNN gave the Haiti operation good coverage.

However, when the OJ Simpson trial began, CNN shifted almost all of its attention to that trial. After not being asked to appear on the anchor desk for a number of days, I entered Tom Johnson's office and told him that since I had no role to play, it was time for me to head back to Augusta. I thought hour by hour coverage of the OJ trial was sensational, rather than substantive journalism. I felt the Haiti story was much more important This was one of the first times that CNN disappointed me, but there would be more.

In the summer of 1995, a major story developed relating to the chaos in Bosnia. Serbian troops had massacred more than seven thousand Bosniak men from the Srebrenica region of Bosnia. President Clinton was trying to decide what to do, if anything. I was in Washington for a speaking engagement when I was called to the DC CNN studio.

CNN's Frank Sesno was interviewing Senator Joe Lieberman of Connecticut and me. Frank asked me if the United States had a strategic interest in the Bosnia area. My response was as follows: America has no strategic interests there; however, the United States would be diminished as a nation if we allowed the massacres to continue. Frank then turned to Senator Lieberman. Rather than making some additional points, Senator Lieberman said that he agreed completely with me. It was one of the nicest compliments I have ever received on the air.

Shortly thereafter, NATO initiated a bombing campaign against Serbian military targets in Bosnia. In August, 1995 and again in the spring of 1999, I served as a military analyst during two air campaigns. In both cases Bill Clinton was president. Both campaigns were successful. The first campaign was over Bosnia. It lasted for just three weeks and led to the successful Dayton Accords. These agreements ended the war in Bosnia and the massacres by the Serbian military.

The second campaign, over Serbia and Kosovo, commenced in March of 1999. It lasted for seventy-seven days. The Serbia/Kosovo campaign ended with the arrival of Russian peacekeepers in June, 1999 at the airport in Kosovo. By 1999, I was no longer working for CNN. I was providing commentary for NBC TV, MSNBC and CBS radio. The story of why I resigned from CNN in 1998, follows.

CNN's "Valley of Death" Debacle Followed by Five Favorable Outcomes

In June, 1998, CNN made a major mistake - a foul up that was so bad, the founder of CNN, Ted Turner, called it the biggest mistake of his life. Turner later said, "Nothing has upset me as much in my whole life." Two CNN reporters had produced a special entitled, "The Valley of Death." This TV special, which was narrated by Peter Arnett, examined a highly classified military operation, "Operation Tailwind," which had taken place during the war in Southeast Asia. This was a four-day operation in September, 1970 in the nation of Laos.

CNN accused the soldiers and airmen of war crimes including dropping sarin, a lethal nerve gas, attacking American "defectors" and massacring large numbers of civilians. None of these charges were true. One week after the Valley of Death special aired on CNN, I resigned from CNN. I told Tom Johnson, the CEO of CNN, three things. I was resigning from CNN, I could not stand the ethics and I would never work for CNN again.

Operation Tailwind was carried out by an Army Special Forces unit. A small number of highly trained US Army special forces soldiers led the operation. These soldiers were accompanied by about one hundred allied troops (Montagnard tribesmen from South Vietnam). From the moment that these troops were inserted into enemy territory they came under heavy enemy fire. On the last day of this operation, United States Air Force pilots provided support while large Marine helicopters rescued the embattled soldiers. Operation Tailwind was successful both in the intelligence information collected but also in the "extraction under fire" operation. Every American warrior soldier was wounded but each one survived. However, three of the allied troops were killed.

I blew the whistle on this story by CNN a number of times: three times before the special was broadcast, a number of times during the week following the broadcast (urging a retraction and an apology to the soldiers and airmen who had been accused of war crimes) and twice after I left CNN.

It seemed clear to me that the reporters had gone into the story with an intended outcome, to discredit the American military during the Vietnam conflict. These CNN reporters had cleverly manipulated their sources and their video, used hearsay versus actual documented fact. They tainted the reputation of some real heroes.

Going public after I resigned and hitting CNN hard was not a difficult decision. CNN's nerve gas special was so egregious that I felt it had to be highlighted to the world. There were headlines in a number of newspapers throughout America. However, what happened in the aftermath of this media mess was both surprising and uplifting.

There is a lovely saying, first expressed by Elbert Hubbard in 1914, "When life gives you lemons, make lemonade." I prefer a longer phrase, "When life gives you lemons, make lemonade, set up a lemonade stand and bring joy to your neighborhood by giving free lemonade to all the kids."

Once in a while extremely good results emerge after something very bad occurs. This fact is useful to consider when you or the people around you are going through a very difficult time.

Thanks to the persistence of officials in the Pentagon and many retired veterans, CNN's outrageous Valley of Death special led to a number of positive events. First, the Department of Defense declassified

Facing page:
New York Times headline, 1998.

CNN Analyst On Military Steps Down After Report

By The Associated Press

June 18, 1998

The top military analyst for CNN has resigned to protest the network's report that the United States military used nerve gas in a mission to hunt down American defectors in Laos in the Vietnam War.

The analyst, Maj. Gen. Perry Smith, retired, who has been a military expert for CNN since the Persian Gulf war, "leaves with our great respect," Steve Haworth, a CNN spokesman, said yesterday. "I think it's an honest difference of opinion."

General Smith resigned on Sunday after failing to persuade the network to retract its report, first broadcast on June 7.

"It's sleazy journalism," General Smith said on Wednesday.

General Smith, a former Air Force officer who flew missions over Laos during the war, said he believed that no nerve gas had been used.

The report accused the military of using sarin gas during Operation Tailwind in Laos, in which two American defectors were supposedly killed, and in other missions. The report, by CNN and Time magazine, quoted several Special Forces soldiers who said they had been involved in the operation.

General Smith, a 30-year Air Force officer, an author and teacher of ethics and management, flew combat missions over Laos in 1968 this operation and proved that CNN's charges were wrong in every dimension. Second, after receiving great pressure from outraged special forces and special operation troops, CNN produced an on-air retraction (very unusual in the TV world). Third, three years later, at a moving ceremony at Fort Bragg, this Special Forces Unit was awarded the Presidential Unit Citation. Fourth, a few years later, Gene McCarley, who was the ground commander throughout Operation Tailwind and who worked so hard to get his soldiers' heroism properly recognized, was inducted into the Infantry Officer Candidate School Hall of Fame. Finally, on 23 December 2016, President Obama signed into law the 2017 National Defense Authorization Act, which authorized the Medal of Honor for the only medic in Operation Tailwind, Sergeant Gary "Mike" Rose. Thanks to the dogged efforts of an Army veteran, Neil Thorne, and with the help of many others, Mike Rose received the Medal of Honor in 2017. Many of his combat buddies attended the ceremony in the White House.

During the month following my departure from CNN, I received more than two thousand letters, FAXs, phone calls and emails. The vast majority were favorable. A handwritten note from Colin Powell was especially appreciated. "Dear Perry. You did the right thing but you always do." I had not known Colin well either when I was on active duty or later, so his note was quite unexpected. General Powell had been the Chairman of the Joint Chiefs of Staff during the First Gulf War and would soon become the Secretary of State under President George W. Bush.

The Secretary of Defense in 1998 was Bill Cohen. I had known Cohen when he was a Senator from Maine. He had delivered the graduation speech at the National War College in 1984. An excerpt from Secretary Cohen's letter to me in June, 1998 follows. "I just wanted to underscore my deep admiration and appreciation for your courageous act of conviction."

Perhaps the most heartwarming letter came from retired General Andrew Goodpaster. He was in his mid-80s at the time. "...my thanks as a fellow American to you for your decisive action in resigning from CNN and doing that publicly once their egregious and bogus broadcast became public. ... I think the outcome of this has been positive, thanks in key part to what you have done." Goodpaster was one of the few people to highlight that my going public soon after I resigned from CNN was the correct thing to do.

Goodpaster, who had graduated from West Point in 1939, established an outstanding combat record during World War II. He received two awards for heroism, the Distinguished Service Cross and the Silver Star and was seriously wounded in 1944. However, his greatest contributions to America occurred after the war in Washington and later at West Point. As staff assistant to President Eisenhower for seven years, Goodpaster set a standard for objective advice to an American President. This was the standard that Brent Scowcroft and Colin Powell followed during the presidencies of Gerald Ford and Ronald Reagan.

Three years after General Goodpaster retired from the Army, he was called back to active duty. His role was to help the United States Military Academy recover from that institution's worst ever cheating scandal. He volunteered to be demoted to the rank of lieutenant general when he became the Superintendent at West Point in 1977. This three-star rank was the appropriate one for a service academy superintendent. By the way, of all the prominent people I have known, General Goodpaster is very high on my list. His sense of duty as well as his contributions to America have never been adequately highlighted.

To return to the CNN story, I should point out that the CEO of CNN, Tom Johnson, wrote me a handwritten note the day I resigned. The first paragraph follows. "Thank you for seven years of splendid service as CNN's Military Affairs Analyst. I am very grateful to you for your professionalism and your dedication. You brought your wisdom, your vast network of armed services contacts, your loyalty and your time (nights, weekends, multiple trips between Augusta and the CNN center)."

LESSONS LEARNED FROM CNN'S NERVE GAS STORY

When I conduct my workshops on leadership, I tell the story of CNN's nerve gas debacle. I point out that what happened at CNN can occur in any organization if the proper safeguards are not in place. I then highlight what I feel are the greatest lessons. I always stress that more can be learned from failures than from successes.

So here goes with the lessons.

1. Do not hire someone who has a poor ethical background.
2. If someone shows up in your organization with questionable values, give that person close adult supervision.
3. Do not tolerate intimidation and do not be someone who intimidates others.
4. Make sure your organization has an inspector general and/or an ombudsman.
5. Provide your folks with an 800 number which will allow them to raise ethical issues anonymously.
6. Encourage criticism.
7. Make sure your organization has regular leadership and ethics educational programs.
8. In the aftermath of a failure find ways to turn the setback into something positive.

The Congressional Medal of Honor Foundation

For a period of twelve years, I had the privilege and pleasure of serving on the board of the Congressional Medal of Honor Foundation. For ten of those years I served as secretary of the Foundation board. I also served on the executive committee of the board. In 2002, I was asked to join the board by Medal of Honor recipient Jack Jacobs. Jack had been on the faculty of the National War College during the three years (1983-1986) I served as commandant. Since I had published a book on Medal of Honor recipient, Jimmie Dyess, Jack felt that I could assist with the first major new project of the Foundation - the creation and publication of a book, *Medal of Honor.*

Medal of Honor was published in 2003. This large tabletop book highlighted the stories of the living recipients of the Medal of Honor. Workman Press took on the project. Of the seven publishers I have worked with through the years, Workman Press was the best.

It was great fun working closely with Peter Collier, the author of the book. Peter, an award-winning author, did not have a military background. He seemed to value my background in military operations, particularly combat operations. My job was to go through each article and ensure that the information was accurate and easy to understand.

This gave me a chance to chat on the phone with many Medal of Honor recipients and to get to know them a bit. The book was a huge success. In the first ten years, more than 300,000 copies were published. Every high school in America received one or more copies. In addition to assisting with the editing of *Medal of Honor*, I helped with marketing and sales.

In addition to the work on the book, while I was on the board, Connor and I attended two Medal of Honor events each year: a fundraising dinner at the New York Stock Exchange and the annual Congressional Medal of Honor Society's conferences at various American cities. The Society, which consists exclusively of recipients, has held its annual meetings in American cities including Shreveport, Branson, Boston, Louisville, Chicago, Phoenix, Simi Valley, California, and Charleston, South Carolina. At the Louisville gala dinner, Connor performed as a soloist. The sustained standing ovation she received after her performance was a salute to her talent and to her father, Medal of Honor recipient, Jimmie Dyess. That evening the Governor of Kentucky presented Connor with a framed certificate. As of 2011, Connor Dyess Smith is an official Kentucky colonel.

HONORING JIMMIE DYESS AT CLEMSON UNIVERSITY AND IN PITTSBURGH

In 2004, two events took place which honored Jimmie Dyess in meaningful ways. At Clemson University, President Jim Barker presented Connor with an honorary degree for Clemson graduate, Jimmie Dyess. Honorary degrees which are presented at college and university graduations are quite common. However, it is rare for someone to receive a posthumous honorary degree. I was asked to give the graduation address. More than two thousand undergraduate, graduate and professional degrees were awarded that day. Thirteen thousand were in attendance.

Clemson University president Barker told me that I must restrict my address to eight minutes. In that short period of time I was able to tell the Jimmie Dyess story and to thank Clemson for honoring him in such a meaningful way. The person who came up with the idea of this award for Connor's father was Randy Smith, a close friend. Although Randy did not know Jimmie Dyess, he was familiar with his remarkable story. Doctor Smith was a distinguished graduate of Clemson and he served on the board of trustees of Clemson University for many years. Randy Smith was able to convince the board that Jimmie Dyess rather than journalist Tom Brokaw should be honored.

*Honoring Jimmie Dyess with Clemson
University's President, Jim Barker, 2004.*

In the fall of 2004, Connor and I flew to Pittsburgh. The Carnegie Hero Fund Commission was celebrating the 100th anniversary of the Commission. The renowned historian, David McCullough, was the afternoon speaker. A two-time recipient of the Pulitzer Prize as well as the recipient of the National Book Award and the Presidential Medal of Freedom, McCullough's topic was heroism. Much of his talk focused on his recently published book, *1776*.

I was chosen to be the banquet speaker that evening. In an audience of about four hundred were twenty-six recipients of the Carnegie Medal. In my short presentation, I told the Jimmie Dyess story. I emphasized the unique nature of Lieutenant Colonel Jimmie Dyess's accomplishments. I introduced Connor and pointed out that she was eight years old when she lost her father.

During the evening I took the opportunity to speak to a number of Carnegie Medal recipients. Two stories follow.

Carolyn Kelly was eighty-three years old when I spoke to her that evening. Two years earlier, at age eighty-one, she had climbed over a fence, swam out in a lake and rescued a woman who had gone under three times. I asked her why she had done it. She told me that her husband was too old and feeble - he could not get over the fence.

At this banquet a middle-aged man was kind enough to tell me his Carnegie Medal story. He had saved the life of a woman by pulling her out of a burning van. Both front doors were jammed so he had to pull her out from the back seat. He lifted her over the top of her seat and pulled her out a back door. I asked him if that was difficult. He smiled when he told me that she was disabled and could not assist him with her rescue. Also, she weighed more than three hundred pounds.

In 2004, the book, edited by Douglas Chambers, *A Century of Heroes* was published. In that book is a chapter which tells the Jimmie Dyess story. The following is a book review which I submitted to the amazon.com website.

"In 1904, Andrew Carnegie established the Carnegie Medal to recognize civilians who at great risk to their lives saved or attempted to save someone in grave danger. Carnegie wanted not only to recognize heroism but to help people who hurt themselves badly during the heroic act. Many great stories. In my judgment this book and the new book, *Medal of Honor* by Peter Collier should be in every home, every school and every library. We need role models and here they are. Both books are highly recommended."

MARK ALBERTIN AND FIVE VIDEOS

An Augusta resident, Mark Albertin is a producer of many fine videos. His skills with cameras, lighting, and drones are impressive. Mark and I have worked together to produce videos on Jimmie Dyess, Don Holleder, Hervey Cleckley and the Triple Nickel Fighter Squadron. The production of these videos is a creative experience in many dimensions.

This is how we tackle the task at hand. I write a rough script; Mark searches the internet to find the best videos, films and photos which relate to the story. He also finds narrators and appropriate voices for characters like Margaret Mitchell (who appears in the Cleckley video).

As the video comes together, Mark and I sit down, side-by-side in his office. Second-by-second we review the draft video and make dozens of adjustments. Once the video is complete and the front and back covers are designed, we send the disc off to have it reproduced. Most videos are given away. For instance, the Cleckley video was given to hundreds of psychologists who are especially interested in the psychopathic personality.

In 2020, during the corona virus lockdown period, Mark and I produced an eighty-minute video on executive leadership. This video was designed to assist Emory University and it's highly ranked Goizueta Business School. After the students had viewed the video, they had a chance to join me in a couple of Zoom sessions.

With the exception of the Triple Nickel video, all of Mark's videos are available on YouTube (see Appendix).

Chapter 13:

PRESERVING LEGACIES
AND OTHER PROJECTS

SINCE MOVING TO Augusta in 1990, I have been involved in many projects. I have written and/or updated my books, including the Jimmie Dyess book, my leadership book (along with my co-author, Jeff Foley) and *Assignment Pentagon* (out in its 5th edition in 2020 with co-author Dan Gerstein).

I am a regular contributor of articles for our local paper, *The Augusta Chronicle*. I help organize the annual Jimmie Dyess Symposium which is held each January at the Augusta Museum of History. The purpose of the Symposium is to preserve and enhance the legacy of Jimmie Dyess. I have assisted in increasing the monetary value of the Jimmie Dyess Symposium Endowment. With a corpus of more than $225,000, this endowment should ensure that the annual event which honors Connor's father will continue on for many decades into the future. In addition to highlighting Jimmie Dyess, I continue to work to preserve the legacies of Don Holleder, and Hervey Cleckley.

I continue to teach on a regular basis for Jeff Rosensweig's classes at the Goizueta Business School at Emory University. On one occasion, I taught for a class that my granddaughter, Dyess, was attending.

I love to play tennis and as long as it isn't too hot outside, during the autumn, winter and spring, I get on the court three times a week with some fine players. Interestingly, a study out of Europe concludes that playing tennis, on a regular basis, adds 9.3 years of healthy life - this may actually be true. Having played tennis for more than seventy years, I still jump (not very high) with joy when I hit a winner.

Shortly after moving to Augusta, I was encouraged by a close friend, Tom Kelleher, to join the Kiwanis Club of Augusta. One of the largest Kiwanis Clubs in the world, this club meets each Monday at the River Room at Saint Paul's Church. Many friendships have been established at these meetings. In addition to listening to fine speakers, I find opportunities to quietly raise funds for worthy causes at the weekly Kiwanis meetings. Connor is also a member of Kiwanis.

THE GENERAL PERRY SMITH PARKWAY

In 2008, I received a call from a good friend from Augusta, Cobbs Nixon. He told me that there was going to be a new parkway constructed in the vicinity of the Augusta Regional Airport. Cobbs then informed me that the parkway would be named in my honor. My immediate reaction - bad idea. I reminded him that I was not an Augusta native and, more importantly, I did not deserve the honor.

Also, I informed Cobbs that I believed that no public facility should be named for anyone who still is alive. The reason is quite simple. The

Perry Smith, Cobbs Nixon and Jay Forrester at the
General Perry Smith Parkway dedication, 2011.

honored person might get in big trouble. For instance, having a facility named after a person who ends up as a convicted felon is an embarrassment to the community.

Cobbs disagreed with me. He told me that the Augusta Airport Commission had approved the parkway and how it would be designated. He also explained that it was fitting that it be named for a military person. This was a good way to salute the tens of thousands of military personnel who call Augusta their home. He also stated that since I was a military airman, it was logical that a parkway circling part of our main airport should be named for me.

The General Perry Smith Parkway is short - less than two miles long. It connects the Doug Barnard Parkway to an industrial park. Unfortunately, the industrial park has not yet been built. The resolution by the Augusta Aviation Commission may be found in the Appendix.

AUGUSTA MUSEUM OF HISTORY: PERFORMING HISTORICAL CHARACTERS

For more than fifteen years, I have served on the board of trustees of the Augusta Museum of History. My first association with the museum took place in the 1990s. I was asked to make a significant financial contribution to a capital campaign which the museum was conducting. I agreed to lend support but I asked a favor in return. "Please construct a permanent exhibit honoring Jimmie Dyess." To the delight of the entire Dyess/Smith/Ewing family, a fine exhibit was built. Located on the second floor of the museum, this exhibit honors Marine Lieutenant Colonel A. J. Dyess and two ships, the USS Augusta and the USS Dyess.

A few years later, at the urging of a friend, Monty Osteen, I became a member of the board of trustees of this fully accredited museum. Later, I served as the chairman of the board. I now hold the position of chairman, emeritus of the board of trustees. Working with members of the board as well as the museum director, Nancy Glaser, and her fine staff has been a rewarding experience.

One of the most delightful activities I have participated in at the museum is as an actor. Each spring the museum hosts a popular fundraising event. *The Night at the Museum* is modeled after the movie which starred Robin Williams as Teddy Roosevelt.

Ten local individuals play roles of distinguished citizens who have had a close connection to Augusta in the past. Some examples are iconic baseball player, Ty Cobb, famous golfer, Bobby Jones, actress, Butterfly McQueen, and groundbreaking musician, James Brown. Each actor is given four minutes to perform as the historical figure.

Every year I volunteer to play a different role. It was fascinating to conduct the research and then play the role of former President Dwight David Eisenhower, World War II prisoner of war and top American held in Stalag Luft III, Colonel Charlie Goodrich, the famous Augusta psychiatrist, Doctor Hervey Cleckley and Confederate General James Longstreet. Of course, I knew Goodrich (Connor's stepfather) and Cleckley (Connor's uncle).

In 2020, I played the role of Augusta native and Civil War General, James Longstreet. Six weeks before the date, I started to grow a beard so that I could be "in character" for my performance. Needless to say, Connor was not pleased with the beard. The morning after the event, the beard departed the scene - never to return.

I especially enjoyed playing the role of General Longstreet since it gave me the chance to emphasize Longstreet's efforts after the Civil War to assist former slaves. No former Confederate general did more to fight against Jim Crow activities throughout the South.

Perry Smith playing the role of General James Longstreet, 2020.

Keeping a museum in solid financial shape is quite a challenge. For a history museum to maintain accreditation from the American Alliance of Museums, it must meet and maintain a number of specific standards This requires certain staff expertise, strict storage standards, and specific heat and humidity controls. With only modest support from the Augusta/Richmond County Commission, the Augusta Museum of History must be very aggressive each year with its fundraising efforts.

The Augusta Museum of History, 2020.

In recent decades, my role has been to help raise funds for the annual Jimmie Dyess Symposium. The first $50,000 raised each year goes directly into the budget of the museum. The next $10,000 goes into the Museum's endowment, the remainder of the funds (about $10,000) goes directly into the Jimmie Dyess Symposium Endowment. Raising $70,000 year after year has been quite a challenge.

The purpose of the Jimmie Dyess Symposium Endowment is very specific. This endowment guarantees that this Symposium will continue for many decades into the future. In this way the legacy of Augusta's greatest hero will be preserved.

Among the individuals who have received the Dyess Symposium's Distinguished American Award are noted journalist Judy Woodruff, the granddaughter of President Eisenhower, Susan Eisenhower, former Georgia Governor Carl Sanders, Congressman Doug Barnard, noted football coach and athletic director Vince Dooley, and wounded veteran and former major league baseball player, Lou Brissie. All of these citizens have a close connection to the Augusta area.

Other civilian recipients of the Distinguished American Award include Ann Boardman, Dick Daniel, Jane Howington, Brian and Neita Mulherin, Doug Hastings, Terry Elam, Julius Scott, Barbara Dooley, Gloria Norwood, Fred Gehle, Beverly Barnhart, Theodore R. Britton, Jr. and Billy Morris.

A living Medal of Honor recipient is honored at every Dyess Symposium. In the first eleven years of the symposium the following Medal of Honor recipients who received the Distinguished American Award were: Jack Jacobs, Bruce Crandall, Tom Kelley, Hal Fritz, Sammy Davis, Al Rascon, Barney Barnum, Roger Donlon, Joe Marm, Jim Livingston, and Mike Rose.

These men are saluted both for their heroism and for their lifetime commitment to worthy causes. Augusta is the only city in America

Dyess Symposium honorees, University President Julius Scott, Journalist Judy Woodruff, and Medal of Honor recipient, Sammy Davis, 2017.

The River Room at Saint Paul's Church, 2010.

which hosts an event where a living Medal of Honor recipient is honored each year.

The most rewarding activity which I have been involved in since moving to Augusta took place in the summer of 2007. It was a capital campaign in support of Saint Paul's Church. Because of the lack of sufficient funding, the upper floors of the large Children's Ministry Center had been unfinished for many years.

In the spring of 2007, the contractor, who had previously committed to complete the construction project, presented the leaders of Saint Paul's church with an ultimatum. He stated that he could not stick with the price he had quoted a number of years previously. This contractor needed a construction go-ahead decision within three months or his price would go up.

A major decision was made by the leadership team of Saint Paul's

Church - a crisis capital campaign would be waged. We would, by golly, raise the $1.2 million and we would do it in three months. One million dollars were already available from a previous capital campaign. Hence the total cost of the project would be $2.2 million.

Since an earlier capital campaign was still underway, this goal seemed to be wildly ambitious. In a moment of recklessness, I agreed to be the co-chair of this campaign. I had no experience in raising funds for capital campaigns. Lee Robertson, who was more familiar with how to raise funds for worthy causes, agreed to be the other co-chair. She had been involved in previous fundraising campaigns at Saint Paul's.

My research took me to a wonderful book, *Megagifts*. It taught me how to ask for large donations. The basic thesis of this book was "always ask BIG." If you think someone can give $50,000, ask for $100,000. Also, always ASK. Never leave a fund-raising meeting without asking.

Initially, our committee tried to get one of the wealthy parishioners to commit to $500,000. The leadership of Saint Paul's would agree to dedicate the main room to that person, and, if necessary, name the room in his/her honor. That approach failed. No one was willing to make such a large financial commitment.

The fallback plan was to visit with a number of wealthy parishioners and ask for contributions of $100,000. If we could get six folks to agree to that number, the church leaders felt the rest of the needed funds could be raised. By meeting with people individually, this approach worked out quite well.

One parishioner agreed to $100K in less than one minute. Others took a bit longer. Within about a month, five folks had contributed $100,000 and three folks, $50,000. This took us past the halfway mark; the rest of the commitments came in within the next three months. People were asked to pay up front and most did. Hence the construction loan was quite small and was paid off quickly.

My favorite story during this exciting period was as follows. I approached a widow who was in her late 70s. She did not attend St. Paul's but two of her children did. When we met for coffee, she knew that I was going to ask for a contribution to Saint Paul's Upper Room Capital Campaign. Just as we sat down, she said, "Perry, my husband's estate has just settled. I want you to help me decide how to give money away." What a delightful surprise and a marvelous opportunity.

She then told me that her children were all in fine shape financially, so she could be quite generous. She wanted to confine her contributions to good causes in the local area. I immediately asked for $100,000 for St. Paul's. I don't think she thought I would ask for such a high number - but she said, "I will give you $50,000 and I will get my son to give another $50,000."

In another one-on-one meeting I asked parishioner, Pen Mayson, this question, "Which parishioners are capable of giving $100,00?" I gave him a list I had previously prepared. He liked the list but then he said. "You do not have everyone on your list." I asked him who I had left off. Pen said, "you and me."

Shortly thereafter a meeting was held with a small group of parishioners from Saint Paul's. In the meeting was a good friend, Dudley Baird, who had spent his professional life as a stock broker. Dudley, when he heard my story, was very frank. He said, "Pen is trying to tell you something, Perry. He is telling you that he wants to give $100,000. He just wants to be asked." Sure enough, I went back to Pen's house and asked him for the big number and he agreed.

After Pen suggested that I should be able to contribute at the $100K level, I gave his idea considerable thought. I then raised the issue with Connor. She immediately broke into tears. Her tears were tears of joy - she was delighted that we were able to make such a large contribution. St. Paul's had meant so much to her ever since she heard Father Charles Schilling preach when Connor was still in college. We had married at St Paul's, as had our daughter. Our two granddaughters were both baptized at St Paul's. The church had been an important part of our lives for many years.

In three months of active campaigning, $1.2 million was raised and construction started soon after. The upper rooms at Saint Paul's Church were opened with great fanfare in the summer of 2008. These rooms consist of a large banquet hall (the River Room), a smaller meeting room (the Berlin Room) and a commercial grade kitchen. The River Room is an ideal venue for wedding receptions. It is the most elegant large meeting room in the entire Augusta/Aiken area.

At this point I would like to highlight a number of aspects of Saint Paul's church. In the early years of the 21st Century, Saint Paul's went through a difficult ten year period. The rector was so substandard in his performance that the senior warden, Vince Shivers, asked me to make the case for this departure. After doing so in an oral presentation to the vestry of Saint Paul's, the rector, in a letter to the Bishop, stated that I was an evil person. The rector also stated that he was going to deny communion to Connor and me. Since we no longer felt

The Rector of Saint Paul's church, George Muir and his wife, Susan, 2020.

welcome at Saint Paul's Church, Connor and I left Saint Paul's and began attending the Church of the Good Shepherd.

The arrival of a new rector, George Muir, in 2014, was a godsend. Within a few months Connor and I returned to the church that had meant so much to us for so many years. George and Susan Muir had planned to stay for eighteen months but they fell in love with Augusta and with Saint Paul's. The Muirs will stay in Augusta after he retires. I am sure they will play important roles in our church and with the greater Augusta community.

When word got around Augusta that I had skills as a fundraiser, I was approached by folks, some of whom I did not know. Very soon, I was raising funds for the soon-to-be constructed Fisher House. This five-million-dollar facility was constructed within walking distance of the large VA hospital on Wrightsboro Road in Augusta. Pete Caye, who was leading the campaign, asked for my help. The campaign had slowed down and Pete asked me to help give it a boost.

The story of Fisher Houses is worth telling. In the 1980s the wife of the Chief of Naval Operations, Mrs. Carlisle Trost, was visiting the Naval Hospital in Bethesda, Maryland. As she walked through the parking lot, she noticed a young woman sleeping in her car with a young baby in her arms.

Mrs. Trost inquired about the woman's situation and was told that her husband was undergoing long-term care in the hospital and she could not afford a motel. This led Mrs. Trost to tell the story to a wealthy real estate developer from New York, Mr. Arnold Fisher. Soon thereafter Mr. Fisher initiated a program that was to provide houses within walking distance of military hospitals. These "Fisher Houses" provide free lodging for family members like the lady in the car.

The rules for the Fisher Houses were established as follows. The Fisher Foundation would provide half the cost of construction and furnishings. The other half would have to be raised by the local community. In Augusta in 2008 there was already a Fisher House near the Eisenhower hospital at Fort Gordon. However, there was no Fisher House near either of the VA hospitals in Augusta.

Soon after agreeing to assist, I decided to write a hand-written thank-you note to everyone who had already contributed $1000 or more. I wrote about twenty-five notes. I stressed that more funds were needed (we were about one million dollars short of the goal).

One generous person had already contributed $50,000. Soon after he received my note, he contributed another $50,000. One of the lessons I have learned is that there are people who give and give and give. Although there is certainly a problem with "donor fatigue" in the Augusta area, some folks never suffer from this syndrome. Over time, I have learned who many of these people are.

Returning to the topic of raising funds for the Fisher House, I contacted the CEO of Lockheed Martin, Bob Stevens, by email. At this time Bob and I were serving on the board of the Congressional Medal of Honor Foundation. I asked Mr. Stevens for support for the Fisher House. A commitment of $250,000 was soon forthcoming.

This large contribution led to great excitement among many in Augusta. There was so much momentum behind the campaign for the Fisher House that the goal was exceeded by about $200,000. This led to some unplanned additions that made the Fisher House on Wrightsboro Road in Augusta one the very best in America.

In the second decade of the 21st Century, I spent much of my time working to support ForcesUnited (formally called The Augusta Warrior Project). Fundraising was a real challenge for the President, Kim Elle, and the entire board. Although I no longer serve on the board, I continue to be an advocate for this cause and to lend financial support each year. ForcesUnited provides support for many of the sixty-six thousand veterans in the Augusta-Aiken area. Areas where help is provided include housing, education, health, and financial support.

In 2019, I worked closely with the officials at Christ Community Health Services (CCHS) as they considered the creation of an endowment. This fine Augusta institution is committed to serving those low-income people and families who cannot afford high-priced medical care. With facilities at two locations in downtown Augusta, CCHS has demonstrated impressive growth in its first ten years. An endowment was initiated in July, 2019. Assisting in this effort has been another of my pleasurable activities in recent years.

As I Entered the World of Geezerhood, I Got Involved in Various Projects

In 2016, an effort was undertaken to preserve the legacy of Dr Hervey Cleckley, Connor's uncle. Mark Albertin worked his magic and, in 2018, the DVD (*Hervey M Cleckley: A Man for All Seasons*) was released. Cleckley, a true polymath, lived a remarkable life (see Appendix). Doctor Cleckley was a pioneer in two areas of psychiatry: the psychopathic personality and the multiple personality. Two of his books were best sellers: *The Mask of Sanity* and *The Three Faces of Eve.*

In 2016, I was invited to a dinner in Las Vegas. The United States Air Force's 555th Fighter Squadron had deployed from its permanent base in Italy to Nellis Air Force Base in Nevada. This squadron was spending three months of extensive training at Nellis. The commander of the squadron invited me to be the dinner speaker at a "Dining Out" at the Nellis Air Force Base's Officers Club. Having flown with the Triple Nickel Fighter Squadron during the Vietnam War forty-eight years earlier, I decided to tell some combat stories. That evening it was clear that there was great interest among the young pilots in the stories of life at Udorn, Thailand.

This event in Nevada led to the creation of a 55-minute video, *Flying Combat with the Triple Nickel.* (see Appendix B). I had one thousand DVDs produced. Many were handed out as gifts to former "Nickels" and to every pilot currently assigned to the Triple Nickel.

Thanks to the assistance of my computer guru here in Augusta, Dan Doughtie, a website (genpsmith.com) was created. It includes some of my journal articles as well as details on the Dyess Symposium. Also, information on my books and videos is included. In addition, Dan assisted me in creating and updating my page on Wikipedia.

One of the activities which has given me great pleasure is writing articles for various journals. About once a month an eight-hundred-word article is published in the Augusta Chronicle. In one case, I wrote an article praising the organist and choirmaster at Saint Paul's Church. The rector at Saint Paul's Church was threatening to fire him; I thought this article might help save his job. Happily the organist stayed and the flawed rector left.

When I am trying to gain support for a local worthy cause, I often write an article explaining how folks can assist. Each year, I help raise funds for the Dyess Symposium, Saint Paul's Church, the Christ Community Health Services, the local Boy Scouts, and Heritage Academy.

The Heritage Academy is a private, Christian based, school in downtown Augusta. It provides a first-class and highly disciplined academic environment to children from kindergarten through eighth grade. These children are largely from poor families who are not satisfied with the public schools in Augusta.

Each child must wear a uniform, must not be a discipline problem and must maintain regular attendance. The parents, grandparents or guardians must pay a small monthly fee. The record of performance of these children is outstanding. Observing the enthusiasm of these young children as they learn "Singapore Math" is a sight to behold.

An important event occurred on the 15th of September, 2017 in Portland, Oregon. Our son married a lovely lady, Althea Mina Alabab. This date was a special one. It was three years to the day from when they first met and one year from the day they became engaged. Althea is a delightful, funny, upbeat person - we are delighted that she is a member of our family.

This memoir would not be complete without the acknowledgment of our close friendship of almost thirty years with Jane and Jerry Howington. After we arrived in Augusta, Connor began attending a weekly bible study session led by Jane Howington. Connor soon became Jane's reader and continued that role for many years. Over time Jerry and Jane Howington became our dear friends. They invited us to the mountains for many summers and we became regular dinner partners on Thursday nights in Augusta.

Friendships in Augusta have greatly enriched our lives. These friends include Maggie Chew, Martha Scroggs, Joan Walker, Ann Kilpatrick, Roy and Sarah Simkins, Billy and Sissie Morris, Dan and Linda McCall, Reab and Joy Berry, Edo and Mary Anne Douglass, George and Louise Sheftall, Bowdre and Lynn Mays, Ed and Martha Moody, Pierce and Gina Blitch, Cobbs and Minta Nixon, Rex and Lou Teeslink, Anthony and Ann Ewell, Bob and Pat Crumrine.

Other Augustans who have deeply touched our lives include Ann Boardman, Catherine Boardman, Jeff and Beth Foley, Woody and Ginger Trulock, Steve and Kim Elle, Karen Phelps, Reab and Shell Berry, Turner and Tara Simkins, Billy and Julie Badger, Ashley Wright, Eleanor Taylor, Bob Kirby, Ted and Nancy Hussey, Clay Coleman, Keith and June Shafer, Jed and Heather Howington, Nan Connell, Clay Boardman, Braye and Tori Boardman, Becky Smith, Pete and Anne Way, Jeff Knox, Dudley and Soleta Baird, Monty and Molly Osteen, Craig Bryant and so many more.

The Georgia Aviation Hall of Fame: The 2021 Enshrinement Event

My close friend and West Point classmate, Doc Bahnsen, nominated me to be an inductee in the Georgia Aviation Hall of Fame. He then beat the bushes for votes on my behalf. Members of various organizations were contacted and many voted in support. These included Red River Rats, Daedalians, National War College alumni, West Point graduates, and Augusta Kiwanians.

The Red River Rats are a group of aviators who flew over North Vietnam during the Vietnam War. Formed in 1934, the Order of Daedalians was composed of those commissioned officers who, no later than the Armistice of 1918, held ratings as pilots of heavier-than-air powered aircraft. As these airmen died, they were replaced by others on a one-for-one basis. The River Rats and the Daedalians support many worthy causes - all relating to military aviation.

The 2020 Georgia Aviation Hall of Fame ceremony was scheduled for April, 2020. Due to the Covid-19 pandemic, the event was postponed until 17 April, 2021. On that date, I will join two other Georgia aviators as we are "enshrined" in the Georgia Aviation Hall of Fame.

Many of my family and friends should be able to attend. I was especially pleased that nephews, godsons, and cousins will attend, along with their family members. Also, coming will be West Point classmates, Augusta friends, Air Force friends, Emory friends and many others. Incidentally, the Georgia Aviation Hall of Fame is located at the aviation museum at Warner Robins Air Force Base in central Georgia.

Rendering of Perry Smith at the
Georgia Aviation Hall of Fame, 2021.

Chapter Fourteen:

THE FAMILY OF PERRY
AND CONNOR SMITH

THIS MEMOIR WOULD not be complete without a description of family members who have defined and enriched my life. It all started when I met Connor Cleckley Dyess in December, 1957. I had just passed my twenty-third birthday. Connor was twenty-two.

CONNOR DYESS SMITH

I have now come to the hard part in the writing of this memoir. Connor is a special person in so many ways. I think it is important that I try to explain who she is and how much she means to me, to her family and to so many others. The fact that she is such a lovely person, striking in her beauty, and so talented as a singer and actor, it is easy to overlook her other wondrous intellectual, emotional and spiritual qualities.

Connor comes from a distinguished family. She lived for years in the shadow of the accomplishments of her father, Jimmie Dyess, her uncle, Hervey Cleckley and her step-father, Charlie Goodrich. Her father, Jimmie Dyess was killed in combat when Connor was only eight years old. As an only child she had no siblings to lean on. Her mother was so devastated by the loss of her husband that she was unable, for a time, to give Connor loving support.

When Connor was a very small child she loved to sing with her dad. Jimmie Dyess had a fine voice and he helped inspire her love of music. Connor sang her first solo when she was nine years old. She was in the children's choir at Reid Memorial Presbyterian Church at the time. At Randolph Macon Women's College in Lynchburg, Virginia,

Connor was a music major. She sang as a soloist in a number of musical productions. When she transferred to the University of Georgia at the end of her sophomore year, she planned to be a music major. Although she ended up majoring in English, she continued to sing in many productions. When I first met Connor, she had recently graduated from the University of Georgia and was working as a surgical technician at the Medical College of Georgia, where her Uncle, Dr. Cleckley, was a professor. After we married and moved immediately to Europe, she worked as a staff aide for the Red Cross.

As was common among college educated women in the early 1960s, once McCoy came along, she stayed home to raise the kids and later to support the social obligations of an Air Force officer's spouse.

One of my special recollections of Connor was when she was a soloist in a Junior League production in Englewood, New Jersey in 1965. Connor was performing as a soloist on stage. Sitting in the audience just in front of me was a man who leaned over to his friend and said, "I am in love with that lady." I leaned forward and whispered in his ear, "So am I and I am her husband."

In Colorado Springs, Connor played and sang the role of Gretel in Hansel and Gretel. I was sitting in the audience with our daughter Serena, who was three years old at that time. When the witch was about to throw Hansel into the fire, Serena screamed out loudly "Don't throw my Mommy in the fire." An audience of 800 burst into laughter. After the production, I took Serena backstage to meet some of the performers. Upon seeing the witch, Serena screamed in terror.

Our son, McCoy, had a different reaction when he watched Connor perform. We were living in Florida and McCoy was six years old. Connor was rehearsing for a variety show based roughly on a weekly TV show, "Laugh-in." Starring Dan Rowan and Dick Martin, "Laugh-in" was really silly but wildly popular. During each show, the actress, Goldie Hawn, would suddenly appear on stage, shouting/singing out "Sock it to me, sock it to me, sock it to me."

In her rehearsal, Connor did the "sock it to me" routine to the tune of Wagner's *Song of the Valkyrie*. McCoy, from the back of the audience, spoke out quite loudly, "That sounds silly Mommy." Everyone at the rehearsal laughed heartily.

The same age as Julie Andrews, Connor was often mistaken for Julie when she was on stage or sometimes out in public.

One of Connor's notable talents is her grasp of the English language. She has been the editor for my seven books and for hundreds of my magazine and newspaper articles. When I wrote my dissertation in 1966, she was able to read my scribbles. She was also a fine typist during the early years of our marriage.

Family vacations were so important to Connor. She felt the best vacation was our 50th wedding anniversary trip to France in 2009. Carefully planned by our daughter, Serena, we spent a week in Paris and a week in the Loire Valley.

PERRY McCOY SMITH, III

Our son, Perry McCoy Smith, III, arrived on July 10th, 1962 at Saint Francis Cabrini Hospital in Alexandria, Louisiana. McCoy was a sweet boy from day one - such a joy. McCoy was an early talker and reader and to this day ranks among the list of the smartest people I know. Quiet, serene, loving and remarkably intelligent, McCoy has brought us happiness in so many ways.

When McCoy was three years old, our family was visiting our good friends (the Charlie Mays) in their home in New Town, NY. McCoy went off happily to play with the many May kids. As darkness approached, McCoy was nowhere to be seen. The entire May and Smith families spread out all over the neighborhood. We found McCoy quietly exploring the quiet neighborhood with no idea that he might be lost. He was greeted with great relief by all of us. His reaction was - what is all the excitement about?

During the year I was in Thailand, Connor and the kids lived in our home at Woodmoor in Colorado. She took great care of McCoy and Serena. They made one memorable trip during that year. Along with Connor's aunt, Louise Rigsby, Connor and the kids flew to Jackson Hole.

When they were visiting Yellowstone, Louise gave McCoy and Serena five dollars each to spend in the park. Six-year-old McCoy, instead of purchasing something for himself, bought a small ceramic figure of Bambi. It was a present for his mother. Connor was very touched by his thoughtfulness and generosity. That event, in many ways, defined the life that McCoy would lead. McCoy also came up with a fine quote. When he smelled the Sulphur fumes coming out of the ground at Yellowstone, he said, "It smells like somebody did not find all of their Easter eggs."

McCoy did well in his schoolwork as he attended schools in many locations. He was salutatorian of his high school class and graduated with honors from college (Colorado State University). He was invited to be a member of Tau Beta Pi. This society honors engineering students in American universities who have shown a history of academic achievement as well as a commitment to personal and professional integrity.

After graduating from college in 1984, McCoy's work pattern was as follows. One year working as a mechanical engineer for the US Navy at Point Magu, California was followed by three years as an examiner at the US Patent Office. In the evenings, he commuted to Baltimore to pursue a master's degree in liberal arts.

He saved up enough money to pay for law school at the University of Virginia. After graduating in 1991, he worked in Washington, DC and then New York for the patent law firm, Kenyon and Kenyon. From his office at #1 Broadway, he had a spectacular view of the Statue of Liberty and the great expanse of water where the Hudson River and the East River empty into the Atlantic Ocean.

In the year 2000 McCoy was off to Portland, Oregon to work for the Intel Corporation as a patent and intellectual property attorney. Twenty years later, at age 57, he retired from Intel and hung out his shingle as an attorney. His small firm, Lex Pan Law, is a full-service technology and intellectual property law firm, based in Portland, Oregon.

His marriage to Althea in 2017 has been a real blessing. McCoy and Althea have two children, Jacob and Perry McCoy Smith IV.

SERENA CONNOR VERFURTH

Our daughter Serena arrived on Augusta 7th, 1964, at Holy Name Hospital in Teaneck, New Jersey. She weighed a robust nine pounds, three ounces.

Here are some stories of Serena's youth. When she was 18 months old, she was asked, "Who was George Washington?" Her answer - "a bridge." We gave her high marks, after all she was less than two years old. We lived in New Jersey and I drove across the George Washington Bridge daily to get to graduate school at Columbia University. She must have heard us having the regular discussion about what the traffic was like on the George Washington Bridge.

When she was about 20 months old, a woman was visiting us at our home in Teaneck, New Jersey. The woman lit up a cigarette (not an unusual act in 1966). Serena said quite loudly and boldly, "IT'S A MATTER OF LIFE AND BREATH." Clearly Serena was learning lots of important stuff from watching TV.

On arrival at the Air Force Academy in the summer of 1966, our small family moved into a house on the base. Our next-door neighbor was our friend, Bob Kelley. Bob was an All-American lacrosse player from Rutgers University. He and I played in the North-South Lacrosse All Star game in June, 1956 and were fellow fighter pilots.

Bob and his wife, Marty, had nine children including two-year-old Diane. Diane and Serena soon became fast friends. One day, upon returning from work, I was greeted by Diane Kelley. She came up to me and said quite loudly, "Where Rene, where Rene?" That is how Serena got her nickname. Two-year-old Diane could not pronounce Serena, so Rene (pronounced *ree nee*) had to do.

Like her brother, Serena was a fine student. She attended three high schools in three separate countries (Germany, the Netherlands and America). She made friends easily and enjoyed every school with the exception of the all-girls Catholic school, Saint Mary's Academy in Alexandria, Virginia.

At Saint Mary's she found the administrators and many of the nuns very rigid and cold. In addition, it was difficult to transfer in the middle of your junior year of high school to a place where many of the girls had been together since kindergarten.

Saint Mary's was a private college prep school in the excellent academic environment of Northern Virginia. Serena didn't like it, but she learned how to study! After a year and a half of the rigors of Saint

Mary's, Serena found the academics at college to be quite manageable.

On graduation Serena hoped to attend the University of Virginia but I had maintained residency in the state of Ohio and out of state admission for UVA was very exclusive. Having been turned down by UVA, she decided to attend the University of the South in Sewanee, Tennessee. It was a way to explore her southern roots, since she had never lived in the South, but she was "half southern."

Serena was a member of the women's soccer team. Her skills were her speed and her passing ability. Even as a freshman she got lots of playing time.

Serena spent her junior year on scholarship in Germany at the University of Heidelberg. Shortly before graduation from the University of the South in 1986, Serena Smith was invited to become a member of Phi Beta Kappa, following in the footsteps of her great uncle, Hervey Cleckley. Serena graduated Magna Cum Laude with a degree in psychology. What an exciting time for the whole family!

After graduation from college, Serena pursued a master's degree at the Georgia Institute of Technology in Atlanta, Georgia. Her field was industrial engineering with a focus on human computer interaction. She interned for James River Corporation in Neenah, Wisconsin and Richmond, Virginia. While in Richmond, she started dating Robert Verfurth, whose father I had known since I was a West Point cadet. Rob and Serena married in Augusta in September, 1990.

After graduate school, Serena worked for Andersen Consulting helping companies move from text-based computer systems to more user-friendly graphical user interface. These projects and several promotions for both Serena and Rob took them to Atlanta, Chattanooga, TN, Hartford, CT and Manhattan. After being certain that she did not have the disposition to be a stay at home mom, she had her first child in late 1995. Dyess couldn't talk but convinced Serena to stay home and raise her.

Serena moved 26 times before she got married and another five times after that. But she, Rob and the girls have been in San Diego, CA since 1998. Although Serena never went back to paid work, she has served as a parent-teacher club president, on the local land use planning board, as a room mom, art teacher, soccer and cross country team manager to name a few of her many volunteer roles. She volunteers at the local animal shelter in San Diego to this day.

We are so proud of our two children - they are very different in many ways. McCoy is a serious hard-working attorney who excelled as a corporate attorney for the Intel Corporation. Serena has been a loving mother to two special ladies, Dyess and Porter. She has been a great help with this book. She taught me how to use Google Doc and is a first-class editor.

DYESS MCCOY VERFURTH

Our first grandchild arrived on October 17th, 1995. She was born in the Norwalk Hospital in Norwalk, Connecticut. When she was two years old Dyess moved with her family from Darien, Connecticut to San Diego, California. A serious student and a fine athlete, Dyess was recognized as the Female Student/Athlete of the year when she graduated from Westview High School in 2014. She was captain of her high school cross country team both her junior and senior years. Her first choice for college was Emory University.

Having taken many AP courses in high school and scoring high on the tests, Dyess was able to validate a semester's worth of courses at Emory. She ran all four years on the cross country and distance track teams at Emory. She was captain of the team her senior year.

In 2018, after just four years at Emory, she graduated with both a bachelor of business administration and master's degree in professional accounting. She was invited to be a member of Beta Alpha Psi, the accounting honor society. After passing the four parts of the CPA exam in the summer of 2018, she joined the audit practice of the large public accounting firm, Deloitte, in October 2018. We are so proud of Dyess.

PORTER CLECKLEY VERFURTH

Porter was born on November 20th, 1997 at the Norwalk hospital in Norwalk, Connecticut. Just a few months after she was born, she was off with her family to San Diego where she would spend her youth. After an early interest in soccer and lacrosse, Porter shifted her attention in high school to cross country and long-distance track. Like her sister Dyess, Porter was a fine student, a good athlete and a natural leader. Out of her high school class of more than 600 she graduated in the top thirty.

Porter followed in her sister's footsteps and was Female Scholar/Athlete when she graduated from Westview High School in 2016. Westview is one of the most outstanding public schools in San Diego County. Porter headed to her first choice, Emory University in 2016. Again, following in the footsteps of her sister, Porter ran for the Emory varsity cross country and long-distance track teams.

In 2017 Porter decided to leave Emory and launch herself into a number of adventures. In the fall of 2017, she created her own "semester abroad." First, she participated in a fifty-day Outward Bound instructor's course in the Pacific Northwest, learning to teach sea kayaking in the San Juan islands and backpacking, mountaineering, rock climbing and orienteering in and around North Cascades National Park. She also obtained a Wilderness First Responder certification. This was an extremely rigorous and demanding course but Porter came through with flying colors. Next, Porter flew to Asia to attend a 22-day, 200 hour, Yoga Teacher Training course in Bali, Indonesia.

Porter returned to the United States where she spent the spring of 2018 attending Santa Barbara City College. Her next college experience was two years at the University of Colorado at Boulder. She graduated with distinction with a degree in philosophy in May, 2020. The graduation ceremony has been postponed because of the Covid-19 pandemic. Like her mother and great uncle, Hervey Cleckley, Porter was invited to be a member of Phi Beta Kappa. A gifted writer, a vegan, a deep thinker and an adventurer, Porter amazes us with her willingness to take on tough challenges. We are so proud of her.

PERRY McCOY SMITH, IV

Perry was born in Portland, Oregon in the fall of 2010. A happy child from birth, Perry was diagnosed with autism before his second birthday. Since that time, he has received high quality therapy, first in Denver and, since age seven, in Portland. He has a first-class mind and is especially good with numbers. He loves being with his Dad and shows great affection towards him.

JACOB ALABAB MOSER

Jacob was born in 1998 in Hawaii. A fine student through his youth, he showed at an early age that he was gifted in the arts - dancing, singing, painting, and photography. He attended Brown University on a scholarship. During his college summers Jacob served as an intern to the State Department in Mexico and in Washington DC. With international relations as his major, Jacob graduated with honors in 2020. Also in 2020, he was invited to be a member of Phi Beta Kappa. Just prior to college graduation he earned a Fulbright Scholarship. Jacob's future is very bright indeed.

*Six family members at Dyess's graduation
from Emory University, 2018.*

Sock hop in San Diego, 2003.

The Robert Verfurth family with kitties, 2020.

*McCoy and
Perry IV, 2013.*

*McCoy and
Perry IV, 2020.*

McCoy, Althea and Jacob, 2020.

In Conclusion

At this point I will conclude this memoir by summarizing the major insights I have gained from the setbacks and failures I have encountered in my event-filled life of more than eight-five years.

1. Recovering from failures. My failures have taught me that recovery cannot take place without the assistance of many talented and dedicated people.
2. Having failed so often and in so many ways, I have learned to tolerate the failure of others.
3. If I had not failed, my life would probably not have been as worthwhile and fulfilling. For example, failing in my job in the Pentagon led to my assuming the very best possible job only two years later. Also, my failure on the lacrosse field taught me how to deal with intimidation. Finally, my failing to stop CNN from making a major mistake led to a number of benefits to the warriors who fought so heroically in Operation Tailwind.

Appendix A:

PUBLISHED BOOKS

One of the challenges of book publishing is marketing the book widely. In 1988, I was fortunate to find an ally and friend, Bill Donnis. Mr. Donnis works for Byrrd Enterprises, the book wholesaler for Army, Air Force Exchange Service (AAFES). Bill not only loves books he also has a keen understanding of which books will be of interest to military professionals and their families.

Bill Donnis has been helpful to me with my leadership and Pentagon books. For many years he has displayed them prominently in hundreds of AAFES stores around the world. He is responsible for the sale of tens of millions of books and at least 20,000 of my books.

Most of my published books have died a quiet and early death. One of my favorite stories relates to the non-success of my first book, *The Air Force Plans for Peace: 1943-1945*. Three years after publication I received a royalty check for fifty-seven cents. A year later, I was offered the opportunity to purchase a large number of copies for ten cents per pound. Since the book weighed less than a pound, I purchased a few copies for five cents each - what a bargain.

On the other hand, three of my books did reasonably well.

Assignment Pentagon

Assignment Pentagon has remained the only substantive guide to the Puzzle Palace for more than thirty years. With the publication in 2020 of the 5th edition, it should remain useful well into the fourth decade of the 21st Century. This book is helpful to new arrivals in the Pentagon and to scholars of Defense Policy and National Security Policy. Also, those interested in how to get things done in large, bureaucratic organizations may find this book of interest.

Assignment Pentagon was first published in 1988. More than 50,000 copies are in circulation. For the 4th and 5th editions I joined up with a recently retired army colonel, Dan Gerstein. Since I had not served in the Pentagon for more than twenty years, I needed help with the later editions. Gerstein is a brilliant writer and a joy to work with.

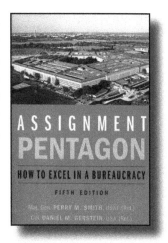

Courage, Compassion Marine: The Unique Story of Jimmie Dyess

Another of my books is a biography of an American hero. *Courage, Compassion Marine: The Unique Story of Jimmie Dyess* tells of the life of the only person to have received America's two highest awards for heroism. As a young undergraduate at Clemson College, Jimmie Dyess saved the lives of two swimmers who were in desperate shape off the coast of South Carolina. He earned the Carnegie Medal that day. Sixteen years later, as a Marine Corps battalion commander, Dyess's heroism in combat earned him the Medal of Honor. An Eagle scout and an All American college marksman, Marine Lieutenant Colonel A. J. Dyess is honored every January in his hometown of Augusta, Georgia.

Rules and Tools for Leaders

With more than 350,000 copies in print, *Rules and Tools for Leaders,* has been my most successful book. It was given a big boost in 1999 when Katie Couric interviewed me on the Today Show. The interview went well, and Katie recommended the book to the television viewers. By the end of that day, the

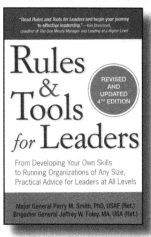

book had reached number two on amazon.com. It has been used for many years at the Goizueta Business School at Emory University. Each year, every scholar in the Executive MBA, the MBA and the BBA programs receive a signed copy. It is also used at West Point.

My three other books are of lesser interest: *How CNN Fought the War: A View from the Inside, Long Range Planning for National Security* and *The Air Force Plans for Peace: 1943-1945.*

Appendix B:

___

FOUR VIDEOS WITH MARK ALBERTIN

Twice a Hero: The Jimmie Dyess Story

This sixty-minute video includes combat footage from the World War II battle for the Marshall Islands. It also includes interviews with people who knew Dyess as a boy scout, as an undergraduate at Clemson and as a Marine. An interview with the president of Clemson, Jim Barker, is also included.

When Duty Calls: The Life and Legacy of Don Holleder

Don Holleder of Rochester, New York was an Eagle Scout and a graduate of West Point. He was a first team All American football player and is a member of the College Football Hall of Fame. He had a distinguished military career in the Army receiving the Soldiers Medal and the Distinguished Service Cross.

Hervey M. Cleckley: A Man for All Seasons

Hervey Cleckley of Augusta, Georgia was an outstanding athlete in four sports, a Rhodes Scholar, a distinguished physician, an inspiring teacher, the author of two best-selling books and a pioneer in the study of two significant psychological disorders: Psychopathy and Dissociative Identity Disorder (formerly called Multiple Personality Disorder).

Flying Combat with the Triple Nickel

This video tells the story of one year of combat during the Vietnam War. The 555th Fighter Squadron was the recipient of three Presidential Unit Citations during its eight years of combat. This video tells stories of aerial combat as well as various activities at Udorn Air Base, Thailand from August, 1968 through August, 1969.

All of these videos are available on YouTube with the exception of the Triple Nickel video. If you wish a free copy of the Triple Nickel video, send me via email (genpsmith@aol.com) a good snail mail address. I will be happy to pay for the postage.

Appendix C:

THE WEST POINT CLASS OF 1956, SOME HEALTHY HIGHLIGHTS

PERHAPS THE MOST remarkable aspect of the West Point class of 1956 has been the state of the health of its graduates. More than half of our graduating class of 480 was still alive sixty years after graduation.

When we were plebes in 1952, all of us became guinea pigs. The "West Point Study" was a cardiovascular examination of a group of healthy young men - which continued for many decades. Every two years each of us filled out a questionnaire and had our local medical facility send vials of our blood to the School of Aerospace Medicine in San Antonio, Texas. In return, each of us got individualized feedback and analysis. The researchers were trying to determine if the analysis of a young man's blood could determine the likelihood of cardiovascular disease while he was on active duty.

As early as 1958, the research scientists in San Antonio warned us of the health dangers of smoking, obesity, high blood pressure, bad cholesterol ratios and the lack of exercise. They also gave us recommendations on specific things we might do to insure a long and healthy life. If we were doing poorly, as compared to our classmates, this was pointed out in these biennial reports. Thirty years after our graduation each of us were invited to San Antonio. We were given a thorough two-day physical. Each one of us met with a cardiologist, who explained in great detail what the various tests had uncovered. For instance, my tests showed that I had a calcium build up in the lining of some of my arteries. Ever since, I have been careful about calcium intake in my foods and beverages.

As a result of the information we received, many in our West

Point class gave up smoking, watched our weight and continued (or increased) our exercise regime. This constructive pattern is called "the Hawthorne effect." The Hawthorne Effect is defined as "a phenomenon in which individuals alter their behavior in response to being observed, and usually refers to positive changes."

My father, who was a heavy smoker and did little vigorous exercise, had died when I was a cadet. He was just fifty-five years old. I decided to follow a different pattern in my life. The West Point Study and its bi-annual feedback helped me reinforce this commitment. When this book was published in 2021, my West Point classmates ranged in age from 85 to 90. I expect that a few of them will be alive when our 80th class reunion rolls around.

There are a number of other aspects about the West Point Class of 1956 that are worth highlighting. Seventy four percent of the graduates of our class served in the military for a full career (twenty years or more). A large number of my classmates have been recognized as being Distinguished Graduates of West Point. We are tied with one other West Point class with eight honorees. Eighteen classmates have become authors of published books including two who published seven (Dave Palmer) and nine (Bob Sorley) books respectively.

Appendix D:

~~~

TWO SPECIAL GROUPS IN AUGUSTA, GEORGIA

IT IS IMPOSSIBLE for me to compile a complete list of the friends who have become such an important part of our life here in Augusta. However, two groups should be highlighted (The Ten Group and the tennis group).

Sometime in the 1980s a group to ten Augusta men began meeting every month to discuss items of interest. I was asked to join soon after I arrived in Augusta. This group is called "the ten group" but it consists of fourteen folks. This assemblage of men includes a journalist, an architect, a college professor, a college administrator, a TV anchor, a credit union executive, a pastor, an insurance expert, two attorneys, a university athletic director, a fighter pilot, an art museum director, and a computer whiz. But you may ask, "If it is the 'Ten Group' why are there fourteen members?" The answer is because about ten folks show up at each meeting.

Each month, one member makes a presentation. This is followed by a robust discussion. As of 2021, the members are David Hudson, Jim Puryear, Lowell Dorn, Richard Rogers, Bob Woodhurst, Gene Norris, Perry Smith, Cobbs Nixon, John Bell, Ed Presnell, Steve Hobbs, Kevin Grogan, Clint Bryant, and Dennis Sodomka. This interaction is a marvelous way to stay intellectually active. They are generous in their support of worthy causes in the Augusta area. For instance, many of them lend financial support, year after year, to the Jimmie Dyess Symposium. Also, they are helpful to me in another way. I sometimes check in with them after drafting an article for the Augusta Chronicle. Candid inputs arrive by email. In future years, I hope this group becomes more diverse. Women, Hispanics and

Asian-Americans would enrich our interactions.

Members of "the tennis group" have enriched each other in four ways. We strive to be role models in integrity - no bad calls. We agree to be exemplars in the non-use of profanity (fiddlesticks and dang are acceptable). We try to be archetypes of positivity even when losing. Finally, we feel that tennis has given us some extra years of healthy lives.

Our ages range from the early 50s to the mid-80s. The caliber of the play is quite high considering the number of geezers and super geezers in the mix. Teams are lined up as follows - the worst and the best take on those in the middle of the skills spectrum. I am especially fortunate. Being the oldest and the worst, I always get a strong partner. Incidentally, my favorite expression on the court is "YOURS."

A big breakthrough with our tennis group took place in 2018. Our all-male group invited the delightful Susan Muir to join us. She enhanced our group with her fine tennis skills, court savvy, a killer cross-court backhand, and good cheer. As of 2021, the group consisted of Ed Gillespie, Richard Slaby, Preston and Libby Sizemore, John Thompson, Mary Helen Hull, Susan Muir, Cobbs Nixon, Dennis Bell, Perry Smith and Al Metzel. On occasion, "ringers" join us including Kim Kelly and Bob Rollins. Never to be forgotten is the amiable Menard Inhen who coordinated the schedule for many years. Menard played with good humor and skill until age 89.

Tennis pros, Pete Collins, and, more recently, Marc and Carolina Blouin have been marvelous. They treat us with loving care. Each one has become a good friend to everyone in the tennis group. The soft courts at the Augusta Country Club are well designed, drain well and are carefully maintained. The tennis venue at the Augusta Country Club is the best I have encountered anywhere in the world.

Appendix E:

A SAMPLE ARTICLE FROM THE AUGUSTA CHRONICLE

THE FOLLOWING ARTICLE appeared in the Augusta Chronicle. Dear reader, I encourage you to check out my website (genpsmith.com) where you will find more of these published articles.

The Courage of Children (2010)

Recently I had a wonderful experience at an elementary school near Augusta. I had been invited to teach the entire fifth grade (about 150 students). The topics were leadership, service to others and courage. I stressed that there are extraordinary individuals who can serve as role models for us all.

To kick the session off, a portion of a video on Augusta's hero, Jimmie Dyess, was shown. This video was followed by stories of heroism on the part of both civilians and members of the military.

In describing the Carnegie Medal, I explained that it was the highest award for civilian valor and that it is awarded every year to about eighty heroic Americans. I then told the true story of an eleven-year-old boy who volunteered to go down eighteen feet into an abandoned cesspool. A baby had fallen through a concrete opening. The opening was so small that no adult could fit through it.

After getting permission from his mother, the boy squeezed through the tiny opening, and descended, upside down, until he reached the crying baby. Firemen, who had tied the boy's feet with a rope, then slowly pulled the boy and the baby up. Just as the boy reached the opening, the boy dropped the slippery baby, who fell back into the dank, smelly muck.

The boy insisted - he had to try again. Back down he went with a basket in his hands so he would not drop the baby during the second rescue effort. This attempt was successful and the crowd cheered as the boy and the terrified baby emerged. The boy was so embarrassed by all of the praise that he was receiving that he ran home. For this act of courage, this boy became, at the tender age of eleven, one of the younger recipients of the Carnegie Medal.

After telling this story, I asked this group of children how many were eleven years old. Most held up a hand. I then asked, "Would you have done what that boy did that day?" Slowly a few hands were raised. When asked why, the answers were fascinating. One said that it was the right thing to do. Another said that if she woke up the next morning and learned that the baby had died, she would feel really bad. A third child said he learned in Sunday school that we should try to help others. Another said that his dad would be mad if he had not given the rescue a try.

Later that day, the students were asked to write down their thoughts on the session. Here are three: "I know now without a doubt that heroes can be all sizes, colors, ages and backgrounds and that makes me hopeful for my chance to be someone's hero." "Heroes aren't always grand people, they're not always destined for heroism, they're not always strong, but I do think they all have something special." "Heroes can be as close as a friend or a family member, but they can also be a passing stranger."

Powerful lessons can be drawn from this session. Children at a young age usually learn the difference between right and wrong. They also understand how important it is to look out for others, especially those who are in trouble. If all of us who are parents, grandparents, uncles and aunts can emphasize these values with our young people, our community and our nation will be well served.

274

Appendix F:

GENERAL PERRY SMITH PARKWAY

By The Augusta Aviation Commission
A Resolution

WHEREAS, Perry M. Smith served our country for thirty years in the United States Air Force flying over 180 combat missions with the 555th Tactical Fighter Squadron, commanded a fighter wing in Europe as a North Atlantic Treaty Organization Commander, served as Commandant of our Nation's prestigious War College, retired with the rank of Major General and currently serves as the Secretary of the Congressional Medal of Honor Foundation; and

WHEREAS, General Smith sits on the Augusta Museum of History Board of Trustees and is currently the President of that Board; and

WHEREAS, General Smith has served as senior warden of St. Paul's Church, where he was instrumental in the building of the prestigious River Rooms; and

WHEREAS, General Smith has been active in his community in assisting the Boy Scouts in fund raising and developing new facilities, been awarded the George Barrett award from the Augusta Kiwanis Club in recognition of the service and leadership to the club and to the community; and

WHEREAS, General Smith has dedicated countless hours to the Wounded Warrior Care Project, the Fisher House at Fort Gordon and The Salvation Army Kroc Center.

NOW THEREFORE, BE IT RESOLVED that the Augusta Aviation Commission out of respect for his service to our nation and this community hereby designates its newest roadway as the General Perry Smith Parkway; and

BE IT FURTHER RESOLVED that the Augusta Aviation Commission gives due credit to General Perry M. Smith, a highly respected leader in our community, who continues to serve tirelessly, devoting his talents and efforts for the betterment of our community and that a copy of this Resolution becomes part of the official Record of the Augusta Aviation Commission Minutes. General Smith is to be commended for his untiring efforts and the legacy he continues to leave for us all to enjoy.

ADOPTED in the City of Augusta, in the County of Richmond, and the State of Georgia, this 27th day of October in the Year of Our Lord Two Thousand and Eleven.

The Honorable Jay Forrester, Chairman
Augusta Aviation Commission

Appendix G:

~~~

DATES, AGES AND PLACES I LIVED
AND SOME HISTORICAL CONTEXT

Year	Age	Location	President	Major Historical Context
1934-35	0	USMA Faculty house, West Point, NY	Roosevelt	Depression
1935-37	1-3	Army housing, Panama Canal Zone (2 moves)	Roosevelt	Depression
1937-39	3	Fort Monroe, VA	Roosevelt	Depression
1939-40	4	Fort Leavenworth, KS	Roosevelt	Depression
1940-42	5-7	Army housing on Fort Ruger, then Fort Kamehameha, and then civilian house in Honolulu, Territory of Hawaii (3 moves)	Roosevelt	Depression, WWII
1942-42	7	San Francisco, CA, then St Cloud, MN (2 moves)	Roosevelt	WWII
1942-43	7-8	Houses on beach and in town, Wilmington, NC	Roosevelt	WWII
1943-46	8-11	6903 Emondstone Ave., Richmond, VA	Roosevelt, Truman	WWII
1946-47	12	Quonset hut on grounds of Palace of Caserta, Italy	Truman	Postwar
1947-47	12-13	Principe di Piemonte Hotel, Viareggio, Italy	Truman	Postwar

1947-49	13-14	Cleveland Avenue, NW, Washington, DC	Truman	Cold War
1949-52	14-17	Quarters 66 West Point, NY	Truman	Korean War
1952-56	17-21	Cadet at West Point, USMA	Eisenhower	Cold War
1956-57	21-22	Marana, AZ	Eisenhower	Cold War
1957-57	22	Big Spring, TX	Eisenhower	Cold War
1957-58	23	Luke AFB, AZ	Eisenhower	Cold War
1958-58	23	Las Vegas, NV	Eisenhower	Cold War
1958-58	23	Stead AFB, NV	Eisenhower	Cold War
1958-59	24	Nancy, France	Eisenhower	Cold War
1959-61	25-26	Married Officer Apartment, Hahn Air Base, Germany	Eisenhower	Cold War
1961-64	26-29	Alexandria, LA	Kennedy	Cold War
1964-66	29-31	Teaneck, NJ	Johnson	Vietnam War
1966	32	Air Force Academy Faculty housing	Johnson	Vietnam War
1967-68	32-33	1635 Oakwood Dr., Monument, CO	Johnson	Vietnam War
1968-68	33	Perrine, FL	Johnson	Vietnam War
1968-69	34	Udorn, Thailand	Johnson, Nixon	Vietnam War
1969-70	35	1635 Oakwood Dr., Monument, CO	Nixon	Vietnam War
1970-71	36	Springfield, VA	Nixon	Vietnam War
1971-73	37-38	1635 Oakwood Dr., Monument, CO	Nixon	Vietnam War

1973-76	38-40	7217 Van Ness Ct. McLean, VA	Nixon, Ford	Cold War
1976-77	42	Colonel's Apartment, Hahn Air Base, Germany	Ford	Cold War
1977-79	42-43	Vice Wing Commander duplex, then Wing Commander house Bitburg Air Base, Germany (2 moves)	Carter	Cold War
1979-81	43-45	Brigadier General's Quarters, Rheindahlen Royal Air Force Base, Germany	Carter	Cold War
1981-83	45-47	Bolling Air Base, Washington, DC	Reagan	Cold War
1983-86	48-51	Quarters 5 Fort McNair, DC	Reagan	Cold War
1986-90	51-55	7217 Van Ness Ct., McLean, VA	Reagan	Cold War
1990-present	55-86	Augusta, GA	Bush, Clinton, Bush, Obama, Trump	Post Cold War

Appendix H:

NAME OF RANKS IN THE UNITED STATES AIR FORCE

Officer		Enlisted	
O1	Second Lieutenant	E1	Airman Basic
O2	First Lieutenant	E2	Airman
O3	Captain	E3	Airman First Class
O4	Major	E4	Senior Airman
O5	Lieutenant Colonel	E5	Staff Sergeant
O6	Colonel	E6	Technical Sergeant
O7	Brigadier General (1 star)	E7	Master Sergeant
O8	Major General (2 star)	E8	Senior Master Sergeant
O9	Lieutenant General (3 star)	E9	Chief Master Sergeant
O10	General (4 star)		

THOSE WHO HELPED

I am deeply appreciative of the contributions that my wife, Connor, and my daughter, Serena, made to this enterprise. Connor edited, story by story, the entire manuscript. Soon afterwards, Serena joined in the effort. Her contributions were huge. She went through the manuscript on four separate occasions during the summer and autumn of 2020. She placed the manuscript on google docs and the pictures on google photos. Serena taught me so much about how to use modern technology to improve a book. She also created the front and back covers. Towards the end of the process, Connor carefully edited the entire manuscript one more time.

Others who helped improve the manuscript include Rob Verfurth, Don Rice, John Warden, Charlie May, Dick Hallion, Mike Carns, Mike Dugan, Lissa Young, Dave Deptula, Mike Ryan, Hal Hornburg, Jamie McIntyre, Jerry Amlong, Lee Denson, Al Renshaw, Doc Bahnsen, Bob Sorley, Dave Palmer, Butch Harbold, Rennie Hart, John Barry, John Snodgrass, Cole Miles, JJ Winters, Ron Hintze, Kathy Bonk, Roger Sublett, Juliette Mofford, Dick Klass, David Kozak and Frank Klotz.

Published when I am well past my 86th birthday, *Listen Up* is my swan song. The book is not a commercial enterprise. Most books will be given away. The profits from books which are sold will be contributed to my favorite worthy cause: the Jimmie Dyess Symposium.

About the Author

Perry M. Smith, Jr. is a teacher, speaker, TV and radio commentator and best-selling author. Hundreds of millions of television viewers world-wide came to know him during the 1991 Persian Gulf War. He appeared on camera more than 100 times as a military analyst for the Cable News Network (CNN).

A retired major general, Smith served for 30 years in the U. S. Air Force. During his career he had a number of leadership experiences, including command of the F-15 fighter wing at Bitburg, Germany where he provided leadership to 4000 personnel. Later, he served as the top Air Force planner and as the commandant of the National War College. He flew 180 combat missions in the F-4D aircraft over North Vietnam and Laos during the Vietnam War.

A graduate of the U. S. Military Academy at West Point, he later earned a Ph.D. in International Relations from Columbia University. His dissertation earned the 1967 Helen Dwight Reid Award from the American Political Science Association.

Smith's published books include *Rules and Tools for Leaders, Assignment Pentagon,* and *Courage, Compassion, Marine: The Unique Story of Jimmie Dyess.* After Smith was interviewed on the Today Show, *Rules and Tools for Leaders* reached #2 on the amazon.com bestseller list.

In 2016, The General Perry Smith Parkway near the Augusta Regional Airport was opened. On April 17, 2021 in Atlanta, Smith will be inducted into the Georgia Aviation Hall of Fame. Smith is married to the former Connor Cleckley Dyess. The Smiths have two children, McCoy and Serena, and four grandchildren, Dyess, Porter, Perry IV and Jacob.

Smith's email address is genpsmith@aol.com and his website is genpsmith.com.

CPSIA information can be obtained
at www.ICGtesting.com
Printed in the USA
JSHW031538180121
10962JS00003B/9